Measuring to Improve

Practical Measurement to Support Continuous Improvement in Education

EDITED BY
PAUL G. LeMAHIEU
PAUL COBB

HARVARD EDUCATION PRESS
CAMBRIDGE, MASSACHUSETTS

Continuous Improvement in Education
Series

Copyright © 2025 by the President and Fellows of Harvard College

All rights reserved. No part of this publication may be reproduced or transmitted in any form or by any means, electronic or mechanical, including photocopy, recording, or any information storage and retrieval systems, without permission in writing from the publisher.

Paperback ISBN 9781682539675

Library of Congress Cataloging-in-Publication Data is on file.

Published by Harvard Education Press,
an imprint of the Harvard Education Publishing Group

Harvard Education Press
8 Story Street
Cambridge, MA 02138

Cover Design: Ciano Design
Cover Image: shutter_m/iStock

The typefaces in this book are Minion Pro and ITC Stone Sans.

Contents

Foreword   v

1 Practical Measurement in the Context of Improvement Research   1
Paul G. LeMahieu, Angel Yee-lam Li, and Paul Cobb

2 Practical Measurement: Foundational Concepts in Practice   17
Sola Takahashi and Jon Norman

3 Developing and Using Practical Measures to Inform Instructional Improvement in Mathematics at Scale   51
Kara Jackson, Paul Cobb, Marsha Ing, June Ahn, Thomas M. Smith, Nicholas Kochmanski, Starlie Chinen, and Hannah Nieman

4 The National Writing Project's Using Sources Tool: A Practical Measure for Informing Instruction and Building a Shared Vision of Argument and Student Capacity   93
Linda D. Friedrich and Rachel Bear

5 Using the Freshman Ontrack Indicator to Improve High Schools in Chicago   129
Elaine Allensworth

6	Designing an Instructionally Focused Practical Measurement System Centered on Equity *Adrian Larbi-Cherif, Anna Premo, Christian Schunn, and Jennifer Lin Russell*	157
7	Validity and Technical Quality of Practical Measures *Thomas M. Smith*	189
8	Practical Measurement in Action *Paul Cobb and Paul G. LeMahieu*	213

Notes	239
About the Editors and Contributors	259
Index	265

Foreword

It is my pleasure to welcome this volume, *Measuring to Improve: Practical Measurement to Support Continuous Improvement in Education*, to the Harvard Education Press Series on Continuous Improvement in Education. The catalyst for this series was the publication in 2015 of *Learning to Improve: How America's Schools Can Get Better at Getting Better.* That book identified six core principles that form a distinctive paradigm for helping educational organizations improve what they do. Over the past ten years, many different groups have drawn on these principles to guide their change efforts. We have learned that vitalizing the third of these principles—we cannot improve at scale what we cannot measure—often proves especially challenging. As improvers formulate working theories for how to address specific problems, they encounter a lack of measures for the core processes, roles, routines, and norms that are the immediate targets for change. Consequently, they remain hampered in addressing the core improvement question: "Are the changes we are introducing, actually generating improvements in how classrooms, schools, and district operate, and do these changes in turn link to the higher and more equitable outcomes desired for students?" I have personally experienced this challenge in improvement efforts led by the Carnegie Foundation for the Advancement of Teaching and have also witnessed it in the work of a wide range of other organizations engaged in various practice improvement initiatives.

This observation may at first glance seem odd, as the education field has become awash in data over the last twenty years. Much of these data, however, have been generated to address a very different use case—to support various accountability agendas. Evidence created for accountability purposes typically shares several general characteristics. It tends to be very global in its content. For example, measures for accountability typically categorize teachers and students into aggregate performance levels, but with little specificity about what these individuals actually know and can do (and even less about how to help them learn to do better). However, this is essential information for informing the next round of continuous improvement. Accountability indicators are also regularly summarized as overall mean differences. Even when these data are disaggregated by various demographic characteristics, extensive variability in outcomes remains within these groups. This ties directly to a second core improvement principle—variability in performance is the problem to solve, and yet the existing measures provide little useful information about that variability or how it might be meaningfully reduced. Furthermore, accountability data generally take the form of lagging indicators. That is, the evidence become available only well after practitioners' work on the processes targeted for change has been completed. Taken together, such data typically provide little insight into how a system of processes, roles, norms, and routines are producing the observed lagging outcomes. Improvers lack the kinds of practical evidence needed to inform dynamic ongoing inquiry processes, such as the Plan, Do, Study, Act (PDSA) cycles, that are central to continuous improvement.

This evidentiary conundrum lives within a larger educational context. We hold high aspirations for what we would like to achieve, and there is typically great excitement about the next new policy, program, or change initiative to be tried. While these intentions are worthy, educators confront an inadequate evidentiary infrastructure to guide them on the journey from noble improvement aspirations to organizational systems that reliably advance quality outcomes equitably at scale. And so a common reform story plays out, one of going fast and learning slow. Absent regular feedback of evidence that illuminates the ongoing results of improvement efforts, the individual and organizational learning that is necessary to transform a promising idea into changes that work reliably for different educators in varied contexts and with diverse groups of students too often fails to mature.

This volume details five cases that have advanced meaningful improvements affecting student learning and progress through schooling. In each instance, improvement teams invented practical measures to inform their efforts and organized regular reflections on these data in pursuit of their outcomes. The goal was to generate usable evidence, in the least intrusive manner, which might constructively inform the improvement efforts of the participants engaged in the work. Their practical measures are anchored in research-based evidence that aligns with improvers' clinical and practice-based understandings; provide regular timely feedback of data connected to their improvement framework; have sufficient signaling capacity to guide individual and collective professional reflection and action; and operate within social processes that support learning from data.

Also key, these teams effectively challenge a prevailing organizational norm that has been inherited from the accountability age, when data often came with a "gotcha" character. Practical measures, rather than being used to make accountability judgments *about* practitioners, are designed *for* practitioners to inform their efforts to improve something that they care deeply about. We see in each of these accounts how establishing and protecting this normative stance proves essential to the improvement enterprise.

Engaged in these ways, practical measures can achieve the status of a boundary object that organizes both individual reflections and the collective learnings of an improvement community. They enable the making of a common language among the disparate voices that initially form around solving a specific improvement problem, provide regular feedback organized around a working theory that is specific to this problem, and create meaningful contexts for collective conversations that deepen participants' shared connections to advancing change.

The practical measures introduced in these chapters are noteworthy for their clarity, ease of use, and salience of their content to their respective user communities. In these ways, they seem simple. However, while good practical measures may look straightforward and easy to use, they are often far from straightforward to design and refine. Developing a practical measure that truly informs improvement often requires a colleagueship of expertise that is capable of blending conceptual research-based knowledge, practical wisdom and experiences, understanding of local contexts, and statistical, psychometric, and visualization skills. The case examples in this book amply demonstrate this, offering much practical guidance to readers regarding how they might do so as well.

Ten years ago, *Learning to Improve* heralded a new paradigm in how educators might work with their local communities and engage with external partners to advance how their educational systems work. Each case in this volume, anchored in that improvement paradigm, has advanced significant changes toward equity at scale in educational outcomes. Each offers detailed, concrete accounts of how the "right" kind of evidence can truly make a difference. I am pleased that Harvard Education Press is bringing their work forward as exemplars of how we can all learn to get better at getting better.

Anthony S. Bryk
President Emeritus, Carnegie Foundation for the Advancement of Teaching
Series Editor, Improvement in Education

1

Practical Measurement in the Context of Improvement Research

Paul G. LeMahieu
Angel Yee-lam Li
Paul Cobb

On an otherwise typical Wednesday morning, Mr. James R. Gray has arrived early at Ward High School. A veteran English teacher with a teaching load that primarily includes first- and second-year students, Jim Gray is an early riser and often among the first to come to school. Today, this is especially true, as he has some unusual activity in his classes to prepare for, so he is making sure that he has a little extra time to do so. Throughout his career, writing has been a singular and enduring passion. He has even counseled colleagues across content areas on how they might improve their teaching of writing and the use of writing in their teaching. So it would be no surprise that he readily joined a group of teachers from across his district, working with longtime colleagues from a nearby university to develop activities to serve as a basis for the improvement of writing in their classrooms, and ultimately across his district.

He had participated in this sort of professional colleagueship many times before, in small professional learning groups that come together to learn from, with, and through each other. But this time is different in several ways. This effort has been guided by university colleagues who seek to use improvement science methods coupled with the social structures of continuous improvement to develop, test, refine, and spread practices that successfully address longstanding equity gaps in the writing performance of students at Ward High School.

Mr. Gray and other members of the English department at Ward High had examined data from the district's annual evaluative assessments and noticed sharp differences in the writing performance of different groups of students. Closer inspection revealed that the writing of several groups of historically underserved students was markedly shorter pieces that included considerably less detail to support their claims. This resulted in less well elaborated arguments. The problem of how to better support these students seemed to clearly be a high leverage problem. The current curriculum and instruction were not serving these students well enough, and Mr. Gray and his colleagues were eager to develop and spread instructional routines that would better serve them. Working with an instructional coach from the district office and two researchers from the local university, they analyzed why this situation might exist—and what changes in classroom practices might address the problem.

The result was what the university researchers called a "theory of improvement," an articulation of possible factors that, if addressed, might resolve the problem. They believed that lessons might be improved by the development and integration of instructional activities such as formal listing and clustering of supporting evidence, early private writes, and high-interest and engaging topic selection. This theory of improvement also included ideas about practices that might "move the needle" on factors that improve students' idea generation and incorporation into their writing. Mr. Gray had long been interested in the early stages of the writing process, in which (before they start to write connected text) students enumerate relevant ideas and organize those ideas into the flow of a logical argument. He and research colleagues from the local university had many thoughts about classroom activities that might better support students in generating initial ideas. It was these practices that Mr. Gray and his colleagues then prototyped in the form of new instructional activities that they planned to test. This testing included developing simple, direct measures that would inform them of whether the new practices were successfully implemented, whether they had the desired impact on students' writing, and if or how they might be adapted to ensure success for their students.

Never before had the university experts so actively sought Mr. Gray's views on the nature of instructional problems and challenges—or his ideas on what might improve the situation. Never before had his views and those of his colleagues been so fully accommodated in a plan to improve instruction or in the contribution of ideas about classroom practice that might lead to meaningful improvement. And never before had he been so directly involved in the development and testing of those ideas to determine what works, for whom, and under what conditions. If their testing could provide information that addresses these questions, what they would reveal not only would help Mr. Gray and his colleagues directly, but also provide improvement ideas that could benefit others throughout his district and beyond. At least this was the promise of the improvement methods that the university researchers brought their collaboration. In short, never before had Mr. Gray been involved in an improvement effort that was so genuinely a partnership: pursuing a common aim, holding shared values, sharing equal power, and committing to long-term engagement.

This is why Mr. Gray is so early to work on this day. For the first time in his career, he has been directly involved in determining the ideas that will be tested, using methods and assessments that he helped to build—methods and assessments unlike any that previous researchers have brought to his classroom. Today, he will test these ideas about practice using methods and assessments that he helped to develop to study things he genuinely cares about. He has a feeling that he will learn something important about his teaching today, something that will benefit him, his colleagues, and their students. After twenty-one years, Mr. Gray is genuinely excited: for the *first time, the education researchers seem to believe that he has something important to say, that his expertise matters.*

In their 2015 book *Learning to Improve*, Tony Bryk and his colleagues put forward a vision of just such a science of improvement in education.[1] Seeking to establish a more mutually beneficial relationship between research and practice, their vision articulates both the intellectual substance and the social organization and processes of improvement science. Reluctant to advocate for any singular model or methodology, their view of improvement in education is grounded in six core principles:

- Make the work problem centered and user focused.
- Attend to variability in performance as the problem to solve.
- See the system that produces the current outcomes.
- Embrace measurement to inform judgment and validate improvement knowledge.
- Use disciplined inquiry to drive improvement.
- Accelerate learning through collaborative work with colleagues.

The consequence of a commitment to these principles is a genuine scientific endeavor, one that prizes shared definitions of foundational concepts and the relationships among them; offers forms of inquiry that are commonly understood, transparent, and open to public inspection, critique, and replication; and provides the communal curation of the scientific knowledge produced.[2] Each of these core principles is essential to accomplish this, and attention to them establishes a form of collective learning in which knowledge is rigorously warranted to ensure that the changes actually are improvements—that they are effective (producing the desired outcomes), reliable (providing improvements by all practitioners and especially for diverse groups of students), and scalable (realizing the improvements across diverse contexts and settings).[3]

This book focuses on the fourth of these core principles of improvement—practical measurement for improvement. But the work described in each of the five cases presented in the following chapters provides an authentic application of improvement science as defined by its attention to all these principles. While each case pursues them in its own way, each is genuinely attentive to most, if not all, of the six core principles.

While the core principles of improvement science are best understood (and pursued) as a collective whole, the fourth is in many ways foundational to the rest. Sound measurement produces the evidentiary basis upon which several of the principles are founded. Understanding problems from multiple perspectives (principle 1), understanding and addressing variability in performance (principle 2), seeing the system that produces current outcomes (principle 3), and using rigorous methods of discipline inquiry (principle 5) all require sound evidence secured through measurement for improvement to adequately substantiate meaningful inferences, insights, and conclusions.

PRACTICAL MEASUREMENT FOR IMPROVEMENT: DEFINITION AND DESIDERATA

Just as its name suggests, practical measurement for improvement is, first and foremost, practical. It is relevant to practice. It is useful to practitioners. It is informed by a theory of practice and how to improve it. It is designed to accommodate practice—and even to be embedded within it. For all these reasons, it is distinct from more typical forms of assessment used throughout education.

Numerous authors have explored the relationship between purpose and appropriate forms of assessment.[4] Across many sources, a general consensus has emerged that describes three primary purposes: accountability, research, and improvement.[5] Not surprisingly, the form, format, and substance of assessment vary considerably to address these purposes adequately. Assessments for accountability tend to be externally imposed, assessing content that is reflective of standards established by an external authority such as a state commission, and infrequently administered. As such, they tend to measure lagging indicators—outcomes that are exclusively and primarily realized only after extended periods of time. Accountability concerns are very often addressed by assessments that are abstracted from the natural rhythms of schooling. Results often arrive long after the administration of the assessment, and it is not at all unusual for the processes of schooling to be suspended to administer accountability measures. While accountability measures can inform and shape decisions about programs and practice, this is more often asserted in rhetoric than realized in action. Mr. Gray and other teachers encounter many accountability measures in their work, including his district's and then the state's annual performance assessments. In a limited way, they can sometimes be helpful for educational planning; for instance, for Mr. Gray, they led to an awareness of a performance problem with implications for practice, particularly for chronically underserved students.

Measurement for research purposes, by contrast, is carried out almost completely on an ad hoc basis, only when called for in a research investigation. This type of measurement is conducted by researchers in the context and for the purposes of their research. They often measure constructs more aligned with researchers' interests than practitioners' needs, and there is frequently a tendency to cast a wide net. Mr. Gray has a certain familiarity with measurement for research as well. On several occasions, he has administered batteries of assessments in reading and writing at the request of university researchers who were exploring theories of how students learn to write. While he accepted the assessments as somehow valuable, they never seemed to examine anything that mattered to him or his students. As Solberg and colleagues put it, where measurement for accountability measures "just what is of interest," measurement for research tends to measure "just in case."[6]

Practical measures, as opposed to those for accountability and research, are assessments applied at the level at which work is carried out. They are practical, in that they can be collected, analyzed, and used within the daily work of practitioners, both as they engage in practices and as they attempt to improve those practices. Practical measures for improvement are used to identify improvement goals, much as Mr. Gray in our example used measures of students' idea generation early in the writing process to identify an improvement target for how to better support groups of students who were currently being underserved. These measures allowed him to assess progress toward that goal and to learn whether the changes he introduced are improvements that were helping to realize that goal.

Given the strong tie between the purpose of assessment on the one hand and its form, format, and structure on the other, it is possible to enumerate essential attributes of practical measurement for improvement. These will be further elaborated in chapter 2, with several illustrated in the five case chapters that follow and then revisited in the final two chapters. For now, however, it is important and useful to see them all together as an initial set. Practical measures for improvement should be:

- Closely related to a working theory of practice (and its improvement) that informs an improvement effort;
- Acceptable to and accepted by improvers and practitioners as relevant to their work;
- Actionable by producing evidence that explicitly triggers the provision of appropriate resources, coaching, professional development, etc.;
- Minimally intrusive, burdensome, or disruptive of educative processes; and
- Timely, both in the sense of the frequency or timing of administration and in the sense of the timeliness in which results are returned for use.[7]

PRACTICAL MEASUREMENT FOR IMPROVEMENT: FACING SOME MYTHS

Over the past decade, we have seen increasing interest in and spread of improvement concepts and methodological approaches in the field of education. It has become more common for people working in various areas of education and at different levels of the education system to incorporate core ideas of continuous improvement into their work—for example, causal system analysis, theories of improvement, iterative testing of changes, and measurement for improvement. As a growing community of improvers actively engages in improvement activities, they are getting better at achieving positive change. However, four common misunderstandings about practical measurement have emerged along the way, misunderstandings that can distract from and even be counterproductive to the pursuit of impact and equity. The first two misunderstandings pertain to the design and development of practical measures, and the remaining two have to do with their use:

1. Practical measurement is "quick and dirty."
2. Researchers design practical measurements, and practitioners use them.
3. Practical measurement can be used for both accountability and improvement purposes.
4. Any data is better than no data.

Myth 1: Practical Measurement Is "Quick and Dirty"

Regarding practical measurement as "quick and dirty" has the effect of reducing concern about the quality of the measurement. But poor measurement is never defensible, and it can be especially problematic if it is guided by a belief that because the purpose of the assessment is improvement, they do not have to be as rigorous as measures for either research or accountability. Rather, good-quality practical measurement requires an effort equal to or greater than that required for measurement for other purposes. Good practical measurement is the result of painstaking effort, often involving several iterations of testing and refinement. Improvement measures often assess constructs that are new and differ greatly from the typical focus of other forms of measurement. For example, Mr. Gray might want to measure not just learning outcomes, but also his students' engagement with and response to the new instructional practices that he is testing. Moreover, it is essential that the evidence produced by practical measures predicts the outcomes that we seek when introducing the changes suggested by our theory of improvement. In Mr. Gray's case, he will want to know immediately whether the new practices help students generate more (and more relevant) ideas. But ultimately, he also needs to know that enhancing the generation of ideas early in the writing process is predictive of better writing. Thus, Mr. Gray is testing the impact of changes in practice and simultaneously assessing the theory of how to improve his instruction and thus better support his students. Sound measurement for improvement must do all this with instruments that can be used with minimal disruption of normal educational processes and can deliver useful evidence in a timely manner in practical settings. This is a tall order indeed. But as we will see in the chapters that follow, it is not impossible when measurements are properly conceived and pursued.

The development of practical measurement is an iterative process. When we construct a new measure and test it for the first time, we may discover that it has very limited predictive power. What if the practical measures that Mr. Gray uses to assess the changes that he makes to his practice demonstrate increased generation of ideas, but not necessarily improvement in the final written product? This might suggest that it is also necessary to attend to the relevance or quality of the ideas (or how they are used in writing). Prescription: adapt, revise, and test again, quite likely with measures that are refined to be more sensitive to Mr. Gray's focus on better supporting specific groups of students. This observation suggests that we might need to add some new items or rewrite existing ones (or both), and then test again. Even then, despite careful revisions, we may still find that more work needs to be done to refine the measure (e.g., some items do not work for a particular subgroup of respondents, or the measure is now too long and disrupts Mr. Gray's instructional practice). Similar to iterating on improvement ideas, iterating on practical measures is itself a form of disciplined inquiry. It requires that those developing the measure have a sense of what rigorous measures look like, possess the capability and commitment to realize that vison, and do so in a form of assessment that is brief enough to fit unobtrusively into the ebb and flow of practice. This book both offers and illustrates a vison of rigorous practical measurement for improvement and also provides a process for developing such measures.

Myth 2: Researchers Design Practical Measurements, and Practitioners Use Them

Given the challenges of good practical measurement as identified previously, it is tempting to conclude that only measurement experts can develop them—or worse yet, that they should do so entirely on their own. When thinking of people who have the expertise to design practical measures and guide their use, the first group that comes to mind is probably researchers. In many fields including education, it is often assumed that researchers should produce knowledge and practitioners should use it—all with a strongly implied intellectual hierarchy established by the distinction. While this is generally true, it is especially the case in an area with a technical character like practical measurement. This leads to the conventional wisdom that there should be a division of labor such that researchers design and develop measures and practitioners use those measures. Although this schism continues to be very much the norm, it does not have to be this way. More pointedly, it cannot remain this way when the measures that we are trying to create and refine are practical measures that must be deeply informed by the circumstances and conditions of practice. Improvement sciences challenge this distinction with its very first principle (i.e., make the work problem-centered and *user-focused*). Rather than accepting that researchers are the sole producers of knowledge and practitioners are only the users, improvement science would have it that all are improvers, and as improvers, all must both produce and use knowledge. Good practical measures, by extension, are the products of authentic and mutually influential collaborations between practitioners and researchers.

One way to know who should be actively engaged in the development of practical measures and the processes for using them productively is to think through the two questions that are at the core of equity-centered improvement in education: Who is involved? Who is affected?[8] More often than we want to admit, those who are closest to practice, such as frontline teachers and school leaders, are those least involved in constructing measures that can have significant impacts on their way of working. This kind of exclusion is often done in the name of not wanting to overburden practitioners by asking them to do "just one more thing." Yet practitioners have the relevant expertise to contribute to a developmental collaboration. They know best whether the proposed assessments will fit within their practice, what sort of processes for using them might be feasible, and how to ensure that they are. The point to note here is that these different forms of expertise are complementary—and that all of them are needed to produce practical measures that are both valid and useful. Practical expertise makes an important contribution, along with content expertise and technical measurement expertise, and all these forms of expertise are necessary for the development of high-quality measures for improvement.

To be clear, we are not advocating that practitioners should develop expertise in research and psychometrics. Instead, we are proposing a shift in power dynamics such that researchers act as "analytic partners," listening to, learning from, and building trusting relationships with practitioners, and thereby ensuring that practice is authentically and centrally situated as they use evidence to achieve improvement.[9]

In the practical measurement cases that follow, you will find examples that illustrate how including the voices of practitioners and attending to them in the process of constructing and testing measures can improve the rigor and value of the measures, bringing about impactful change in practice.

Myth 3: Practical Measurement Can Be Used for Both Accountability and Improvement Purposes

Observing and understanding variability in performance constitute one of the core principles of improvement science, and practical measurement is a tool that can help enact this principle with integrity. Seeing the range in student performance and knowing whether efforts to improve are not just helping on average, but are also diminishing the range between the most and least successful students is essential to knowing whether genuine improvements are being made. However, observing variability alone does not necessarily advance improvement work unless we also make explicit the factors, and even the causes, that generate this variability. We see this as Mr. Gray and his colleagues drew upon their practical expertise to hypothesize that inadequate support for generative ideation early in the writing process explained the observed pattern in the performance data, even as it suggested ideas for changes to practice that might address this identified explanatory factor.

The critical question is: For what purpose will these measures be used? As noted above, measuring for accountability aims to use measurement to demonstrate how performance is distributed to determine who to reward, pressure, or penalize. Alternatively, measuring for improvement, emphasizes the importance of using measurement to understand variability in performance—what works, for whom, and under what conditions—to facilitate the kind of learning that is essential for changing a system for the better.

These two purposes stand in stark contrast. In fact, it can be argued that the more appropriate a measure is for one of these purposes, the more ill suited it is for the other.[10] Everything about the form, structure, and conditions of administration of assessment for accountability contributes to its inadequacy for improvement purposes. Length, timing, and timeliness all conspire against accountability assessment as a useful improvement tool. The overwhelming emphasis that arises when a measure is used for accountability militates against many of the most important necessities of good assessment for improvement. Ironically, much of the useful information that benefits sound instructional practice and its improvement lies in incorrect, inadequate, or socially undesirable responses. The same is true for other forms of improvement as well. Observing and understanding undesirable outcomes or performance (and formulating actions to address them) require information about what is *not* working every bit as much as information on what is. Yet measurement for accountability creates pressure that distracts from practices (whether established or in development) that support deep learning or the improvement of processes, by privileging correct or socially desirable responses above all else. By contrast, measurement for improvement is entirely inappropriate if used for accountability purposes. Its narrow focus on very particular practices and outcomes (some of which may be unique to certain classrooms) undermines the ability of an assessment for improvement to support inferences that can be generalized to broad domains, as is appropriate for accountability measures.

The prudent course is to recognize that healthy systems need both and to encourage the development and use of both—as is appropriate to their respective purposes. This constitutes the essence of the evidence-based culture that supports a high-performance system and serves as the driver of the systemic change needed to achieve it.

Myth 4: Any Data Is Better Than No Data

While evidence is fundamental to the advancement of improvement work, gathering the wrong data or using data for inferences that they cannot properly support can lead improvers to act on the basis of inaccurate signals, resulting in misinformed judgments and actions. This situation can be worse than having no data at all, as the act of using data may foster a misleading sense of confidence that decisions are data driven. It may also distract from genuine improvement. For example, if Mr. Gray and his colleagues had access to only traditional measures of fluency (e.g., word counts or even syllable counts) and accepted them as indicative of idea generation, then rather than making informed judgments about what constitutes individual and distinct ideas, they might have concluded that lengthy exposition of fewer points defines quality. However, this is not always the case, and assuming that it is can lead to unfortunate maladaptations of practice.

In consideration of the critical importance of having the right data and using that data judiciously, the five case chapters that follow attend to issues of validity as they relate to practical measurement. This examination of validity calls for a nuanced differentiation between validity for use and validity in use.[11] The former refers to the extent to which a measure assesses its intended construct, while the latter concerns the appropriate use of a specific measure for a defined purpose. The illustrative cases presented here not only expound upon this distinction but also illuminate ways of studying and, in turn, improving the validity of practical measures.

WHAT LIES AHEAD FOR THE READER

This book aims to provide a comprehensive look at practical measurement for improvement in education. It explores issues related to the purpose, development, forms of practice, and systems of use for such measurement.

It also identifies and elaborates on several challenges in conceptualizing and executing measurement that supports formal efforts at improving policies, programs, and practice.

Following this introductory chapter are five cases of practical measurement developed for and used in the context of efforts that are explicitly intended to foster improvement. Each case describes the purpose and context for the measures, the processes of their development and application, as well as the improvement routines for using the measures in each case. While the cases are clearly distinct, they all address the defining characteristics of practical measurement for improvement that we discussed here and that are elaborated in greater depth in chapter 2. Each qualifies therefore as a bona fide instance of practical measurement for improvement. Collectively, their similarities strengthen our definitional sense of the enterprise, even as their differences illustrate the range of legitimate expression within practical measurement.

In this book, each of the case chapters is structured to do the following:

- Provide background information on the improvement context, including the extent to which it attends explicitly to issues of equity, thereby clarifying the goal or purpose for developing the practical measure.
- Describe the practical measure and the process of its development with attention to its technical properties, including validity of the measure for its intended purposes and the outcomes that it predicts.
- Explain how the use of the practical measure contributes to the improvement effort, together with clarification of the cadence of data collection, analysis, and feedback, as well as routines for making sense of data and the role of data representations in supporting this sensemaking.
- Discuss the conditions that are necessary for the productive use of the practical measure, including both the classroom, school, and district conditions that need to be in place, as well as the types of support that users might require to develop the capabilities needed to use the measure productively.

While none of the cases address all these issues in a comprehensive manner, all five address the essential characteristics of practical measurement for improvement. Each illustrates good measurement practices, and collectively, they have much to teach us about how to engage in practical measurement well and wisely.

Following these five chapters, chapter 7 explores the technical quality and other qualities of sound measurement for improvement. As identified in the previous discussion, practice in this area can be challenging, and labeling something as "practical measurement" increases rather than decreases the level of challenge. This chapter offers a framework for examining the validity of the evidence used to inform improvement efforts. It sets out criteria for examining practical measures and illustrates them, drawing from the examples developed in the case chapters. Although the final practical measures may appear simple, developing high-quality indicators is a demanding process requiring skillful orchestration while balancing several competing demands. Specifically, the framework directs attention to validity in use, defining quality in practical measurements as the extent to which the evidence they produce stimulates and meaningfully informs the improvement of practice.

It could be argued that developing and appropriately using practical measurement for improvement pose a greater, not a lesser, challenge than assessments for the more common purposes of accountability or research. It must achieve a level of technical rigor equal to any other type of assessment, but it must do so in a form that is unobtrusive in practice or, in the best of cases, seamlessly embedded in practice.

Finally, chapter 8, the concluding chapter of the book, pulls together themes and insights from the five case chapters, consolidating what we can learn from them. Several of these themes are identified in the previous discussion and include:

- the essential elements and attributes of high-quality practical measurement for improvement and the ways in which they can be realized;
- the process of creating practical measures, including the types of expertise that are required to do so well;

- the role of practical measurement in reducing inequities in students' educational opportunities and accomplishments;
- the challenges of and opportunities for enacting rigorous and productive practical measurement at scale; and
- the contextual conditions and types of support that practitioners will likely need if they are to use different types of practical measures productively.

In this concluding chapter, these themes will be revisited and used to create a clear, consistent, and comprehensive vision of practical measurement for improvement. We hope that understanding of and attention to such a vision will position measurement for improvement within the reach of all improvers.

2

Practical Measurement
Foundational Concepts in Practice

Sola Takahashi
Jon Norman

Jeff Giles, assistant principal at Warren High School in Downey, California, likened his data experiences in the Carpe College Access Network (Carpe Network) to a physical exam by a doctor, in which you look to diagnose a problem, try potential solutions that might resolve the problem, and then check the data again to see if the solutions are working. This is in stark contrast to the typical data experiences that he had in his ten-plus years as a school administrator, which he compared to "an autopsy." These typical ways of using data were often after the fact—after the school year was over or after students had graduated—where he saw that there had been a problem but could not make things better for the students who had been affected by that problem. The commonly available lagging data often fail to provide educators with the timely and regular information that enables them to monitor and make adjustments to programs, interventions, or other changes that they have made in their schools for the purpose of improvement. But using data in the Carpe Network is different.

The Warren High School college guidance team is excited about and committed to the work that they are doing as part of the Carpe College Access Network.[1] This network of high schools in southern California, led by the High Tech High Graduate School of Education (HTH GSE), is applying continuous improvement methods to increase college-going rates for students who have historically been underserved by the US educational system, including those who are Black, Latinx, Indigenous, and/or experiencing poverty. The Warren team is enthusiastic about using real-time data to inform their work. As the first steps in this effort, the Carpe Network has focused on increasing the rate at which their students complete the Free Application for Federal Student Aid (FAFSA), which is a critical step for students who need financial assistance to attend college. It is also one that many students never complete. The Warren team explained that their access to frequently updated data about FAFSA completion has enabled them to be "more intentional in our work" and to "pivot quickly... when we see things that we don't like in the data," according to Jeff. Using these data, they have been innovative in their strategies for targeting students who need additional support to complete the FAFSA. Jeff proudly explained that through their continuous improvement efforts, they far exceeded their original goal of 74 percent of their seniors completing the FAFSA in the 2019–2020 academic year, with 89 percent of their seniors successfully completing this important step in their college application process. This was a remarkable achievement, Jeff noted, for a large public high school like Warren, with 3,500 students, mostly from low-income backgrounds.[2] It was also an important step for these students to be able to attend college—many of whom will be the first from their family to do so.

When educators engage in this type of improvement work—the type that Jeff and his team are engaged in and that is described in chapter 1 of this book—they use targeted measurement that is embedded in their daily practice and informs their ongoing improvement efforts. We refer to this type of targeted measurement as *practical measurement*. Continuous improvement, as practiced by Jeff and his colleagues, involves identifying key parts of a system that are essential to some problem that educators are trying to solve, as well as testing and improving possible solutions through iterative inquiry cycles.³ In the case at hand, elements of the relevant system include the structures and processes through which students access financial resources, gain knowledge of, and complete the college application process, develop a sense of belonging at their school and as a college goer, and persist in college matriculation after high school graduation. Good practical measurement, such as the FAFSA completion data that the Warren team used in their work to improve access to financial aid, is specific to the parts of the system that improvers are working in and timely enough to inform the direction of improvement work.

Practical measures provide evidence relevant to a number of aspects of the improvement process. They focus the improvement work on specific goals, raise targeted questions, and foster a shared vision of what a team is working on. The Warren High School counselors described their work prior to joining Carpe as well intentioned, but "kind of all over the place—we were doing so much."⁴ They explained how the Carpe data portal that HTH GSE designed and provided to all participating schools "helped us put everything in a central place where we could all share that information, but also share the same vision." Selecting and using practical measures help a team to articulate precisely what they are aiming to improve—namely, increasing FAFSA completion—and thereby set up individual efforts to pull in the same direction.

Practical measures enable educators to see their own and each other's practices with new insights, challenging poorly grounded assumptions about how their system works and about the individuals who inhabit it. The school teams involved in the Carpe Network are critically examining a key facet of their communication and student support systems through weekly tracking of FAFSA data. They have identified both efforts that were not working particularly well and student groups that were not being served effectively, and they have been spurred in their thinking about how to better serve their students. Regularly examining the FAFSA data pushed some of the Carpe Network members to question their assumptions about why so many students failed to complete the FAFSA—for example, that these families don't care about college or that it's not the school's responsibility to reach all families. Practical measurement illuminates existing processes, thereby providing information about how to approach the problem at hand.

Improvers use practical measures to see if their work is leading to the desired improvements. In Carpe, the FAFSA data has provided critical and timely information about the progress of school teams toward their goals, and they have led to insights about FAFSA completion rates after particular interventions or shifts in practice. Jeff Giles has reflected on how using the FAFSA data has provided "a very intentional way to support students along the way. It's like, we're... using data live to actually support students throughout the process before it's too late." Practical measures complete a feedback loop, which allows real-time adjustments and adaptations to occur as changes are enacted, thereby better meeting the needs of the intended beneficiaries.

The use of practical measurement can promote a focus on the role that current practices play in promoting inequitable educational outcomes, rather than placing blame on students or families for undesirable outcomes. Using the FAFSA data has brought about a mindset shift for the Warren team, who described how their approach to their work of supporting students has changed. In reflecting on their work prior to joining the Carpe Network, one counselor explained, "We were just putting out the message [about FAFSA completion] to the masses and, you know, whoever showed up, showed up, and whoever got the message, got it, you know? But that [approach] was leaving a lot of students behind, a lot of students were falling [through] the cracks because we were just leaving it up to them versus, now with the FAFSA data, it's up to us." Using data that told them who had completed the FAFSA and who still needed to allowed the Carpe team to reach out to students who might not show up on their radar. Rather than placing the onus of responsibility on the students, the Warren team scrutinized their own practices to understand why and how they were failing to reach them, and what they could do to better support those students. In some of the most transformative and impactful moments of practical measurement use, the sense of responsibility, ownership, and hope is deepened among its users. Such mindset shifts are especially important in the face of the long-standing inequities that continue to plague our schools, where students who are Black, Latinx, Indigenous, and/or experiencing poverty have long been underserved and marginalized. All too often, adults in and around schools attribute inequitable outcomes to students and families rather than examining the practices and policies of educational systems.[5] Locating the authority to make a difference in the relevant system is a fundamental necessity for continuous improvement to work, and practical measurement can be a catalyzing tool to spur thinking in this direction.

It is our aim in this chapter to describe what practical measurement for improvement can look like in education and to provide guidance to those in the field who seek to identify, develop, and use these measures in their continuous improvement work. We begin with a definition of practical measurement to ground this discussion. We then highlight how the use of practical measurement has been essential to the work of the Carpe Network. We also describe the characteristics of practical measurement, which include dimensions relating to both what is measured and how it is measured. We briefly discuss the questions of measurement rigor, which will be a topic taken up in greater depth in chapter 7. We then turn to some of the nuts and bolts of doing this work by exploring the kind of data infrastructures that support practical measurement. We delve into the social processes of use, where practical measurement comes to life with meaning and utility in the hands of its users. Next, we bring to the fore some considerations and key elements of an effective social process. Finally, we conclude with some essential lessons from past practical measurement work.

A DEFINITION OF PRACTICAL MEASUREMENT FOR IMPROVEMENT

We define *practical measurement for improvement* as the deliberate gathering, analysis, and interpretation of information that enhances practitioners' learning as they test changes and improve processes that lie at the heart of their work.[6] Practical measures are "practical," in that they can be collected, analyzed, and used within the daily work lives of practitioners, and also that they directly focus on practice. Practical measures are used to identify improvement goals, to assess progress toward those goals, and to learn whether specific changes introduced in an effort to attain those goals are in fact leading to improvement.[7]

Practical measurement is a broad umbrella term, capturing a range of types of measures that can inform continuous improvement in a timely way. These include "process measures," which capture information about processes that are the focus of improvement efforts (e.g., FAFSA completion rates).[8] These processes are the ways in which people and organizations carry out their work, and they stand in contrast to outcomes that are commonly measured (e.g., college enrollment rates). Practical measurement also includes "early warning indicators" that are leading indicators of important outcomes of interest (e.g., measures of teachers' level of burnout in a project focused on teacher retention).

THE CASE OF THE CARPE NETWORK

The Carpe Network was launched in January 2019 by the HTH GSE, to increase college access for historically underserved students.[9] As of now, this network, funded by the Bill and Melinda Gates Foundation, is in its third year. The effort includes teams from nineteen schools in southern California (including High Tech High charter schools and others) that meet as a network periodically throughout the year and receive coaching support from HTH GSE staff in between. This network is working to improve the college-going system in member schools by focusing on school practices, structures, and routines that are directly associated with college application and matriculation. The HTH GSE team, using insights from research and its past networked improvement efforts, has identified four main levers that matter for college access: (1) successful completion of the college application process; (2) access to the financial resources necessary to enable college attendance; (3) students' sense of belonging as a college student; and (4) reducing "summer melt," whereby admitted students fail to attend college. HTH GSE hypothesizes that addressing each of these influential drivers can significantly increase the rates of college attendance among historically underserved students.

In the first years of its work, the network has focused on improving access to financial resources by targeting the completion of the FAFSA process, which is a critical step for families who need help affording college.[10] FAFSA completion enables access to federal grants and loans, but the FAFSA is a long and cumbersome form—it is not easy to understand or complete. This is especially true for the students targeted by Carpe, many of whom are students whose primary language is not English or whose caregivers have not been through the college entry process themselves. Students experiencing poverty and students of color are less likely than other students to complete a FAFSA, and a lack of financial aid often prevents them from attending an institution of higher education even when they are otherwise ready to do so.[11]

The Carpe Network (which served over 7,200 seniors in 2020) increased its FAFSA completion numbers in the first two years of their multiyear improvement effort by approximately 500 students compared to the year prior to the network launch—an increase from 71 percent to 78 percent. The HTH GSE team that is leading the work of nineteen school teams (including Jeff Giles's team at Warren) includes Stacey Caillier, director of the HTH GSE Center for Research on Equity and Innovation, Edgar Montes, codirector of the Carpe Network, and Ben Sanoff, director of data analytics. They have seen how powerful it can be for school teams to have regular access to data that is directly connected to their work. School teams can track the percentage of their students who have completed the FAFSA every week from the fall until the March deadline.[12] They do so using a line graph that updates weekly with the latest data. The teams use the FAFSA completion data to track their progress across all students and for each student subgroup that they are targeting. The Carpe data portal provides information about how many more students they need to reach to achieve the team's aim in total, as well as by week (the total number of students divided by the number of weeks remaining), to support strategizing and planning for the work ahead.

The school teams also use the data to assess the success of new practices for increasing FAFSA completion. These data, because they are updated frequently, provide the teams with feedback that enables them to see if particular outreach strategies and interventions are making a difference; if so, how much of a difference; and for which groups of students.[13] Furthermore, because the data are connected to student rosters, the teams are able to identify and access information on specific students who may need additional support to complete the FAFSA.

The shifts that Stacey, Edgar, and Ben have seen in some of the school teams, however, are even more fundamental than changes in knowledge and practice. The Warren High School team has not been the only one to shift their mindset toward ownership and responsibility for what the data show. Stacey described how "so often we [educators] get so focused on the activities—not the outcome—like, 'we're doing it,' 'I did the presentation,' 'I gave the information.'" She then went on to observe that the data and the way in which they are used have shifted the focus of teams away from just executing actions and toward making a difference for students. Throughout the network, the teams used data about FAFSA noncompleters to decide whether they need to change their outreach or support strategies. For example, rather than relying on robocalls, some school teams recruited tutors and parent volunteers to call families and personally invite them to the FAFSA night events. Other teams created new informational materials and conducted sessions in Spanish to reach Spanish-speaking families. Rather than framing the students and families as failing in their responsibilities to attend the FAFSA support sessions, teams view students who have yet to complete the FAFSA as their responsibility and focus on how they and their school staff can better support these students and their families.

What does it take for data to play this role in a continuous improvement effort—as information for educators to better understand whether their improvement strategies are working, as a tool to spur reflective conversations about practices and their consequences, and as resources for learning that shape the next steps? We take up these questions in the remainder of this chapter. The details of the Carpe Network's achievements provide a valuable launching point for broader conversations about what it takes for practical measurement to provide relevant and timely feedback that can inform a continuous improvement effort. The nature of the data is important—what the data are, how they are connected to the continuous improvement effort, and the mode of collection and analysis. But just as important are the ways in which data are used. The routines for making sense of the data (e.g., who participates, when, and around what data) and the norms of participation make or break the potential for practical measurement to fulfill its role in continuous improvement. We start by discussing the characteristics of practical measures.

CHARACTERISTICS OF PRACTICAL MEASURES

Measures that are effective in informing continuous improvement efforts are marked by several key characteristics of what is measured and how it is measured.[14] First, practical measures are closely tied to a theory of improvement—that is, they measure key ideas about how to achieve the aim of an improvement effort. Second, practical measures are actionable—improvers can use the measures to inform their next steps and decisions. Third, they are meaningful—what is measured makes sense to those doing the improvement work. Fourth, the administration of practical measures is minimally burdensome to those on the ground level and minimally disruptive of their work. Fifth, improvers can access data from practical measurement in a timely way—timely in the sense of having data at the right time to decide on an appropriate course of action.

We unpack each of these characteristics of practical measurement in the text that follows, and in doing so, we include examples both from the Carpe Network's work and from other improvement efforts to illustrate the diversity of expression of these characteristics across a range of practical measures. It is also worth noting that practical measures evolve over time, and we do not intend to suggest that these characteristics are all in place in the initial stages of an improvement effort. Furthermore, given the context of the improvement effort, some of these characteristics may be more critical than others. We offer these characteristics as an ideal set to work toward, with an acknowledgment that most improvement efforts will need to prioritize and sequence the development measures with all these characteristics.

Practical Measurement Is Closely Tied to a Theory of Improvement

At the foundation of continuous improvement is the idea that "every system is perfectly designed to get the results it gets."[15] When improvers focus on solving seemingly intractable problems, they seek to understand the system that currently produces undesirable results, rather than blaming individuals for lacking skills, knowledge, or effort. Improvers articulate a theory of improvement that identifies the practices and aspects of a system that are pivotal in producing the outcomes that they are trying to improve.[16] For example, in the Carpe Network, the HTH GSE team investigated impediments to their overall aim of increasing college matriculation and postsecondary degree attainment for students who are Black, Latinx, Indigenous, and/or experiencing poverty. They developed their theory of improvement through research and reflections on their past work in this area (including leading a prior network focused on postsecondary readiness). The Carpe Network determined that four key aspects of the college application and matriculation process are amenable to change, and when improved, will collectively contribute to increased college-going rates for target student groups. These were described before, but we will repeat them here: (1) successful completion of the college application process; (2) access to the financial resources necessary to enable college attendance; (3) students' sense of belonging as a college goer; and (4) reducing summer melt, (whereby admitted students fail to attend college).[17] Over time, the initial theory of improvement gets refined as improvers learn more about how the system on which they are focusing works.

The theory of improvement deconstructs a complex system into its component parts. This enables improvers to take meaningful collective action in pursuit of improvement, even across very large networks. In the case of the Carpe Network, this system includes the people, processes, policies, and tools that shape the college application and matriculation processes, including a focus on the guidance counseling work that takes place in high schools as a key lever for change. It encompasses students and families, guidance counselors and other school staff, and how they relate to and engage one another as students access financial assistance, and select, apply for, and matriculate in college. Illuminating the black box between *inputs* (e.g., students entering junior or senior year) and *outcomes* (e.g., college attendance) is key to understanding how this system works, and thus how to improve it. But existing measures in education often do not capture information at this level of granularity—and even when it is captured, the data are rarely analyzed and the results provided to educators quickly and in a form that is easy for them to use.

Practical measurements offer a way to see into the black box. Specifically, it illuminates the theory of improvement—the parts of the system that improvers have identified as mattering to their improvement efforts. This also means that the measures must be sensitive to change—that they have to be able to signal improvements in the corresponding parts of the system when they occur.[18]

The Carpe team chose first to tackle the aspect of their theory of improvement that relates to students' access to financial resources by attempting to increase financial aid applications, with the FAFSA process as a singularly important access point across a number of sources. The Carpe Network utilized FAFSA completion as a practical measure of access to financial resources. The measure is informative in a number of ways: guidance counselors then know exactly which students to target at an individual level, the school team members know how their interventions are working generally, and when disaggregated by student subgroups, they also have a better understanding of the equity challenges at their site. For the HTH GSE team leading the network, the FAFSA data, including both overall averages and disaggregated by site, supports their understanding of how the network is performing as a whole, which bright spot schools are implementing effective strategies that others can learn from, and which school teams are struggling and need additional support.

Knowing the challenges that many students face in obtaining a degree, the Carpe Network focuses on two outcomes to signal their commitment to not only getting students to college, but getting them to colleges that will likely support them to degree completion. The outcome measures for each high school, therefore, are the college enrollment rate for seniors and an indicator of support offered at the colleges in which seniors enroll, captured as the average predicted graduation rate across all enrolled colleges.[19] The network also tracks measures at key milestones of the college application process, including whether students have a balanced list of colleges to apply for—which includes colleges with a range of graduation rates, as well as Barron's selectivity index—college application completion, and college acceptance and enrollment. In addition, a survey of high school seniors captures their perceptions of the support that they have received from their school in the college application process, and their sense of being a college goer.

As the work of the network evolves, Ben Sanoff, who leads the measurement and analytics work of Carpe, continues to explore what constitutes the essential set of measures that will guide the network's development of strong processes that can improve college access. A system of measures, like the set used by the Carpe Network, includes measures of outcomes, as well as of key processes thought to shape those outcomes.[20] The theory of improvement, which identifies the key processes that matter for the desired outcome, serves as a foundation with which practical measurement is integrated.

Practical Measurement Is Meaningful to Key Stakeholders

The successful use of any practical measurement is done by those who seek to learn from that measurement. It is therefore essential that the measure reflects something meaningful about what matters to the different stakeholders who use it, as they are the ones making changes in their practices. Educators' belief that a measure gets at something important to their practice is critical to the effectiveness of the measure. When a measure is meaningful, educators are more likely to want to use it to inform their thinking and their next steps, and it can support educators in being motivated to do the hard work of improvement. That said, meaningfulness can develop over time—a measure may come to be accepted as educators experience its use. Some users of a measure may not initially view it as meaningful, but attending to users' perceptions during the development of the measure and working to make it meaningful will make a difference over its long-term use.

For the schools in the Carpe Network, the FAFSA measure has worked well as a meaningful measure for the school teams. The measure is clearly connected to an aspect of the college application and matriculation system that matters (it is integral to the process of getting their students to apply to and attend college), and it is easily understandable (i.e., it is a simple percentage that can be disaggregated to show data for subgroups and individuals). Edgar, the Carpe codirector, relays how the school teams came to "see [the FAFSA completion data] as, 'we own this, this is our work... this is something that we're responsible for.'"

Practical Measurement Yields Actionable Information

Practical measures for improvement provide information that can guide improvers' actions. An example from the Carpe case involves network schools using the FAFSA data to assign staff members to support specific students who still need to complete the FAFSA form. Schools have also tried several strategies when they have noticed insufficient progress on the FAFSA completion metric, including reaching out directly to the families of focal students to invite them to school events designed to support FAFSA completion.

Moving from data sensemaking to action often requires further inquiry and learning for those who are charged with taking the next steps. An example of this is the Carnegie Math Pathways (CMP) program, which aims to increase the number of students successfully completing required college-level math courses so they can earn a two- or four-year degree. In working to overcome the problem of students not earning the appropriate credentials in mathematics to graduate from college, the CMP program found it essential to consider student agency as a driver of student success in courses.[21] Drawing on extensive research in the area, the CMP team developed a short, nine-item survey designed to assess students' experiences in these courses, including a student's sense of belonging in the classroom. For many students who have had little academic success or are the first from their families to attend college, their sense of identity and belonging in college generally and college mathematics courses in particular is a powerful determiner of their agency as college students. The belongingness measure informed instructors about the extent to which they were—or were not—fostering their students' sense of community, peer support, psychological safety, and connection.[22] When belongingness was identified as a weakness of a class, the next steps that instructors took included talking to students to better understand their experiences and solicit their input, and gathering ideas from both research and faculty colleagues who had been successful in promoting a sense of belonging in their classes. The information about what action faculty members should take is not inherent in the data, but the belongingness data signal both the need to take action and the nature of the problem to be addressed. In this regard, the proximity of data to action varies from one measure and context to the next.

Practical Measurement Is Minimally Burdensome

Practical measurement calls for data to be collected and processed in ways that impose the least amount of burden on educators who are working to improve their practices and to students engaged in educational processes. Nonetheless, measurement is likely to include some additional work, and this burden has to be justified by the benefit of the information that is gained, but educators are often stretched thin across their own responsibilities and do not have time for substantial extra data collection, entry, or analytic tasks. Practical measurement is most practical and sustainable when it demands little additional work for practitioners. Furthermore, it is important that the disruption caused to the core work of educating students is minimized. Measures that take time away from the work of teaching and learning must be carefully considered so disruption is either eliminated or reduced.

These concerns for the effort that measurement might require affect the sustainability of the continuous improvement work. Measures that require burdensome data collection, such as lengthy surveys or extensive training for data collection, will be less likely to be taken up and sustained than measures that can be quickly administered, with limited disruption to routine practices. Improvers can eliminate or minimize the data collection burden by using data that are already collected, or by finding ways to embed data collection in existing work routines. Some strategies for minimizing the burden may not be readily apparent or available when a practical measure is first used. In some cases, technological support can be employed to automate data processing and analysis, but in these instances, measures are often used at a smaller scale first, in order to test their value before any investment is made to develop the supporting infrastructure.

For the Carpe Network, FAFSA completion data serve as an example of minimally burdensome measurement. The FAFSA completion data are collected automatically by the federal government when students submit the form, and they are publicly available. The high school staff were not required to spend any extra time collecting and entering FAFSA completion data. Ben Sanoff and his team developed a process to access the data on a weekly basis to populate school-level dashboards (see figure 2.1). The school staff contributed to this process by completing a discrete task—uploading student roster data that is then linked with the FAFSA data so they can identify which students have and have not completed the FAFSA. School teams were also able to regularly access key details about the students who have not completed the FAFSA, including if they have started the application process, if there were technical issues that prevented the acceptance of their application, and their grade point averages and credit completion information (see figure 2.2).

Ben and his team also developed a second dashboard designed to give the HTH GSE team a networkwide view of the FAFSA data. This dashboard displays data from all the school sites (see figure 2.3) so team members can see which schools are making good progress and which are struggling, thereby informing their coaching efforts. Developing the two dashboards required substantial work by Ben and his team when the network was first established. However, the work was streamlined as processes were honed, and the burden on individual school teams and their members was minimal. They could therefore focus on making sense of and acting on the data.

Practical Measurement Provides Timely Feedback

A characteristic that is essential if feedback is to be useful in any improvement endeavor is that it be timely. When improvers know immediately after

Figure 2.1 Carpe dashboard—single school

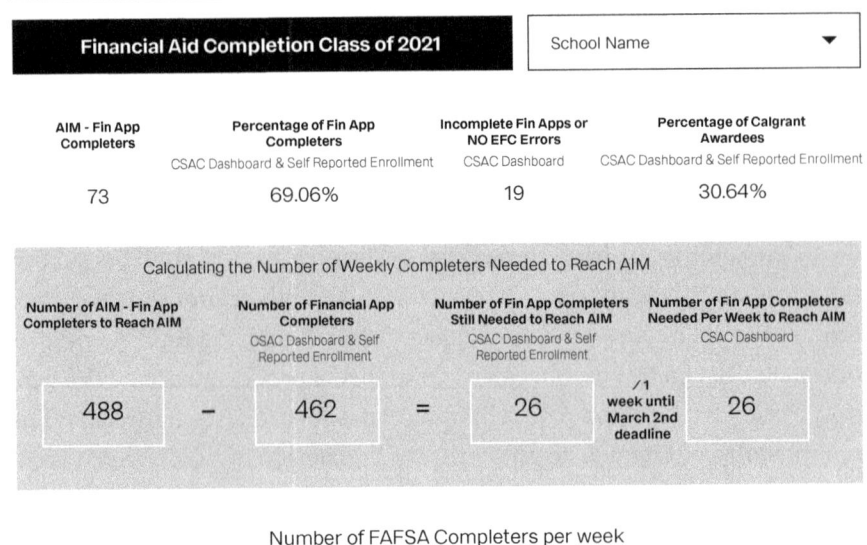

Figure 2.2 Snapshot of Carpe data: Details for students who have not completed the FAFSA application

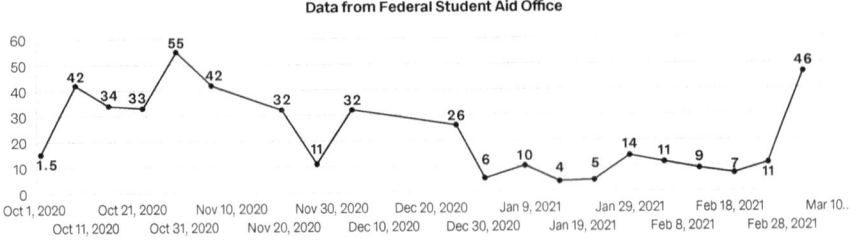

Figure 2.3 Snapshot of Carpe data: Display of school trends for FAFSA completion rates over time

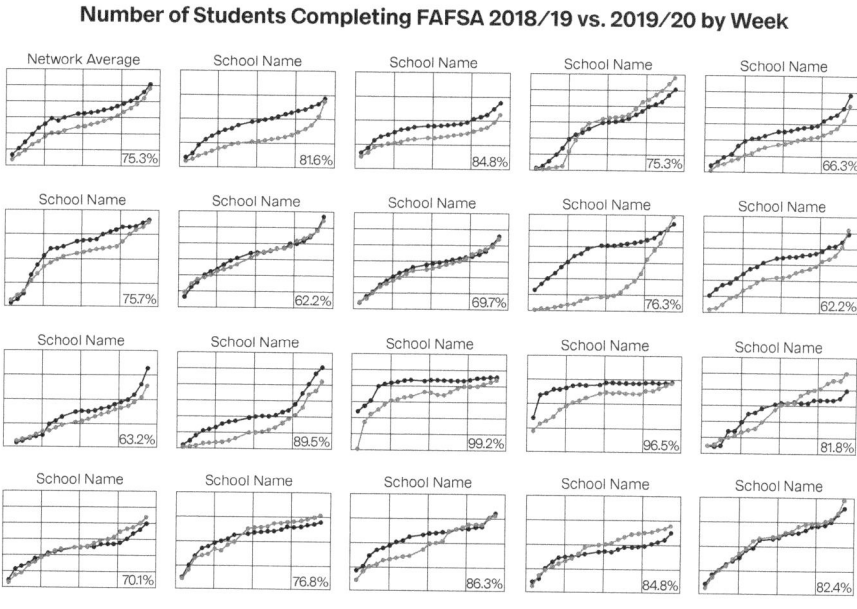

they try an intervention whether, for whom, and to what degree it worked, they are in a better position to quickly adapt and make informed decisions about the next steps. Practical measures are also useful for improvers when data are collected as regularly as needed so they can understand if and how the changes are having a positive impact. The definition of *regularly* will vary by process and context. For example, FAFSA completion data are made available weekly to schools. This timing works for school teams, as they can include a review of the data in weekly meetings in which they plan strategies for the week ahead. In contrast, it is sometimes important to measure some processes daily, such as absenteeism or the number of minutes of independent writing time students spend each day, while other processes may need to be measured less frequently, such as data from weekly administrative meetings or biweekly, one-on-one meetings between school leaders and coaches. The frequency of data collection must be considered in conjunction with the burden and concerns such as survey fatigue, wherein survey takers are less attentive (or even refuse to complete the survey at all) when responding after repeated administrations of the measure. The data infrastructure plays an essential role in these efforts to provide timely feedback and is discussed further later.

UNDERSTANDING THE DEGREE TO WHICH PRACTICAL MEASURES ARE "RIGHT" FOR THEIR PURPOSES

Since practical measures are intended to be used by practitioners, it is important that they perceive and accept the measures as relevant, useful, appropriate, or right for their intended purpose. How do we know if our practical measurements are right—whether they are doing the work that they need to do to give educators insight into the system they are trying to improve, and a sense of whether their work is moving in the right direction? The question of the validity of practical measures will be taken up in depth in chapter 7. However, our discussion of the work of practical measurement would be incomplete without raising two issues that should concern measurement developers: Is a practical measure connected to the hoped-for outcomes of an improvement effort? Does a practical measure get used by improvers in ways that meaningfully inform their continuous improvement work?

The first question concerns the idea that an effective practical measure captures an aspect of the system that matters for the ultimate aim of an improvement effort. In the Carpe case, for example, the HTH GSE team drew on research on US postsecondary educational attainment to identify FAFSA completion as a key determinant of college attendance, particularly for students from low-income backgrounds. There are also ways to examine the relationship between practical measurement and the outcome of interest through quantitative analysis.[23] Returning to the CMP example about students' sense of belonging in developmental math courses in community colleges, one way in which the researchers ensured the credibility of the student survey as a practical measure was to analyze the relationship between students' responses to the survey and their course success. Once improvers saw that a greater sense of belonging was related to course success, they were more confident that the survey was the right tool to use.

Analyses like this are typically post facto, and generally the relationship of a practical measure to a desired outcome must be hypothesized, initially, from scholarly and practical theories and the available evidence base.

The second question concerns assessing whether we have the right practical measurements based on an understanding of how improvers are using them.[24] It is in the use of the measures that we see whether the practical measurement enterprise (not just the measurement instrument itself, but the larger process that includes its use) is actually stimulating and supporting reflective and constructive conversations. As Stacey, one the HTH GSE leaders of Carpe, watched the high school teams examining line graphs depicting FAFSA completion rates for their school over time in an early network meeting, she noticed that they analyzed and reflected on their own practices, recognizing moments where FAFSA completion rates increased or stagnated and identifying aspects of their own practices that may have made a difference—or failed to do so. It is the teams' productive analysis of their practice that qualifies this as a constructive use consistent with the aims of the improvement effort. "They were linking what they had done directly with the results," Stacey explained. These observations of school teams' use of FAFSA data were early indications that the use of this measure had the potential to enhance the improvement effort, given the right context and supports.

A final observation: ensuring that a practical measure is connected to the hoped-for outcomes and is being used in productive ways can be time- and labor-intensive work. The investment of resources into this work, therefore, should correspond to the potential importance of a measure in the improvement work. For example, if a teacher will use a measure to decide whether to recommend a relatively small tweak in practice to a few of her colleagues, this would not call for the level of scrutiny that another measure with longer-term use and larger-scale impact might.[25] The degree of investment in gathering evidence about the use and consequentiality of a measure should be considered in light of the potential negative consequences of using a measure that is ill suited for the purpose in question. If the potential costs of an ill-suited measure are high, this calls for a more thorough collection of evidence.

THE PRACTICAL MEASUREMENT DATA INFRASTRUCTURE

Effective use of practical measurement requires constructing an infrastructure that supports the social, analytic, and technical aspects of data collection, analysis, and use. This infrastructure is developed and adjusted over time, as improvers learn what measures are valuable for their improvement efforts, as well as how to collect, analyze, and use the resulting data to inform their continuous improvement work. In the Carpe Network, HTH GSE staff are primarily responsible for accessing the FAFSA data, analyzing it, and sharing the results through a technically and visually sophisticated dashboard that allows each school team to see in real time whether it is making progress and to know which students have not yet completed the FAFSA form. It also allows the school teams to look at differences among groups of students (such as by race/ethnicity, gender, or multilingual learners) and thus to identify groups that need additional support. Ben Sanoff at HTH GSE had the analytic know-how and technical skills to develop this data infrastructure, and he continues to work with school teams to determine the ways of presenting the data that are most useful for them. Ben and the HTH GSE team are working on how to make data about other milestones in the application process (in addition to FAFSA completion) easy to access and use—data that are not already collected or are not publicly available. Taken together, the routines for collecting and analyzing data and the purposefully designed data representations comprise a data infrastructure.[26]

Most people are familiar with the technical aspects of data infrastructures: the need for computers and servers, or for pens, paper, folders, and file cabinets, for example. These physical aspects of data infrastructure need to be considered for effective practical measurement. For example, decisions need to be made concerning where and on what computer a file needs to be stored, and what mechanisms will be in place to allow multiple people contributing to an improvement effort to access the data. Equally important are considerations about who needs access and through what social processes they will make meaning of the data and take action. Such concerns become elements of an infrastructure insofar as they incorporate ongoing and systematic routines for access and use.

Less often discussed explicitly are the social and analytical aspects of data infrastructures. The social components of data infrastructures refer to the required roles and activities for collecting, storing, analyzing, reporting, and using data. Particularly given that the collection of practical measurement data is often done by people for whom it is an additional task outside their regular work routines and responsibilities, it is essential that improvers think through the social dimensions of data collection. Questions that need to be answered involve, for example, who will enter data into a spreadsheet and who will keep track of where data are stored. Practical measurement may ask students, teachers, instructional coaches, or others within educational settings to collect, manage, and analyze data themselves. Doing so requires new sets of social processes in addition to the technical decisions that need to be made; it may also need people to take on new roles and professional identities.[27]

The analytic part of a data infrastructure entails moving from the collection of data to the development of visualizations that enable sensemaking about the key issues and questions of concern. The sense that people make of data is profoundly shaped by the form in which the data are represented. The right data visualizations can spur meaningful conversations that focus on key issues by allowing all participants (especially those who are not trained in statistics) to notice the characteristics of the data that are most relevant to pressing questions that need to be addressed. Traditional analysis has for too long made statistical expertise the price of admission to the conversation. Especially now, as we seek to expand participation in these conversations, we need to develop ways of representing data that are intuitively meaningful and more accessible.

Thoughtful data visualizations have been developed in the Carpe initiative as a way to support access and interpretation. Ben Sanoff changed the visuals on the Carpe data portal from an initial set of drop-down menus for various demographic categories (e.g., a drop-down menu for race and ethnicity so teams could view the data for each group; see figure 2.4a), to a simultaneous display of the data for key subgroups in a bar graph,

Figure 2.4a Original drop-down menu design for student data

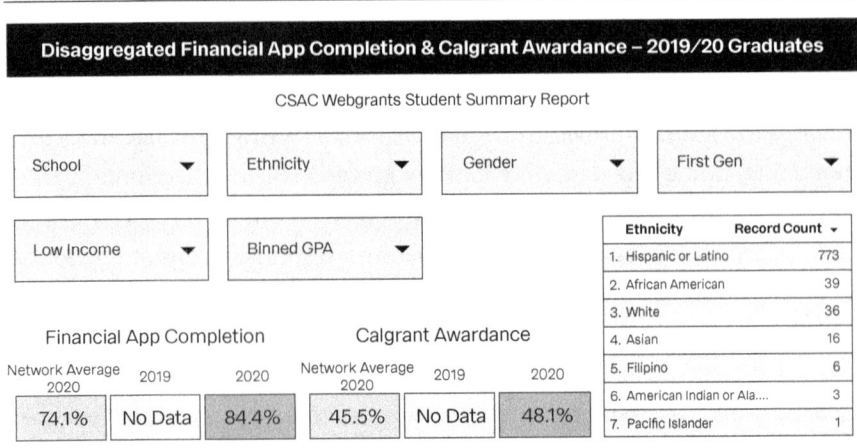

including data for racial and ethnic subgroups disaggregated by gender (see figure 2.4b). He found that the latter display allowed school teams to more easily identify student groups that were not being served well, and to thus set equity aims and develop strategies to better support the

Figure 2.4b Revised student data displays

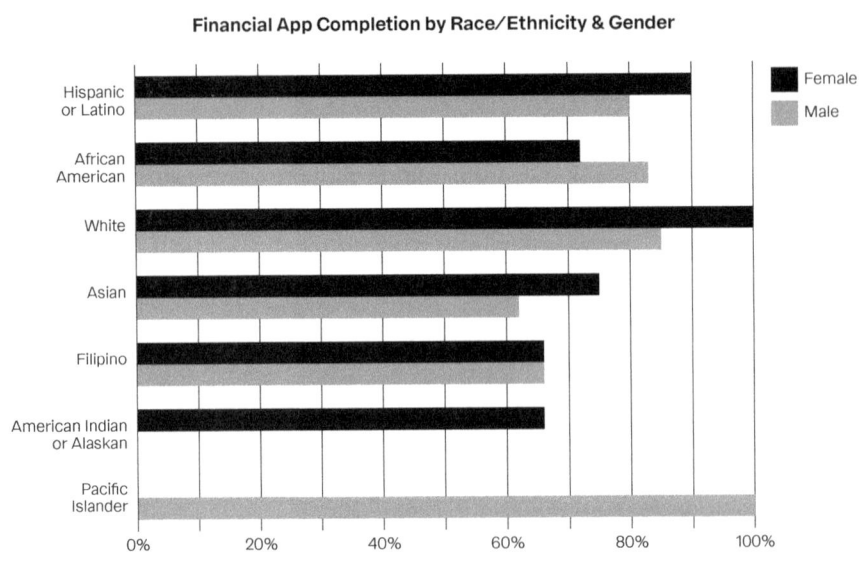

underserved students. Every decision about the design of data visualizations should be shaped by the purpose that the visualizations are intended to serve in the improvement effort.[28] Critical in the context of continuous improvement are data visualizations that can be easily understood by different stakeholders in the system.

SOCIAL ROUTINES OF PRACTICAL MEASUREMENT

While the identification or development of practical measures with the right characteristics matters, it is ultimately when groups of educators and administrators come together to make sense of the data and take action that the gears of continuous improvement turn. Improvers develop social routines for measurement to integrate it into their work. Stacey, Edgar, and Ben at HTH GSE all pointed to data conversations as the places where some of the most powerful moments of shared learning for Carpe school teams occurred. It is in these spaces of shared sensemaking that school teams determine which strategies are and are not working, which subgroups of students they are not serving well and how to better meet these students' needs, and where team members have changed some of their core beliefs. In the process, they transform resignation into ownership and hope. This did not happen by chance—it was the result of paying careful attention to how the teams engage with the data, both within their teams and throughout the larger network.

In Carpe's second year, the HTH GSE leadership team has been more explicit about the importance of locating the source of problems within the school system, rather than with students and their families. Stacey described how she and the HTH GSE team regularly launch the school teams' work by making explicit that their improvement effort must "start with 'we' not 'they.'" Stacey and her team frame their conversations to focus on what the teams can do to make a difference, rather than blaming students or their families for any lack of progress. She recalled school teams who, early in Carpe's work, attributed low rates of FAFSA completion to students' "laziness." Working with these teams, she facilitated their conversations to focus on what they could do, rather than locating the responsibility for improvement with students. In doing so, school teams reflected on the problem they were trying to solve, and one team expressed the insight that "maybe it's us." Stacey pointed to this as a pivotal moment for this team. They identified what they could do to make a difference, executed these ideas, and ended up with one of the highest FAFSA completion rates in the network. The FAFSA completion data played a critical role in this team's work by catalyzing productive conversations in which they reflected on their actions, identified next steps, and changed the ways in which they understood their own roles within the college application and matriculation processes. These types of conversations and actions affirm the HTH GSE team's view that the practical measures that they were using were the right ones for their network.

As the Carpe case illustrates, educators' social routines and processes for making sense of data and determining actions is where the rubber meets the road in the work of practical measurement. Data do not speak for themselves, they often are not self-evident, and practitioners cannot take mindless direction from them. A school team might notice some student subgroups completed the FAFSA at a lower rate than other subgroups and attribute this to students' "laziness," or they could recognize it as indicating failures in their current efforts to support certain groups of students. In social routines of data use, all members of the improvement community make meaning and take action, and in the process, their values shape and are shaped by the community. Effective social processes support individuals to come together to examine data, make meaning of them, and build action from this meaning.[29] In the context of continuous improvement efforts, these processes and routines create a dynamic feedback loop from action to sensemaking and reflection, and then back to action.

In their research to understand how data use in education works, Cynthia Coburn and Erica Turner identified several key features of data sensemaking in schools. We borrow their framework to consider practical measurement work. One of the core features includes *structures and routines for data sensemaking conversations* that support the constructive use of practical measures.[30] Improvers use these routines for interacting with each other around data, determining when, how often, and for how long these interactions occur, and deciding who at the table should talk about the measures and the data that they produce.[31] In a continuous improvement context, regular conversations of this type are essential if educators are to maintain their momentum in tracking their progress and assessing their actions with colleagues as they test ideas through rapid inquiry cycles.[32] As an example, coaching calls between pairs of school team leads and HTH GSE coaches happen on a biweekly basis. The HTH GSE leadership team meets on a weekly basis to examine the data and discuss the network's progress and directions. Other improvement efforts will call for engaging with data more or less frequently, and with different individuals participating in different venues. What remains essential is that sensemaking routines are structured so that they clearly indicate who needs to look at what data when, and for what purpose—and the routines for doing so become embedded in the operations of the community. Improvement efforts are most effective when they consider whose voices are included in data conversations, and how to bring in historically marginalized voices in a data sensemaking process to enable a more complete understanding of what is being experienced by those who are closest to the problem.

Productive sensemaking routines necessarily include *norms of openness, transparency, and innovation*, and thus clash with traditional school norms, in which teachers work as artisans, forging their own individualized teaching practices behind closed doors. Continuous improvement requires that teachers and others work collectively, sharing insights, successes, and failures with one another as part of a learning community. Effectively guiding the use of practical measures requires a sensitivity to norms around data at a particular site, as well as explicit strategies to promote and support norms of transparency and reflective practices. To counter fears that data might be used punitively, improvement teams may share data only at the aggregate level at first, sharing individuals' data but without any identifying information, and asking the innovators and early champions of the work to share their own data and experiences with others in an effort to begin to build new norms. Such strategies can support the building of trust within an improvement community, which then enables openness, transparency, and innovation. The deidentification of data can also enable the conversation to proceed without violating important privacy considerations when that is a concern.

The use of *data conversation protocols* can help improvement teams enact certain conversational norms. Such protocols provide a series of steps and discussion prompts, along with roles and timing, that guide a group through a conversation that focuses on both data sensemaking and determining the actions to take. Conversation protocols do not guarantee a solution in themselves, and their use is best supported by skilled facilitators.[33] Their effective use can support a shift in group norms toward transparency and innovation. For example, HTH GSE uses a "Data for Equity" protocol, which guides team members to first articulate what they notice about the data and what questions the data raise for them, and then to share interpretations in a way that encourages participation of the different perspectives at the table.[34] The inclusion of an equity pause in the protocol pushes team members to step back from their conversation to reflect on what assumptions they are making and consider whether they are engaging in deficit-thinking about students and families, or if they are scrutinizing their own practices and the structures, processes, and norms that make up their system.

While data sensemaking structures and routines help improvers use data to inform the next steps in their improvement efforts, Coburn and Turner also point to *social and political power* as critical factors that influence how data are used. Practical measurement work happens in a context in which power relations are enacted in day-to-day routines and moment-to-moment interactions among stakeholders.[35] These relationships include the individuals within the walls of a school—among teachers and administrators, for example—as well as among a broader range of stakeholders who are part of a school community, including school staff, students, families, and community members. Issues of power matter to measurement work because data are used to articulate what matters to an organization and to shape decisions and actions.[36] In every aspect of measurement work, from decisions about what to measure and how to analyze the data all the way through interpreting them and making decisions about action based on them, there is the persistent risk that some viewpoints and interpretations will be marginalized, rejected, or ignored.[37] When the viewpoints that are sidelined are those of communities with less social and political power, existing power dynamics are reinforced and opportunities to better understand the system and to make progress toward equity are lost. Using practical measurement and continuous improvement to advance equity requires intentional strategies to support the full participation of those who traditionally hold less power in education organizations, and this will require the examination of existing practices, routines, and norms.

In the Carpe Network, the HTH GSE leadership team has been intentional and proactive in having the school teams enlist students in their improvement efforts. All school teams conducted "empathy interviews" early in the work to understand the perspectives and experiences of the students, and thereby strengthen their ability to serve and support them rather than making unquestioned assumptions about the types of support that they need.[38] But student involvement does not end there. In addition, a fellowship program launched by HTH GSE as part of Carpe convened a cohort of twenty-five to thirty first-generation college-going students from five of the Carpe schools in a series of monthly meetings. The students received training about knowledge and skills relevant to college access, and they in turn provided feedback to the HTH GSE leadership team and the Carpe school improvement teams about the strategies and approaches that have emerged on how they could better serve students. As school teams engaged with their FAFSA data and identified strategies and interventions to test, a panel of students gave them feedback on their ideas. Stacey explained, "The students gave really great feedback on what would work, and what wouldn't, and why." She described how the school teams came to value students' involvement in the work, and how in the next phase of the work, school teams will invite seniors to participate in their network meetings. Students bring an important perspective to the Carpe Network, which, as Stacey remarked, "keeps it a lot more real."

In the work of practical measurement, issues of power in and around school organizations are especially salient because the work of continuous improvement compels educators to hear and learn from the experiences, insights, and actions of people who traditionally have little power or authority. They are the people who typically are closest to the problem and/or are affected by the problem. Teachers, for example, traditionally have less positional authority in a school system than school and district administrators, but they play an essential role in instructional improvement efforts as they enact practices that directly shape student learning experiences. Addressing race- and class-based equity issues in schools is a critical focus of improvement efforts. Students and families from historically underserved groups are often the intended beneficiaries, and yet they are among the stakeholder groups with the least power in a traditional education setting even though they hold critical insights that reflect their experience of the system at the ground level.

All this is to say that doing the work of practical measurement well requires a sensitivity to the social and political power dynamics in an improvement context, and an awareness of how the improvement work may clash with those dynamics. It is important throughout the practical measurement process that improvers are mindful of who is making decisions at the table about the measures, whose voices are represented when data are interpreted, and which interpretations gain legitimacy and why. The perspectives and voices that need to be included in a continuous improvement effort are often at odds with the ways in which power typically plays out in education settings. Doing improvement work well calls for explicit efforts to foreground historically marginalized perspectives. The Carpe Network provides a compelling example of how this work might be done.

CHALLENGES AND ENCOURAGEMENTS

Developing and enacting practical measurement in education constitute challenging work. The challenge stems from its purpose of informing systemic improvement efforts in complex organizations like schools, districts, or colleges. A variety of forces both within and outside an organization can derail the best of intentions, and often the best theories of improvement themselves do not fully account for these forces when the work begins. It can therefore be messy work, in which the next steps are not always clear and progress is not linear. But it is also potentially transformative work that allows educators to see better how their systems are working, and that enables them to interrogate and improve practices, policies, and mindsets. Next, we share some key lessons from on-the-ground practical measurement work.

The work of practical measurement for improvement draws on *a variety of forms of expertise*. Specific improvement efforts will require different mixes of expertise but will typically include the following five types of expertise. First, measurement or analytic expertise provides guidance about both how to measure key elements of the system and how to enact an investigative process from collecting data through analysis and sensemaking.[39] Second, content expertise informs the measurement work with insights about a particular problem and can inform decisions about what is important to measure, and how practitioners might make sense of the resulting data, given what we know about the problem itself. Third, expertise about practice provides a realistic and grounded view of what measurement work is meaningful, feasible, and useful in the organizations in question. Practice expertise includes knowledge about organizational constraints, structure, and culture, as well as knowledge about relevant educators' roles, practices, and pressures. Furthermore, because practical measurement is designed to serve the improvement effort, ongoing communication between those working on measurement and the leaders of the improvement effort is critical. Fourth, community expertise provides the knowledge and insights of students, families, and the broader community, who experience and understand their schools in ways that those who run them do not. Including members of these groups in practical measurement gives voice to valuable insights into what matters and what sense to make of data, as well as what next steps may make a difference. Fifth and finally, because measurement work is an integral part of a continuous improvement effort, it should happen in close communication with improvement experts, who understand the methods and processes of an improvement approach. This expertise is useful in guiding an improvement team to articulate a theory of improvement, grounding measures in this theory, and conducting iterative testing of changes. Importantly, we are not suggesting that every practical measurement effort should include a large team—multiple types of expertise can reside in a single person. The collaborative and multifaceted work of continuous improvement benefits from leaders who recognize the need for these forms of expertise and can call on them as the need arises.

Having the right people involved in appropriate ways is just the beginning. There has been some misunderstanding in the field that the work of developing practical measurement should be easy, that measurement instruments should be practical to design, or that the rigor or quality of these measures is less important than it is in traditional educational measurement endeavors. This is not the case—the development of practical measurement is often *time- and resource-intensive work*. The "practical" part of practical measurement is about its day-to-day use by improvers and those who are making changes in their practices. Practical measures are designed with a very particular objective in mind—to inform improvement efforts—and thus they differ from measures designed to investigate relationships between theoretical constructs or those to be used for accountability purposes. But these are distinctions of kind, not quality, and they do not negate the need for rigorous work in adapting or creating practical measures for improvement purposes.

In fact, the work of designing practical measurement instruments and infrastructure requires additional efforts not typically found in traditional educational measurement endeavors to ensure that the measures are practical to use, while simultaneously being meaningful to a range of stakeholders and users. This additional work may include soliciting input early and often from those who will use the measures, streamlining measurement instruments or exploring novel data collection mechanisms to minimize the burden of doing it, and setting up systems that automate timely analysis that is accessible to a variety of users, among others.

Relatedly, practical measurement work is *evolutionary*. In this chapter, we have discussed an ideal set of characteristics and the supporting structures that promote the effective use of practical measures—but practical measurement efforts in real educational settings rarely if ever have all these features at the outset. They evolve over time in conjunction with the development of broader continuous improvement efforts. We identified some of the ways in which this evolution occurs earlier in the chapter, when we discussed how the characteristics of practical measures may develop over time and how the decision to invest in developing and augmenting a data infrastructure often follows small-scale use of the measure. Much of the measurement validity work that we have discussed here takes place during and after a practical measure has been in use for some time. For example, analyses to examine the relationship between practical measures and outcomes of interest need to occur after outcome data have been collected, which could take a year or longer. It is our aim that this chapter delineates a vision for the work, not a checklist of prerequisite criteria.

Many of the challenges of developing and using practical measurement will *vary by the type of measure and context of use.* Some types of measures are easier to develop than others. Measures of behavior, where the indicator of interest is a simple yes/no and can be counted, tend to be relatively easy to develop. These include measures of status attainment, such as FAFSA completion, school attendance, or participation in professional development sessions. The challenges that may arise in these cases involve figuring out how to collect such data within the flow of work, how to manage the data, and how to set up a data infrastructure that leads to timely data analysis. On the other hand, improvers may face greater struggles in developing measures for concepts that are not easy to see or tally. Examples include learning and cognitive processes, the quality of instructional practices, and socioemotional development, as it is often less clear how these concepts can be measured in minimally burdensome ways.

Furthermore, the context in which the improvement work is to be carried out will have profound implications for practical measurement work. For example, does a school already have professional norms of collaboration and of transparency of practice? Is there an existing data infrastructure that can be used to enable practical measurement? Are organizational leaders invested in the improvement effort? These are some of the salient organizational features that are conducive to the uptake and use of practical measurement.

Good practical measurement for improvement stands in contrast to traditional educational assessment, in that it is not adequately addressed by measures that are burdensome or intrusive, and therefore are administered infrequently. Any single practical measure is insufficient to inform a continuous improvement effort, which involves focusing on several parts of a system or perhaps one element of the system repeatedly over time. In the Carpe Network case, as compelling and useful as the FAFSA data have been, the network recognizes that it represents just one aspect of the relevant system that enables college access, and it does not capture the ultimate desired outcomes for students. A *system of measures* is necessary, including measures at the outcome level, as well as at the level of processes, structures, and norms.[40] In Carpe, the system of measures also includes two outcome measures: college enrollment and predicted graduation rates—and numerous measures at the level of processes beyond FAFSA completion: development of a balanced college list, completion of college applications, and students' sense of belonging, among others. Improvement teams use a system of measures to understand the relationship between the strategies that they try, the processes that constitute the system, and the outcome that they seek to improve.

Practical measurement should never be used to evaluate individual practitioners or schools (or other education organizations) for accountability purposes. Such evaluations require a different kind of measurement work to ensure that measures lead to the right conclusions. This is because accountability decisions focus on individuals (not processes) and involve rights with legal ramifications (e.g., maintaining a job, obtaining a degree, or other actions). The minimally burdensome and quick-turnaround characteristics of practical measurement that are essential for continuous improvement purposes makes them particularly ill suited for informing accountability decisions.

CONCLUSION

Practical measurement produces relevant and timely information for educators and administrators who are tackling consequential problems and improving schools and districts. Improvement efforts involve teams learning together to solve problems, and measurements are key to improvers' efforts to marshal evidence and learn from their efforts. The characteristics of practical measures—that they are tied to a theory of improvement, meaningful, actionable, minimally burdensome, and timely—fit the needs of improvement in providing data to improvement teams in (close to) real time so that they can know the impact of changes that they are making. Improvement teams need more than just the measures themselves to be successful; they need both infrastructures that support such measurement and routines that enable their use.

Practical measurement for improvement is both needed and generally lacking in the US educational system. We have looked to health care to learn how continuous improvement can work to transform systems because it is several decades ahead of education in this regard. While there are many more parallels between the two fields than one might assume, we have noticed that the types of data readily available to health-care providers differ from those that are typically available to educators in schools. The frequent data entry routines of doctors, nurses, technicians, and other health-care providers to track their interactions with patients, coupled with the robust data systems in health-care institutions, leads to an abundance of and ready access to the types of measurement that we have been describing as practical measures for improvement. As a consequence, improvement teams in health care are often able to select from available measures (rather than develop them anew at every turn) and can move their work forward faster. In education, we have invested much more of our efforts and resources into accountability and research measures (and their associated infrastructures), which are valuable for many purposes but are ill suited to the purpose of informing improvement efforts on a regular basis. These existing measures are generally too cumbersome and too removed from improvers' daily practices to use them to inform improvement teams about how their change efforts are progressing.

The HTH GSE team faced the challenge of having to develop practical measurements as their work moved forward. While FAFSA completion data were already collected and easy to access, this was not the case for other measures that they sought to use. These included measures of whether students were going to apply to a balanced list of colleges and whether they were making progress in actually applying to these institutions. Stacey, Edgar, and Ben were developing innovative solutions to embed data collection for these measures in existing college application processes.

Four other chapters in this book (chapters 3–6) show ways in which practical measurement can contribute to efforts to transform educational systems. They vary in how they embody the five characteristics of practical measurement that we have described in this chapter, given the context of the improvement efforts in which they were embedded. However, the measurement work in all these cases is driven by a concern about what needs to be learned from the measures, for what purpose, and by whom. In addition, all the cases involve the development of new routines and norms for collectively making sense of data. These new routines empower improvers and enable conversations of consequence to practice between different groups of people within a system—not just among policy makers and leaders. Notable results include improved practices and processes, which ultimately benefit student learning and advance educational equity.

3

Developing and Using Practical Measures to Inform Instructional Improvement in Mathematics at Scale

Kara Jackson
Paul Cobb
Marsha Ing
June Ahn
Thomas M. Smith
Nicholas Kochmanski
Starlie Chinen
Hannah Nieman

A persistent issue in the United States concerns understanding how to improve the quality of mathematics teaching, and thus student learning, on a large scale (e.g., across classrooms, across schools), and specifically doing so in ways that redress long-standing inequities in students' opportunities to learn mathematics.[1] In this chapter, we draw upon our work on the Practical Measures, Routines, and Representations (PMRR) project

(2015–2023) to focus on the contributions that practical measures can make to instructional improvement efforts that aim to address this issue.[2] PMRR consisted of three research-practice partnerships, in each of which a team of university-based researchers worked closely with a large school district to support the improvement of middle-grade mathematics teaching and learning.

In the following pages, we first clarify a research-based vision of ambitious and equitable mathematics teaching that supports students' attainment of rigorous learning goals, and we discuss the types of support that teachers need if they are to develop instructional practices consistent with this vision. We then provide a short overview of the PMRR project before describing the process that we followed to develop a set of practical measures designed to assess key aspects of the mathematics classroom learning environment. We next discuss how our district partners have used the measures in their instructional improvement efforts, and we explain why it is essential that the measures are integrated into supports for teachers' learning, such as one-on-one coaching and collaborative meetings. Against this background, we then discuss three distinct ways in which the practical measures can contribute to ongoing instructional improvement efforts: (1) determining whether instructional changes are improvements, (2) enhancing the effectiveness of various supports for teachers' learning, and (3) enhancing the coherence of instructional improvement efforts. Finally, we will share how we have investigated the validity of these measures.

AMBITIOUS AND EQUITABLE INSTRUCTIONAL PRACTICES

Decades of research suggest the importance of students developing both procedural fluency and conceptual understanding of key mathematical ideas, and also of engaging in authentic problem solving, in which they analyze novel situations to figure out which strategies to use. In addition, research indicates the importance of students learning to communicate effectively about their mathematical reasoning, and of seeing themselves and their peers as people who "do" mathematics.[3] These rigorous goals for students' mathematics learning, represented in documents like the Common Core State Standards for Mathematics, guide most if not all the official standards in states, districts, and schools.[4]

A substantial body of research in mathematics education and the learning sciences indicates how classrooms should be organized to enable students to attain rigorous goals. We refer to the resulting vision of instruction as *ambitious and equitable.* This vision is ambitious both in the sense that it specifies what instruction *should* entail and yet is currently the exception rather than the rule in most US classrooms; and in the sense that it aims at deep, enduring, and personally meaningful understandings of mathematics. It is equitable in the sense that it deliberately aims to support a diverse range of students to substantially participate in and learn from all phases of classroom lessons.

A crucial aspect of ambitious and equitable instruction concerns the nature of the *tasks* that are used as the basis for instruction. In many US mathematics classrooms, and especially in classrooms serving students of color, students for whom English is not their first language, and/or students living in poverty, it is common for instruction to be organized around tasks of low cognitive demand that students can solve by using a procedure that the teacher has explicitly demonstrated.[5] However, if students are to develop deep and enduring understandings of central mathematical ideas, it is critical that all students have regular opportunities to solve tasks of high cognitive demand that closely approximate what it means to "do" meaningful mathematics from a disciplinary perspective. Tasks of this type require students to analyze novel problem situations to figure out what strategies to use and why.[6]

Research also provides guidance on the critical features of specific *phases of lessons* that are organized around cognitively demanding tasks. One crucial phase of a lesson is the introduction, or *launch*, of a cognitively demanding task.[7] In a high-quality launch, teachers ensure that students develop understandings of any linguistic and cultural suppositions that may be unfamiliar in a given task. Just as important, teachers also support students in understanding the key mathematical ideas required to understand what a problem is asking of them, but without suggesting specific procedures for solving it. This phase of a lesson is especially important from an equity perspective. Unless the launch is of high quality, students who are unfamiliar with any linguistic or cultural suppositions of the task, or who have difficulty picturing what is happening mathematically in the task, will likely struggle to begin working productively on it and might well become discouraged, thus limiting their learning opportunities in the remaining phases of the lesson.

Following a launch, students engage in either *individual or small group work* to solve cognitively demanding tasks. If students are working in small groups, it is important that norms and routines have been established such that they see value in sharing ideas with one another, especially tentative and exploratory thoughts, and in asking one another to explain their reasoning so that the group can consider different solution paths.[8] During this phase of lessons, it is important when students work both individually and in small groups that teachers monitor how they are attempting to solve tasks to plan for a productive whole-class discussion.[9]

In the final phase of a lesson, teachers orchestrate a *whole-class discussion*, in which they intentionally select certain students' strategies to be shared, and in what order, to advance students' understandings of the key mathematical ideas.[10] Crucially, in a whole-class discussion that advances students' learning, students do more than share their solution strategies. A key aspect of the teacher's role is to press and support students to explain not merely how they attempted to solve tasks, but also *why* they used a particular approach, thereby making their previously implicit interpretations of tasks visible. In addition, the teacher presses and supports the listening students to make sense of and assess those explanations and to make connections between different solution strategies, thereby highlighting the key mathematical ideas under consideration.[11]

SUPPORTING TEACHERS' DEVELOPMENT OF AMBITIOUS AND EQUITABLE TEACHING PRACTICES

This vision of ambitious and equitable mathematics instruction represents a significant shift from current practices in most US classrooms.[12] For example, achieving this vision requires a fundamental change in the role of the mathematics teacher from showing students how to use procedures to solve familiar types of problems to providing opportunities for students to derive or even invent procedures that they understand conceptually to solve novel tasks. It also requires teachers to shift from acting as the sole arbiter of what's correct and incorrect, to supporting students in evaluating options and deciding what makes sense based on mathematical arguments.

A substantial body of research in professional development and teacher education indicates that making these kinds of changes in the *how* of teaching involves significant teacher learning.[13] This research also makes it clear that most teachers will require two types of support if they are to develop ambitious and equitable instructional practices. One type of support concerns instructional materials that aim at central mathematical ideas and that target both conceptual understanding and procedural fluency. A substantial body of evidence indicates the importance of including cognitively demanding tasks and of organizing these tasks into instructional sequences that are coherent, in that what students learn in one phase of a sequence provides a basis for their learning in subsequent phases.[14]

A second type of support concerns sustained opportunities to work closely with accomplished colleagues to develop their pedagogical content knowledge and instructional practices.[15] *Pedagogical content knowledge* refers to the content knowledge that is specific to the work of teaching mathematics.[16] For example, teachers need to understand not only the meaning of fractions themselves, but also how students tend to make sense of fractions and how to represent key ideas of fractions to support students' development of a deep and enduring understanding of them. Teachers need intentional support to develop this kind of specialized knowledge and to investigate and try new instructional practices, including planning for and orchestrating whole-class discussions that advance students' understandings of key mathematical ideas. Depending on resources in a given school or district, supports for teacher learning might come in the form of one-on-one coaching, teacher collaborative meetings, a series of professional development sessions, or some combination of these. It is important that the types of support are aligned and constitute a coherent system for teacher learning, such that, for example, what teachers are working on with a coach is consistent with and builds on what they are working on in grade-level teacher collaborative meetings.[17]

Over the last fifteen years, we have engaged in long-term partnerships with several large, urban districts to support their efforts to improve the quality of mathematics teaching and learning districtwide.[18] A primary goal of this work has been to support the districts in establishing and improving a coherent system of high-quality supports for teachers' learning.[19] It is in the context of these partnerships that we have come to see that practical measures can make essential contributions to such instructional improvement efforts. To be clear, we do not see practical measures as a stand-alone silver bullet. However, as we will describe in this chapter, we have found in our partnership work that practical measures can play an important role in enhancing supports for teachers' learning.

OVERVIEW OF THE PMRR PROJECT

The PMRR project has two overriding goals. The first is to develop a system of practical measures that are useful in creating and improving supports for teachers' learning. To date, we have developed a set of *classroom measures* that assess students' perceptions of key aspects of the classroom learning environment that prior research findings indicate make a difference for students' learning. They include measures of the launch of cognitively demanding tasks, small-group work, and whole-class discussions. In addition, we have developed a rubric designed to assess the level of cognitive demand of the instructional tasks that teachers use as the basis for their instruction. Alongside these measures, we developed *routines* for administering them and for analyzing the resulting data, and *representations* that facilitate educators' analysis and productive use of the resulting data.

The second goal of the project is to investigate the contributions that the practical measures (and their associated routines and representations) make to our partner districts' instructional improvement efforts. Our partner districts have used the classroom practical measures in initiatives that support the ongoing improvement of one-on-one mathematics coaching, teacher collaborative meetings, and the writing of curriculum guides. Our decision to investigate the use of the classroom measures in three districts was intentional, as our goal was to develop measures that will be useful across schools and districts that are aiming to improve the quality of mathematics teaching and learning.

DEVELOPING PRACTICAL MEASURES OF STUDENTS' PERCEPTIONS OF THE CLASSROOM LEARNING ENVIRONMENT

In this section, we describe the process that we undertook to develop practical measures of students' perceptions of key aspects of the classroom learning environment. Often, there is an assumption that because practical measures are, by intention and design, easy to administer and the resulting data are relatively easy to analyze, they should also be easy to develop. This has not been our experience. Generating conventional measures of key aspects of a classroom learning environment is already a difficult task, and the requirement that it should be relatively easy for practitioners to collect and analyze data while minimizing disruptions to their work are additional design conditions that only increase the challenge.

As we describe here, the process of developing the practical measures of students' perceptions of the classroom learning environment—measures of launches, small-group work, and whole-class discussions—was quite protracted. In an effort to ensure that the administration of the measures would be minimally burdensome to users, each of the three measures takes the form of short student surveys that take one to three minutes to complete.

Initial Design of a Set of Items

Figure 3.1 illustrates the process that we followed to develop measures relevant to the launch, small-group work, and whole-class discussion. For each of these measures, the first step was to review the existing research literature to identify key aspects of ambitious mathematics instruction that were the focus of each of the three surveys developed. We then developed

Figure 3.1 Development process for the practical measures of students' perceptions of the classroom learning environment

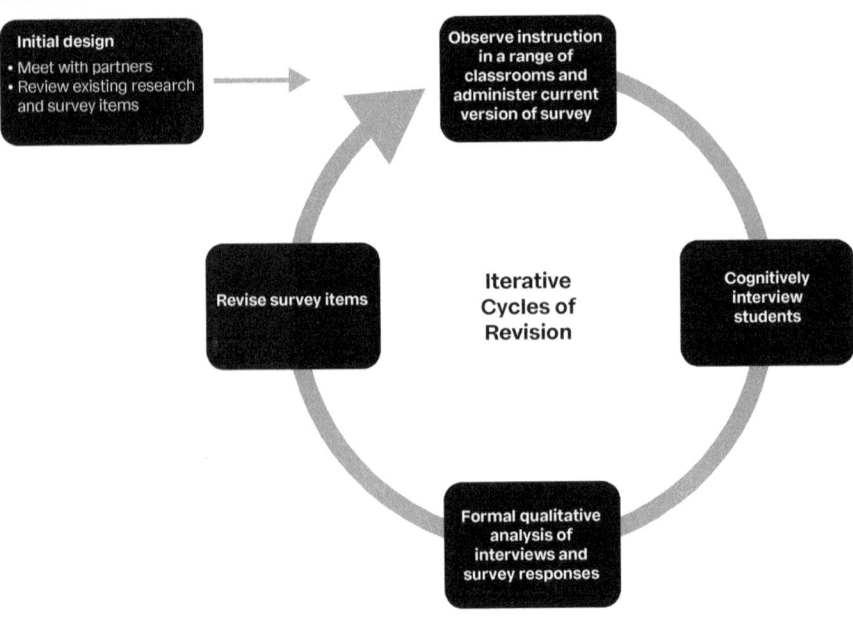

an initial set of student survey items to assess each of these aspects. Importantly, district mathematics specialists and coaches (and teachers, when possible) were involved in the development process, including in the design of an initial set of items. Their insights into what would be both feasible and compelling to a range of users were invaluable.

Iterative Cycles of Design, Analysis, and Revision

Once an initial set of items had been developed, the second step in developing each of the three student surveys was to ensure that the survey items assessed what they were designed to assess. In each revision cycle, a team of five or six researchers and district colleagues from one of the partnerships tested the current version of a survey in at least four classrooms, which varied in terms of the quality of instruction. The team members, all of whom had expertise in mathematics teaching and supporting teachers' learning, observed a mathematics lesson in each classroom and assessed the quality of instruction in terms of student learning opportunities specific to each survey item. At the end of each lesson, one of the team members then administered the survey to the students.

The team then compared students' responses, aggregated for each classroom, with their own assessment of the quality of instruction in each classroom to determine whether the survey was sensitive to those critical attributes and therefore discriminated appropriately between the classrooms in terms of key aspects of instruction that prior research has linked to student learning. In addition, immediately after observing a lesson, each team member conducted an audio-recorded cognitive interview with a student in which they asked the student to explain their response choices and probed the student's interpretations of the items.[20] The researchers then analyzed the cognitive interviews to identify mismatches between the team's assessment of the quality of instruction and students' interview responses. Finally, the researchers proposed revisions to the survey based on these two analyses that included eliminating, adding, and modifying items. We provide an illustration of the revision of one of the items in the following section. On average, we found that five rapid testing and revision cycles were required to develop each of the three surveys, which focus on different phases of ambitious lessons.

Each of the surveys was developed in English. When possible, we intentionally included students for whom English was not their first language in the trials to guide revisions to the items. Once the surveys were finalized, we had them translated into twelve languages, which reflects the diversity of languages spoken by students in our partner districts.

The Resulting Sample Measure: Whole-Class Discussion Survey

Given space limitations, we focus on one of the final set of measures: the whole-class discussion survey. Our review of the relevant research literature resulted in the identification of five aspects of whole-class discussions that affect students' learning. These aspects and the corresponding survey items are shown in table 3.1.

One aspect concerns the cognitive demand of the task as *implemented*. As mathematics education researchers Peg Smith and Mary Kay Stein observed, whole-class discussions that support students' attainment of rigorous learning goals "are unlikely to occur if the task on which students are working requires limited thinking and reasoning."[21] The research base also indicates that even when teachers use cognitively demanding tasks as written in curriculum materials (e.g., tasks that can be solved in several ways), it is very common for teachers to lower the demand of the tasks implemented by suggesting a procedure that students should use to solve the tasks.[22] Our iterative trials resulted in two survey items that provided consistent information about the cognitive demand of the task as it was implemented in the classroom and experienced by students: "What did you need to do in order to be successful in your math class today?" and "Was there only one right way to solve the problem(s) today?" (See table 3.1 for the response options for these and other items.)

The second aspect of productive whole-class discussions that we identified concerns what students are held accountable for. The intent of mathematics discussions is often to evaluate whether students' answers are correct rather than to bring significant mathematical issues to the fore by capitalizing on the range of ways in which students have attempted to solve tasks.[23] Focusing on answers alone does not help students make sense of or deepen their understanding of central mathematical ideas, and thus does not advance their thinking. Further, an exclusive focus on the correctness of answers does not enable the teacher to learn about students' current mathematical reasoning. We found that asking students, "What was the purpose of today's whole-class discussion?" was especially generative in determining whether students were primarily held accountable in discussions for making sense of mathematical ideas or producing correct answers.

In productive discussions, teachers attempt to achieve their mathematical agendas by building on students' current thinking and reasoning.[24] The third and fourth aspects concern the extent to which discussions focus on students' ideas and students have opportunities to listen to, reason about, and make sense of other students' ideas. We found that a simple item that asked, "Who talked the most in today's discussion?" with response options "Students" or "The teacher" provided an admittedly crude, but also illuminating assessment of the extent to which students

Table 3.1 Overview of the whole-class discussion measure

Aspects of the classroom learning environment that impact students' learning opportunities in whole-class discussions	Items (Students select the one best response to each question.)
Cognitive demand of the task as implemented	• What did you need to do in order to be successful in your math class today? ☐ *Solve problems using the steps the teacher showed me* ☐ *Listen to and make sense of other students' reasoning* • Was there only one right way to solve the problem(s) today? ☐ Yes ☐ No
Student accountability during discussion Note: *When analyzing students' responses, we collapse the first, second, and fifth options as "producing correct answers" and the third and fourth options as "sensemaking."*	• What was the purpose of today's whole-class discussion? ☐ *Share how we solved problems using the steps our teacher showed us* ☐ *Learn the way the teacher showed us to solve the problem* ☐ *Learn different ways that work to solve a problem from other students* ☐ *Share a mathematical idea we came up with on our own* ☐ *Check to see if our answers are correct*
Extent to which discussions focus on students' ideas	• Who talked the most in today's whole-class discussion? ☐ *Students* ☐ *The teacher*
Opportunities to make sense of others' ideas	• Did listening to other students in today's whole-class discussion help make your thinking better? ☐ Yes ☐ No • Did you have trouble understanding other students' thinking in today's whole-class discussion? ☐ Yes ☐ No
Extent to which students want to share their ideas and feel their ideas are valued	• Were you comfortable sharing your thinking in today's whole-class discussion? ☐ Yes ☐ No • Would it have been OK to share thinking you were unsure about in class today? ☐ Yes ☐ No • Did you feel like your teacher really thought about your mathematical ideas in class today? ☐ Yes ☐ No ☐ *I did not share today* • Did you feel like other students really thought about your mathematical ideas in class today? ☐ Yes ☐ No ☐ *I did not share today*

shared their thinking in discussions. However, while students sharing their thinking is a necessary aspect of mathematically productive discussions, research indicates that sharing, in and of itself, does not help students to deepen their mathematical understanding.[25] It is also critical that teachers press and support students to explain and justify their reasoning in ways that other students can understand.[26] Two survey items proved useful for assessing the extent to which listening students were supported to make sense of the ideas being shared: "Did listening to other students in today's whole-class discussion help make your thinking better?" and "Did you have trouble understanding other students' thinking in today's whole-class discussion?"

Of course, the extent to which students share their thinking with one another depends on the classroom norms that have been established, as well as whether students feel that their ideas are valued.[27] This fifth aspect of productive whole-class discussions is especially important from an equity perspective. It is well documented that teachers often view students of color, students for whom English is not their first language, and/or students living in poverty as being less capable of participating in rigorous mathematical activity, and these students, in turn, perceive that their ideas are not valued in classroom discussions.[28] We have found that four survey items surface students' perspectives on this aspect of the classroom culture. One item assesses students' comfort in sharing: "Were you comfortable sharing your thinking in today's whole-class discussion?" A second item assesses whether students view the classroom as a setting in which they can take intellectual risks: "Would it have been OK to share thinking you were unsure about in class today?" Two items assess whether students perceive that the teacher and other students valued their mathematical ideas: "Did you feel like your teacher really thought about your mathematical ideas in class today?" and "Did you feel like other students really thought about your mathematical ideas in class today?"

To illustrate the iterative nature of the development process described here and shown in figure 3.1, we briefly describe the history of this last item. In its first iteration, students were asked, "Was your thinking *respected* by other students in class today?" However, in cognitive interviews, four of seven students indicated that they interpreted *respected* as "listened to," suggesting that although the question indicated to these students that listening students were attentive, it did not indicate to them that the listening students *valued* their thinking. In the second iteration, we asked more directly, "Did other students *value* your thinking in class today?" However, six of the fourteen students interviewed indicated they would have checked "No" as the response option if other students had *disagreed* with their ideas, even if their ideas were seriously considered. This was problematic because of the important role that disagreements play in productive mathematical discussions. In the third iteration, we trialed "Did anyone ignore your mathematical ideas in class today?," but six of twelve students reported in cognitive interviews that *ignore* connoted disagreement or personal conflict. In the fourth iteration, we trialed the current item, "Did you feel like other students really thought about your mathematical ideas in class today?" All twelve students whom we cognitively interviewed indicated that *really thought about* communicated valuing and said that the modifier *really* was important in this regard. We then tested this version of the item in another set of contrasting classrooms and found that it continued to communicate as intended and was sensitive to differences in whether students appeared to value each other's ideas, as indicated by the ways that students responded to one another's ideas. Across all the trials of this item, our team conducted cognitive interviews with forty-five students from nine classrooms in three districts.

Each of the three practical measures of students' perceptions of key aspects of the classroom learning environment is intended to assess student learning opportunities in a specific lesson, and therefore predict what students will likely learn in that lesson. They are intentionally proximal, in that they focus on a current lesson, and thus specific instances of practice. For example, students' responses to the whole-class discussion measure predict whether their participation in a specific whole-class discussion supports them in deepening and/or elaborating their understanding of key mathematical ideas. The resulting data provide feedback on how effectively the teacher orchestrated the whole-class discussion in this lesson. For example, imagine that several students indicated that they had trouble understanding other students' thinking in the whole-class discussion. This information can then prompt the teacher to consider why students might have had trouble, and what they could have done differently to help more students to make sense of others' thinking. In the context of instructional improvement work, it is a considerable strength of practical measures that the resulting data are directly actionable.

In addition to the three student surveys that assess the launch, small-group work, and whole-class discussions, we developed a rubric to assess the cognitive demand of the instructional tasks as written, which teachers can use in planning an upcoming lesson. It was adapted from an existing research measure to make it easier for teachers and professional learning leaders to understand and use.[29] The rubric supports users in distinguishing between three types of tasks that differ in terms of what students are asked to do: "using procedures," where students have to use a procedure to solve a familiar type of task; "making sense of procedures," where students have to use a procedure to solve a task and either demonstrate why or figure out why the procedure works; and "problem solving," where students have to analyze a novel task in order to figure out a feasible solution strategy.

INVESTIGATING THE USE OF PRACTICAL MEASURES OF STUDENTS' PERCEPTIONS OF THE CLASSROOM LEARNING ENVIRONMENT

As we have illustrated, the three practical measures of students' perceptions of key aspects of the classroom learning environment target fundamental changes in how most teachers of mathematics interact with students on a daily basis. These types of changes require teachers to develop new forms of practice—ones that often challenge deeply held assumptions about what it means to teach, learn, and understand mathematics. For example, learning to facilitate a genuine discussion in response to students' current reasoning entails a profound shift in how most teachers envision and enact their role in the classroom. Research indicates that developing fundamentally new forms of practice, like facilitating authentic discussions, requires sustained professional learning opportunities in which teachers both investigate their current practices and try new forms of practice with someone more accomplished in the intended form of practice (e.g., a coach).[30] In contrast, research indicates that it is reasonable to expect that teachers can make minor adjustments to their practices after relatively limited professional development. As an example, teachers can learn to use a new pacing guide effectively from one or two stand-alone professional development sessions.[31] The key issue is the depth of the change in practice being called for, and thus the nature of the learning involved for teachers to develop the intended form of practice.

Given that the measures that we have developed target ambitious forms of practice that entail significant changes in most teachers' current practices, we contend that it is essential to integrate the practical measures into supports for teachers' learning. As an example, large-scale studies of mathematics teaching indicate that, in most mathematics classrooms, the typical purpose of whole-class discussions is to evaluate whether students' answers are correct.[32] Orchestrating whole-class discussions in which teachers elicit and build on students' reasoning, while also supporting other students to make sense of their peers' explanations, therefore represents a substantial change in practice for most teachers. Using data from practical measures productively involves interpreting students' survey responses and then deciding on specific changes to practices that might improve students' learning opportunities. Students' responses to the *whole-class discussion* measure may support teachers to rethink the purpose of whole-class discussions. However, even if teachers identify the importance of supporting students to make sense of their peers' solution strategies as an instructional improvement goal, the literature on teacher learning indicates that it is unreasonable to expect that most teachers will be able to determine how to change their practices to attain this goal on their own.[33] It is for these reasons that we contend that administering the practical measures and analyzing students' responses should be integrated into existing supports for teachers' learning, such as one-on-one coaching and teacher collaborative meetings.

In what follows, we describe how two of our partner districts have used the classroom measures and illustrate two distinct ways in which the measures can contribute to instructional improvement efforts when they are integrated into supports for teacher's learning: (1) determining whether an instructional change is an improvement; and (2) enhancing the effectiveness of the supports for teachers' learning. In addition, we discuss a third possible contribution of the measures—namely, that the use of the measures can enhance the coherence of instructional improvement efforts at scale. The two districts in which we ground the discussion, District E and District I, both aimed to support teachers' development of ambitious and equitable instructional practices. However, there were differences in the districts' theories of improvement and in the available resources and structures for supporting teachers' learning. In District E, the whole-class discussion measure was integrated into one-on-one coaching cycles, whereas District I used the measure in a Curriculum Guide Writing initiative to improve the quality of the written mathematics curriculum. Both cases illustrate how the measure can be used to determine whether an instructional change is an improvement. In addition, the District E case illustrates how the integration of the measure into a key support for teachers' learning (i.e., coaching) can enhance the effectiveness of the support.

Determining Whether an Instructional Change Is an Improvement

As Takahashi and Norman describe in chapter 2 of this book, practical measures enable users to get timely feedback regarding whether a change that they deliberately made to their practice is an improvement. There are two ways in which we have found that our practical measures can support practitioners in determining whether an instructional change is, indeed, an improvement: whether a change *in teaching* results in improvements in students' learning opportunities, and whether a change in a *support for teachers' learning* results in improvements in instruction.

Case 1: Using Practical Measure Data to Determine If an Instructional Change Is an Improvement

The overall goal of the partnership with District E was to establish a cadre of accomplished mathematics coaches who could work with teachers one on one to support their development of ambitious and equitable instructional practices. To this end, the researchers and district mathematics specialists collaborated to design and lead a sequence of eight professional development sessions for each of two years for fifteen middle-grade mathematics coaches, each of whom served one school. The goal of the professional development was to support the coaches in enacting coaching cycles effectively, where each cycle consists of the three phases shown in figure 3.2:

- A *coplanning phase*, in which the teacher and coach coplan an upcoming lesson, with particular attention to the aspect of instruction that the teacher is attempting to improve.
- A *lesson enactment phase*, in which the coach either models particular aspects of high-quality instruction while the teacher observes, the teacher and coach coteach the lesson, or the teacher teaches the lesson while the coach observes.
- A *debrief phase*, in which the teacher and coach analyze the impact of instruction on students' learning during the lesson.

Readers familiar with improvement science as it has been applied to education will note the strong parallel between the three phases of a coaching cycle and the four phases of a Plan, Do, Study, Act (PDSA) cycle, with the concluding Study and Act phases of the cycle being collapsed into the final debrief phase of a coaching cycle.

The integration of the practical measures into a coaching cycle involves a coach-teacher pair first identifying the student survey that is aligned with the aspect of instruction that the teacher is attempting to improve (e.g., they select the whole-class discussion survey if the teacher was attempting to improve aspects of classroom discussions). They then administer that survey at the end of the lesson enactment phase and analyze the students' responses during the debrief phase along with other

Figure 3.2 One-on-one coaching cycle

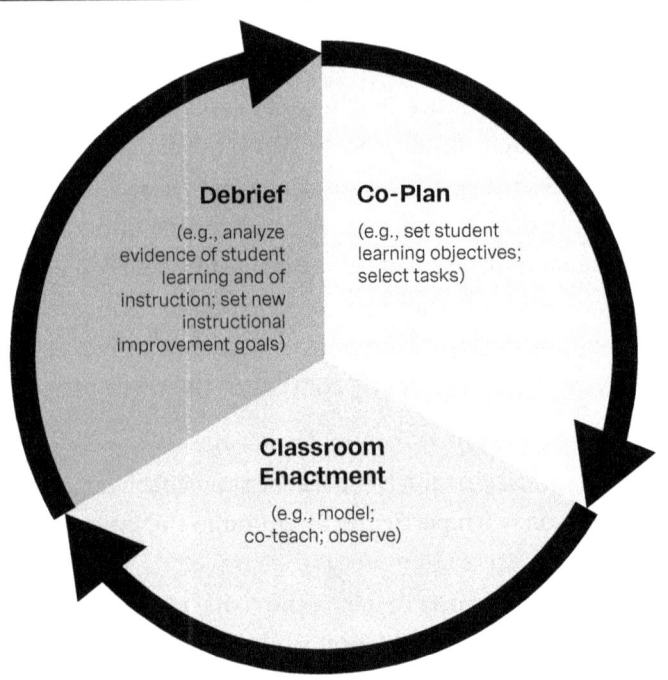

sources of evidence collected to document students' learning, including student work. Using the practical measures data in this way enables them to determine whether a change that the teacher has made to instruction has improved students' learning opportunities. If a coach and teacher judge an instructional change to be an improvement, they might draw on their analysis of the lesson to set a new instructional improvement goal that would then orient their work during the next coaching cycle. However, if the instructional change did not result in the intended improvement in students' learning opportunities, the teacher and coach might propose an alternative instructional change that could have the desired impact.

As an illustration, one coach-teacher pair had administered the whole-class discussion survey in the prior coaching cycle and found it problematic that more than half of the students had responded "Yes" to an item that asked, "Did you have trouble understanding other students' thinking in today's whole-class discussion?" (see figure 3.3; data from February 22, 2018). Crucially, the coach and teacher attempted to understand why the students responded in this way, with the coach observing that the teacher had frequently rephrased students' explanations during the discussion. This led the teacher to suggest that if she encouraged the listening students to rephrase other students' explanations, this might help them understand those explanations:

Coach: I notice when a student will share, you would rephrase what they were sharing. I wonder if—
Teacher: —having another student rephrase?
Coach: Exactly.

In subsequent mathematics lessons, the teacher worked to support her students in restating others' explanations in their own words rather than restating them herself. When the coach and teacher administered the whole-class discussion survey one month later in the next coaching cycle, they found that less than a quarter of the students indicated that they had trouble understanding other explanations (see figure 3.3; data from March 22, 2018). They interpreted these data as indicating that the instructional change that the teacher had made was indeed an improvement, with her commenting, "That's great. Put that on my résumé."

Figure 3.3 Students' responses to whole-class discussion survey item, at two time points

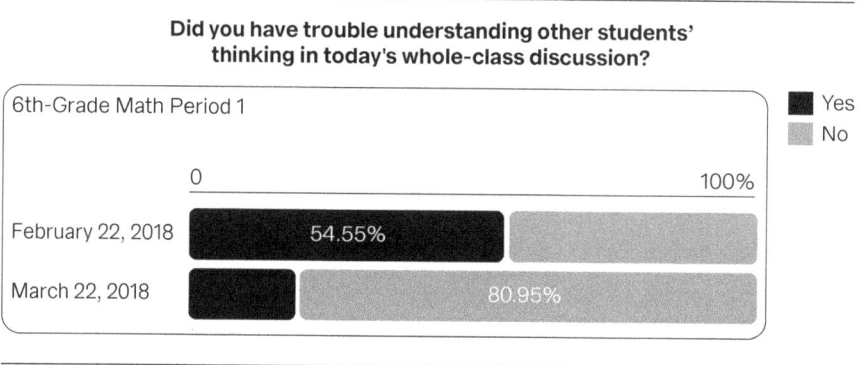

This illustration is representative in that the coaches and their partner teachers increasingly used the practical measures to determine whether a change in teaching was an improvement as the professional development progressed.[34] Integrating the practical measures into coaching cycles enabled them to gauge whether they were making progress in improving students' learning opportunities, and to adjust their work together accordingly. Furthermore, supporting the development of a cohort of coaches who used the classroom measures in this manner as they each worked one on one with several teachers would contribute directly to improvements in the quality of instruction and students' learning at the district level.

Case 2: Using Practical Measure Data to Determine If a Change in a Support for Teachers' Learning Is an Improvement

We now turn to a case of using these practical measures to assess whether a change in a support for teachers' learning results in improvement in instruction. To illustrate this case, we draw on how District I mathematics specialists integrated the classroom practical measures in a Curriculum Guide Writing Initiative.[35] Prior to this initiative, middle school mathematics teachers in District I were expected to use a freely available online curriculum, but they were given little guidance regarding which aspects of the lessons to prioritize and how. District mathematics specialists were concerned that most teachers were selecting tasks of low cognitive demand from the online curriculum, thereby limiting students' opportunities to develop conceptual understanding and procedural fluency. District mathematics specialists also expressed equity concerns; without district guidance, it was likely that the quality of instruction varied widely across classrooms, and very likely in ways that furthered inequities in students' learning opportunities.

In response, the district undertook a Curriculum Guide Writing Initiative, which is summarized in figure 3.4. District mathematics specialists recruited accomplished middle-school mathematics teachers to serve as curriculum guide writers. Writers worked with the district mathematics specialists for a day every four to six weeks to draft new units and to revise previously developed units. Another group of teachers was recruited to

Figure 3.4 Curriculum Guide Writing Initiative

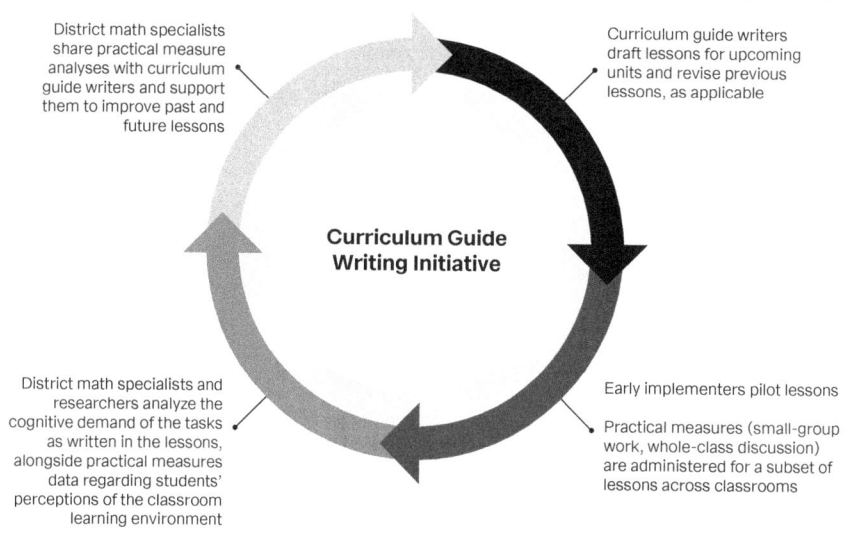

be "early implementers." They were expected to pilot the newly drafted units and to provide feedback to the writers about the materials. In addition, early implementers administered either the small-group work or the whole-class discussion practical measures for a subset of lessons within an instructional unit.[36]

District mathematics specialists and researchers then met to review an assessment of the cognitive demand of the tasks as written in each of the lessons, based on the rubric described earlier, and analyze students' survey responses, aggregated across classrooms for specific lessons in an instructional unit, to gain insight into both the cognitive demand of the tasks as implemented and into students' learning opportunities in small-group work and whole-class discussions in those lessons. In addition, they investigated the relationship between the cognitive demand of a task as written and students' learning opportunities in the lesson as implemented, by looking at the assessment of the cognitive demand of a task as written alongside survey data for specific lessons.

To illustrate how practical measure data was used in this process, figure 3.5 shows students' responses to one whole-class discussion survey

Figure 3.5 Sample practical measure data shared with district mathematics specialists and curriculum guide writers

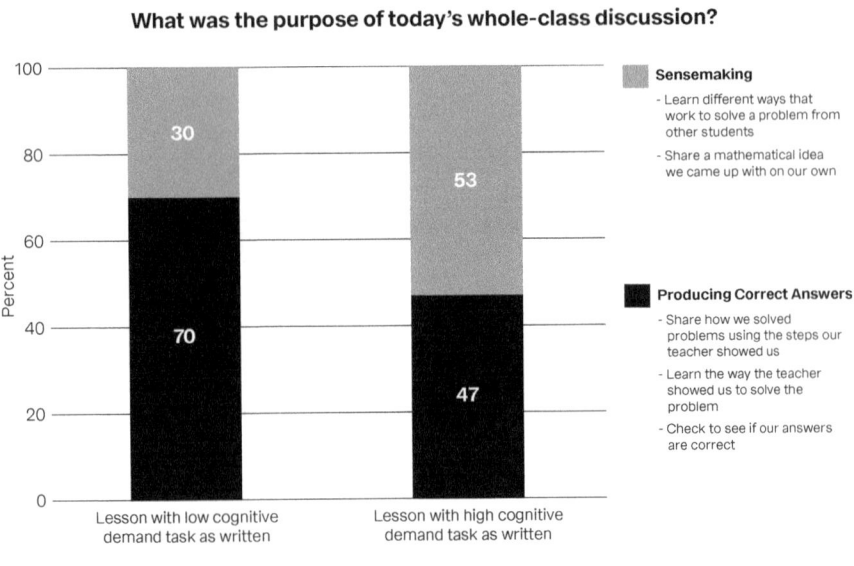

item, "What was the purpose of today's whole-class discussion?" for two different lessons within a unit, aggregated across three seventh-grade classrooms. The bar chart on the left corresponds to a seventh-grade lesson in which the task as written in the curriculum writing guide was judged to be of low cognitive demand, whereas the bar chart on the right corresponds to a seventh-grade lesson in which the task as written was judged to be of high cognitive demand. In the lesson organized around a task of low cognitive demand as written, less than one third of the sixty-two seventh graders' responses suggest that the purpose of the whole-class discussion was to engage in sensemaking. However, in the lesson organized around a task of high cognitive demand as written, more than half of the sixty seventh graders responded that the purpose of the whole-class discussion was to engage in sensemaking. Analyses like this illustrated that the cognitive demand of the instructional tasks as written influenced students' learning opportunities in the whole-class discussion phase of a given lesson. Of course, there were variations in individual teachers' implementation of tasks of high cognitive demand, and thus in students' survey responses at the classroom level. Overall, however, the pattern illustrated in figure 3.5 was evident across several lessons and grade levels.

Informed by the results of analyses such as that shown in figure 3.5, the district mathematics specialists met with the writers and used findings like these to support the writers in understanding how students' learning opportunities in whole-class discussions were influenced by the cognitive demand of tasks as written. The district mathematics specialists pressed and supported the writers to increase the cognitive demand of the tasks as written in the lessons. In addition, on the basis of student survey results indicating that there were some variations in how teachers implemented tasks of high cognitive demand, the district mathematics specialists also pressed the writers to provide more explicit guidance for teachers with regard to planning for small-group work and whole-class discussions (e.g., identification of key ideas to focus on in discussions). The writers then drafted new lessons and revised the previous lessons. In total, the district mathematics specialists, curriculum guide writers, and researchers engaged in the cycle (shown in figure 3.4) four times.

A subsequent analysis of the cognitive demand of the tasks as written in lessons indicated that the cognitive demand of the written lessons improved in all three grade levels during the initiative. For example, figure 3.6 shows the findings of an analysis of the cognitive demand of the tasks as written in sixth-grade lessons and units. The y-axis of each of the bar charts indicates the level of cognitive demand of the main task as written in a lesson. A score of 1 or 2 indicates that the cognitive demand of the main task as written was low, and a score of 3 or 4 indicates that the cognitive demand of the main task as written was high. As figure 3.6 shows, the cognitive demand of the tasks as written in the first half of Sixth-Grade Unit 1 (lessons 1–12) was generally low. The curriculum guide writers received feedback after they had written the first half of Unit 1 for each grade level. With support and pressure from the district mathematics specialists, the writers increased the cognitive demand of the tasks as written in later lessons in this unit (lessons 13–27) and in

Figure 3.6 Improvement in cognitive demand of the main tasks of lessons as written, by unit

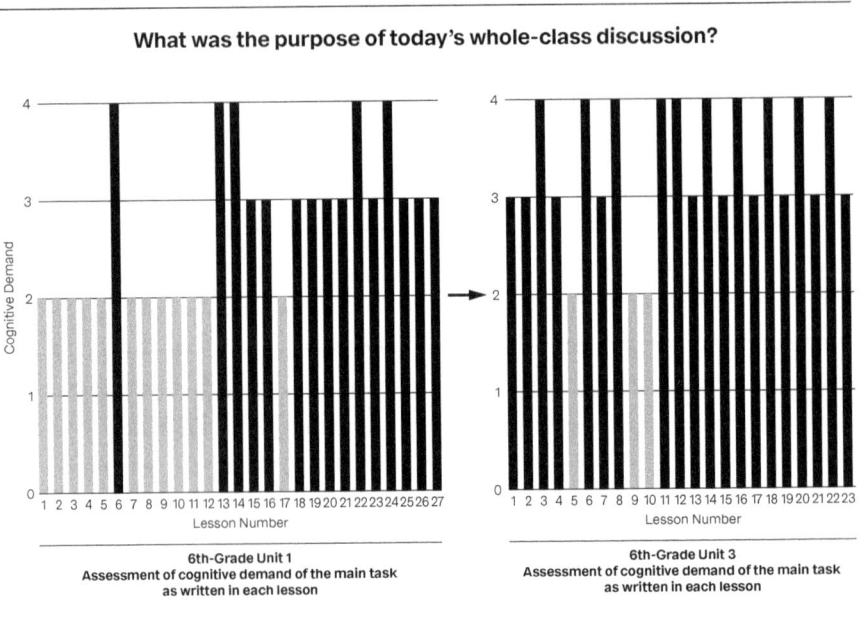

subsequent units, as shown by the cognitive demand of the tasks as written in Unit 3.

More generally, this curriculum guide writing example serves to highlight how these classroom practical measures can enable practitioners to assess whether a change in a support for teachers' learning leads to improvements in instruction. In addition, it illustrates how educators, like district mathematics specialists, who often do not work directly with teachers in their classrooms, may use the practical measure data to gain insight into instructional practice across classrooms, grade levels, and schools, in relation to a district-level professional development initiative.

Enhancing the Effectiveness of Support for Teachers' Learning

The primary rationale for developing practical measures proposed in the literature is that they can provide practitioners with a means of determining whether a change is an improvement, and whether a change effort is producing the intended improvements across classrooms or schools.[37] As we have illustrated, the practical measures served this purpose effectively when they were integrated into a coaching initiative and into a curriculum writing initiative. However, we also found that coaches' use of the practical measures can further enhance their effectiveness in supporting teachers' learning by enabling them to facilitate debrief conversations that are more productive than would have been the case otherwise.

As background, debrief conversations, in which a coach and teacher analyze the enactment of a lesson that they planned together, typically focus almost exclusively on the teacher's instruction. However, the findings of two recent studies indicate that in productive debriefs, the coach and teacher first analyze students' reasoning to agree on whether they attained the learning goals for the lesson, and only then analyze the instruction, not as an end in itself but to understand why the students learned what they actually learned.[38] A major goal of the professional development for coaches that we codesigned with our district colleagues, therefore, was to support coaches' facilitation of debrief conversations in which they and their partner teachers connected student learning goals, students' reasoning, and instruction in this manner. A follow-up analysis indicates that the professional development was reasonably successful, as most of the coaches did begin to support the teachers with whom they worked in making these connections.[39] This analysis also revealed that once this development had occurred, the coaches' use of the practical measures could enhance their facilitation of debriefing conversations in three significant ways beyond determining whether an instructional change was an improvement.

The first of these enhancements was that the use of the data from practical measures supported coaches and teachers in resolving disagreements that arose as they analyzed the focal lesson. In the absence of these measures, they could collect students' work to document their learning during the lesson but typically have no tangible evidence of the quality of instruction. They therefore have to depend on their recollections, which often differ and are sometimes in conflict, and also on any notes that the coaches made. It was therefore noteworthy that the coaches with whom we worked spontaneously spoke of students' survey responses as providing what they characterized as a third, independent, and much-valued perspective on the lesson in addition to their own and their partner teacher's perspectives. Coaches viewed this as a significant advantage, as they no longer had to pit their recollections against those of the teacher but could instead take the students' perspective as a primary point of reference. Thus, they considered it advantageous to use the practical measures precisely because the measures enabled them to bring the students' voice to the fore.

The second enhancement of debriefing conversations was that coaches' and teachers' use of the practical measures could support them in developing more powerful explanations of how instruction influenced students' learning than otherwise would have been the case. This was primarily because the measures oriented them to focus on those aspects of the classroom learning environment that prior research indicates matter for students' learning but that might have otherwise been unnoticed by them. Thus, in the previous example, which illustrates how coaches and teachers can use the practical measures to determine whether an instructional change is an improvement, the extent to which the students understood each other's explanations might well have been invisible to the coach and teacher in question had they not administered the whole-class discussion survey. Most of the other items on the whole-class discussion survey (see table 3.1) and most of the items on the other two student surveys also focus on aspects of the classroom learning environment that are not directly observable and thus might well be invisible to teachers and to less experienced coaches unless they administered one of the surveys. The practical measures, therefore, served a signaling function for both teachers and coaches by emphasizing the importance of those aspects of the classroom learning environment on which the survey items focused. This observation suggests that the practical measures, therefore, might be an important support for coaches' as well as teachers' learning, although further research will be needed to investigate this conjecture.

The third enhancement of debriefing conversations was that the use of the measures could support coaches and their partner teachers in identifying what we term *productive instructional improvement goals*. Our criteria for productive goals are that they are a feasible next step in individual teachers' learning, given their current knowledge and practices, and attaining the goals is likely to result in immediate improvements in students' learning.[40] This third enhancement builds directly on the second because when coaches and their partner teachers analyze students' survey responses to explain their actual learning in a lesson, they identify not only instructional strengths, but also instructional weaknesses that delimit students' learning opportunities (e.g., students have trouble understanding others' explanations). In suggesting an instructional change that might address an identified weakness, coaches and teachers reframe the weakness as an improvement goal (e.g., enable students to understand others' explanations) and propose testable conjectures about how they might attain those goals (i.e., potential change ideas). Crucially, improvement goals formulated in this way are productive because attaining them is likely to result in immediate improvements in students' learning.

It is important to emphasize that practical measures are not silver bullets. The use of practical measures will not inevitably enhance coaches' effectiveness beyond enabling them to determine whether a change is an improvement. Instead, the extent to which the use of the practical measure enhances coaches' effectiveness depends on how coaches facilitate teachers' analyses of and use of practical measures data. More specifically, it is essential that coaches press their partner teachers to relate students' survey responses to their instruction.[41] For example, if a majority of the students indicate that they have trouble understanding other students' explanations, the coach might ask the teacher, "Why do you think most of the students chose that response?" In asking this question, the coach supports the teacher to consider their crucial role in shaping the classroom learning environment as the students experienced it, and thus to connect aspects of their instruction (e.g., the teacher rephrases students' explanations) to students' learning opportunities (e.g., the extent to which students understand others' explanations). It is only when coaches support teachers in making this connection that they complete the links between the teacher's instruction and students' learning, as shown in figure 3.7.

Figure 3.7 Practical measures data as a bridge between students' learning and the teacher's instruction

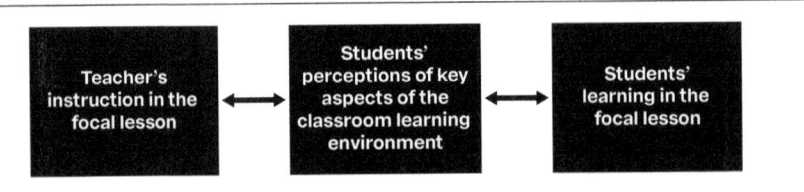

In doing so, they unlock the full potential of the practical measures by making the connection between the partner teacher's instruction and students' learning visible, and thus open to scrutiny.

We strongly suspect that the three ways in which the use of the practical measures can enhance coaches' effectiveness also apply to two other types of support for teachers' learning: professional development sessions and teacher collaborative meetings. As we have noted, high-quality coaching supports teachers to connect student learning goals, students' reasoning, and instruction. Discussions in teacher collaborative meetings and professional development sessions that have the potential to support substantial teacher learning also support teachers in making these connections.[42] It is therefore plausible to suggest that integrating the practical measures into these other types of support for teachers' learning might be similarly beneficial, although additional research is needed to investigate whether this actually is the case.

Enhancing the Coherence of Instructional Improvement Efforts

Thus far, we have discussed two types of contributions that practical measures of the classroom learning environment can make to instructional improvement efforts. Here, we draw on our partner districts' experiences in using the measures to suggest a third contribution. Specifically, we anticipate that the use of the measures by practitioners at different levels of the system (teachers, coaches, and district mathematics specialists) can enhance the coherence of instructional improvement efforts at scale by orienting them all to focus on improving the same key aspects of classroom learning environments, aspects that prior research findings indicate matter for students' learning. Research on instructional improvement at scale has consistently demonstrated the importance of what Fred Newmann and colleagues referred to as "instructional program coherence" in creating supportive conditions for teachers' work and advancing student learning.[43] Instructional program coherence is characterized by a set of coordinated, long-term instructional improvement strategies (e.g., curriculum materials, coaching) that span different role groups (e.g., teachers, coaches, school leaders) and that are oriented by a common vision of high-quality instruction. In schools and systems marked by strong instructional coherence, educators at various levels of the system coordinate their efforts, so, for example, what school leaders hold teachers accountable for is aligned with the instructional materials that teachers are using and with the support provided for them to improve their instruction. Our observations indicate that the use of the practical measures might enhance the coherence of improvement efforts, even though different groups of practitioners pursue improvement goals that are specific to their role within the system (teachers in supporting their students' learning, coaches in supporting teachers in a school or across several schools, and district mathematics specialists in supporting the development of capacity for instructional improvement across schools). Here, we clarify the rationale for this conjecture by drawing on the two cases introduced thus far in this chapter.

In the coaching initiative described here, the coaches integrated the use of the student surveys into the one-on-one coaching cycles that they conducted with teachers. The district mathematics specialists, who supported the coaches, might then review students' responses aggregated across classrooms at regular points in time to assess whether the professional development that they are providing to coaches is having the intended impact on classroom instruction, and also to identify additional areas of instructional weakness. Their review of the resulting data might then lead the specialists to revise their plans for upcoming professional development sessions. In this scenario, the specialists would use the same measures to assess whether changes in the professional development were improvements as the coaches and their partner teachers would use to assess whether instructional changes were improvements. The specialists' work with coaches and the coaches' work with teachers would be tightly coordinated and oriented to pursue complementary improvement goals that focus on the same key aspects of classroom learning environments that research indicates matter for students' learning.

Our second illustration focuses on the Curriculum Guide Writing Initiative described earlier. Once the guides had been developed, a next step was for district mathematics specialists to ensure that all teachers were provided with support to improve their enactment of the cognitively demanding tasks in their classrooms. These supports included regularly scheduled grade-level teacher collaborative meetings that were facilitated by coaches. The coaches might integrate the student surveys into this work, with the participating teachers administering one or more of the surveys in specific lessons that they had planned together. The coaches could then review these data to target the support that they provided in collaborative meetings regarding planning upcoming lessons. And district mathematics specialists could review students' responses aggregated by grade level for specific lessons to inform their support of the coaches' facilitation of the collaborative meetings. In addition, district mathematics specialists could analyze the resulting data to identify patterns in students' responses regarding particular lessons, with the intent of then continuing to revise the lessons in the curriculum guide.

In both these illustrations, the measures themselves (e.g., the items) and the resulting data might serve as *boundary objects* that support coherent work by practitioners at different levels of a system.[44] Although there are differences in the purposes for which users at different levels of the system would analyze students' responses, the use of the common measures can serve to coordinate and align the focus of the various types of support provided to teachers and coaches, and with respect to a common vision of instruction.

Routines of Use and Representations of Data

Before turning to considerations of validity, we highlight two important issues that need to be addressed if practical measures are to contribute to instructional improvement efforts. The first issue concerns the design and maintenance of routines for data collection, analysis, and use that can be integrated into users' current practices relatively seamlessly; and the second concerns the development of visual representations of the resulting data that enable users to address the questions they want to ask of the data.

A defining characteristic of practical measures is that they can be easily integrated into practitioners' current practices. In the case of our classroom measures, we found it productive to work closely with colleagues in each district to design and implement routines for administering the surveys and collecting the students' responses. These routines varied across districts, depending on their technological resources, with the survey being delivered electronically in some districts and through paper and pencil in others.

It is also important to design routines for analyzing the data and for sharing the findings in ways that support the ongoing improvement efforts. As we have indicated, we consider it essential that these analysis routines are integrated into support for teachers' learning.[45] For example, we have illustrated how the analysis of students' responses to the whole-class discussion survey was integrated into the debrief phase of one-on-one coaching cycles. The resulting data analysis routine involved coaches and their partner teachers first analyzing students' work to assess what the students had learned in the focal lesson, and only then analyzing students' survey responses to understand why students had learned what they had actually learned. In the final step of this routine, the results of this latter analysis informed coaches' and teachers' identification of instructional improvement goals that oriented all phases of the next coaching cycle.

In the case of the Curriculum Guide Writing Initiative, district mathematics specialists shared the findings of their analyses of practical measures data with the writers in their regular work sessions. The data analysis routine involved district mathematics specialists and curriculum guide writers (by grade-level team) analyzing both students' responses to the whole-class discussion surveys for specific lessons and the cognitive demand of the tasks as written in those lessons. Based on the findings of this analysis, the specialists pressed the curriculum guide writers to consider how they might increase the cognitive demand of tasks as written in an instructional unit and how they might insert questions in particular lessons to help teachers focus whole-class discussions on key mathematical ideas.

Both examples illustrate the importance of integrating routines for collecting and analyzing practical measure data into ongoing instructional improvement routines, rather than treating the use of practical measure as a separate activity. In fact, in both the coaching and curriculum guide writing examples, the instructional improvement efforts were designed before leaders began using the practical measures. Furthermore, in both cases, district mathematics specialists delayed the introduction of the practical measures until their use could enhance the ongoing instructional improvement efforts. For example, in the coaching initiative, the practical measures were not introduced until the fourth of eight professional development sessions, which focused on facilitating debrief conversations, the phase of the coaching cycle in which teachers and coaches analyze practical measures data. Similarly, in the Curriculum Guide Writing Initiative, district mathematics specialists did not introduce the practical measure data to the writers until after the first sets of lessons had been drafted and the writers were eager to receive feedback on the lessons. Based on our experiences, we cannot underscore strongly enough that considering when and how to introduce practical measurement in an instructional improvement initiative is a critical step in supporting productive use of the resulting data.

The design of visual representations of the resulting data merit as much care as the design of the routines of use themselves. Intentionally designed representations can enable practitioners to conduct authentic analyses in which they examine data to address questions that are consequential for their instructional improvement work without statistical sophistication being the price of entry.[46] Members of the research team with expertise in data visualization partnered with teachers, coaches, and district mathematics specialists in each of the partner districts to codesign an online platform on which the students' survey responses can be viewed and analyzed, and to develop visualizations that would help them make informed decisions that are relevant to their improvement initiatives and purposes for analyzing students' survey responses.[47]

To design productive representations, it was important to understand both the specific theory of improvement in a given effort (e.g., coaching, curriculum guide writing) and the intended users' current practices, as this enabled the research team to anticipate the types of questions that different groups of users would likely want to address by analyzing the data. For example, in the case of the coaching initiative, it was important that coaches could compare students' responses to particular survey items over time to determine whether a change in teacher's instruction was an improvement at the individual classroom level (see figure 3.3). The data representation shown in figure 3.3 reflects many design decisions jointly made between district partners and the research and design team. For instance, we decided on stacked bar chart representations rather than other options, such as a line graph that plotted the frequency for a preferred answer (in the case of figure 3.3, the preferred answer would be the proportion of students who answered "No"). This decision was informed by our codesign sessions with partners, in which they indicated that it would be problematic if the representations focused primarily on the desired student responses as this might lead to gaming those responses. Instead, our partners suggested that coaches and teachers would be more likely to discuss and attempt to explain students' responses if those responses were represented as stacked bar charts.

In the Curriculum Guide Writing Initiative, district mathematics specialists and curriculum guide writers wanted to investigate the relationship between the cognitive demand of instructional tasks as written and students' learning opportunities. They therefore needed representations of students' survey responses for specific lessons that were aggregated across classrooms by grade level, as well as representations that enabled them to compare students' responses to particular survey questions for lessons in which the cognitive demand of the tasks as written differed (see figure 3.5). These two examples illustrate how seemingly small decisions about data representations (e.g., stacked bar charts rather than a line graph) matter, and the value of soliciting input from intended users to inform the design of data visualizations that lead to productive conversations and sensemaking.[48]

CONSIDERATIONS OF VALIDITY

In the context of our work, we have conceptualized the validity of the classroom measures as comprising two aspects. The first, *validity-for-use* of a practical measure, concerns whether a practical measure actually assesses what it was designed to assess and is thus appropriate for its intended uses. For example, the validity-for-use of the classroom measures discussed here concerns whether they actually measure those key aspects of the classroom learning environment that are of interest and can be used to determine whether an instructional change is an improvement. The second, the *validity-in-use* of a practical measure, concerns whether specific *instances of using* a measure are appropriate, and thus whether practitioners, given appropriate skill and processes, can act on the resulting data with confidence. As proposed by several measurement scholars, including Edward Haertel, Michael Kane, and Pamela Moss, determining whether a particular instance of use is valid needs to take account of the purpose for which the measure was used, the context in which it was used, and the user's current knowledge, perspectives, and practices.[49]

Validity-for-Use

The *validity-for-use* of a practical measure is about whether it assesses what it claims to assess.[50] For example, the purpose of the whole-class discussion measure is to assess key aspects of the classroom learning environment that prior research links to student learning. Evidence for validity-for-use of the whole-class discussion measure includes that students' responses predict whether their participation in a specific whole-class discussion supported them in deepening their understanding of key mathematical ideas. The cycles of development and revision described previously (see figure 3.1) were essential to establishing the evidence of the validity-for-use of the whole-class discussion measure and of the other two survey measures. As we have described, we drew on existing research that links key aspects of the classroom learning environment to students' learning to determine what the measure should assess. Having identified these critical foci, it was imperative that the items communicate to students, that the intended users (e.g., teachers, coaches, district mathematics specialists) view the aspects of the classroom learning environment on which the items focus as being relevant to their instructional improvement efforts, and that students' responses to the items, aggregated at the classroom level, reflected differences in the quality of discussions, and thus students' opportunities to learn mathematics. Repeated development cycles in which we tested and revised items were therefore essential to establish the validity-for-use of the measure. We have also found it essential to continue to assess the validity-for-use of the measures in contexts beyond the initial development sites by comparing researchers' observations of classroom instruction at new sites with students' survey responses aggregated at the classroom level to check that they reflect students' learning opportunities.

Validity-in-Use

From a validity-in-use perspective, a practical measure can be used appropriately for some purposes but not others, in some contexts but not others, and by some users but not others.[51] This perspective is not unlike measurement and assessment scholars' efforts to investigate the consequences of using measures as an important aspect of validity.[52] Based on our investigations of the use of the classroom measures in our partner districts, we have identified appropriate (and inappropriate) purposes for using the measures, as well as key aspects of contexts and of users' knowledge and perspectives that influence whether they are likely to act reasonably in response to the resulting data.

Appropriate Purposes and Uses

As described by Takahashi and Norman in chapter 2 of this book, the purpose of practical measures is to support educators' engagement in *improvement*; practical measures are never intended to be used for accountability purposes. In this regard, the practical measures of the classroom learning environment are designed to be used in efforts to improve the quality of mathematics instruction, and thus students' learning. It would be completely inappropriate to use these practical measures to evaluate the quality of instruction, teachers, or schools for accountability purposes. If the measures are used erroneously for accountability purposes, teachers may well feel pressure to suggest to students that they respond to survey items in specific ways, thereby compromising the validity of the data for any purpose. In both the coaching and the curriculum guide writing initiatives, the students' survey responses were used to assess users' current practices and to set improvement goals. The explicit establishment of an improvement frame was essential and nontrivial in both cases, especially given the prevalence of using data for accountability purposes in many districts, including our partner districts. While practitioners might use practical measures for purposes beyond those originally envisioned, those who design practical measures have a responsibility to describe the intended purposes.[53]

Key Aspects of School and District Contexts

A second critical element of validity-in-use concerns aspects of school and district context that enable a measure to be used for the purposes of improvement. Failure to attend to context will likely result in practical measures being used in an ineffective or possibly even a harmful manner. For example, we recommend using our classroom measures only in schools and districts that are implementing improvement initiatives that include the provision of supports for teachers' development of ambitious and equitable instructional practices. Relevant aspects of school and district contexts therefore include that there is a shared understanding of what counts as high-quality mathematics teaching (and thus what counts as improvement in teachers' practice), and teachers are provided with ongoing support to improve the quality of their instruction. As we have indicated, while some teachers may find students' survey responses useful on their own, it is essential for most teachers that the analysis of the resulting data is integrated into ongoing coaching, teacher collaborative meetings, or other professional learning initiatives. It is also important that the school or district has the capacity to respond to practical measures data by improving the quality of supports for teachers. The classroom measures will be most helpful, therefore, when there are district- and/or school-level leaders who have expertise in supporting mathematics teachers' learning and the time to plan and facilitate professional learning. In addition, it is critical that trusting relationships are established in these professional learning settings, such that teachers feel comfortable treating the review of students' responses as an opportunity to raise genuine questions about instruction, as opposed to an evaluation of their current instructional practices. We have also found it is essential that students feel their perceptions are valued. Although they are rare, we have witnessed cases in which students did not perceive that their teachers were genuinely interested in their perspectives and therefore did not provide truthful responses on the survey.

Key Aspects of Users' Perspectives

Another element of the validity-in-use of the practical measures concerns teachers' current perspectives on their students. An investigation of teachers' interpretations of their students' survey responses found that their interpretations are strongly influenced by their perspectives on their students' current mathematical capabilities.[54] In particular, teachers who contend that some or all of their students are incapable of participating in and learning from ambitious mathematics instruction typically explain students' survey responses in terms of limitations in the students rather than limitations in their current instructional practices, and thus do not view students' responses as providing trustworthy or relevant feedback on their instruction. Unfortunately, the findings of a prior study indicate that in the absence of support, a significant majority of mathematics teachers in districts serving large numbers of students of color, students for whom English is not their first language, and/or students living in poverty will likely interpret students' practical measures responses in this way.[55]

Based on these findings, we suggest that the measures are best used by teachers who view their students as capable of engaging in the intended forms of practice, are pursuing genuine questions about teaching, and see value in learning about students' perspectives. However, coaches have reported that examining students' responses with teachers in the debrief phase of coaching cycles has provided them with insight into teachers' perspectives on their students' capabilities—perspectives that they doubt the teachers would have discussed as explicitly had they not examined the students' responses together. The coaches also reported that these insights prompted them to consider how they might support teachers to develop more productive views of their students' capabilities. Consistent with the coaches' insights, we contend that it is critical for professional development leaders to prioritize supporting teachers' development of more productive views of their students' mathematical capabilities, especially in districts serving large numbers of students from historically marginalized communities.

CONCLUSION

Supporting sustained improvements in the quality of mathematics teaching and learning at some level of scale necessarily requires the establishment of high-quality support for teachers' learning.[56] At present, educators at various levels of the system have little means of gaining insight into what is happening between teachers and students in mathematics classrooms, what is happening between teachers and facilitators in professional learning contexts, and whether changes introduced in either classrooms or professional learning contexts lead to the intended improvements. System leaders' use of practical measures can enable them to gain insights that can, in turn, inform their decisions about how to improve the support for teachers' learning, and thus teaching and students' learning.

In this chapter, we have illustrated how the classroom measures that we have developed provide actionable feedback about high-leverage aspects of mathematics instruction. We have illustrated three ways in which they can contribute to instructional improvement efforts. First, the measures enable educators to determine if an instructional change is an improvement. Second, when the measures are integrated into supports for teachers' learning (e.g., a coaching cycle), they can enhance the quality of that support. Third, we have conjectured that use of the measures by practitioners at different levels of the system who are involved in an instructional improvement effort can enhance the coherence of that improvement effort.

We have argued that these practical measures, which can be used to assess teachers' progress in developing ambitious and equitable instructional practices, should be integrated into supports for teachers' learning. However, we also see value in other types of practical measures that focus on whether an action occurred rather than on the quality of the action. For example, it could be useful for coaches and district mathematics specialists to have a practical measure of the proportion of teachers who select and use cognitively demanding tasks as a basis for their instruction, as this information would help them understand the extent to which this aspect of ambitious instruction has become routine and widespread. It could also be valuable to have practical measures that focus on time allocation, for example, the amount of time that teachers devote to the various phases of lessons (e.g., launching cognitively demanding tasks, small-group or individual work, whole-class discussion). We anticipate that, in some cases, teachers might be able to interpret and act productively on data from these types of measures without substantial professional learning support.

In this chapter, we have focused on practical measures of key aspects of the classroom learning environment. However, our long-term goal is to develop a *system* of practical measures, routines, and representations that, in addition to the classroom measures, include practical measures of *teachers' perceptions of aspects of the professional development learning environments* that prior research has linked to teachers' learning. We have developed a measure specific to teacher collaborative meetings, and are currently refining measures specific to one-on-one coaching cycles. We are hopeful that, as with the classroom measures, the professional development measures will allow users (e.g., coaches, professional development facilitators, and district mathematics specialists) to determine whether a change in their facilitation practice is an improvement, thereby contributing to the improvement of the support for teachers' learning. We also hypothesize that most coaches and facilitators will likely need support in interpreting and responding productively to the data. Further, we anticipate that the professional development measures will be especially useful to those people who are charged with supporting the learning of coaches and professional development facilitators, especially district mathematics specialists. For example, a repeated assessment of the quality of coaching cycles or of teacher collaborative meetings would allow district mathematics specialists to make informed decisions about how to target their support for coaches' and facilitators' learning, and might also enhance the support that they provide beyond determining whether a change in coaches' or facilitators' practices is an improvement.

As a final observation, we anticipate that a system of practical measures that assesses key aspects of both classroom learning environments and professional development learning environments will enable district leaders and researchers to distinguish between an inadequate theory of instructional improvement and the inadequate implementation of a theory. A robust theory of instructional improvement specifies clear goals for students' learning and a vision of high-quality instruction, and it also proposes specific forms of support for teachers' learning, together with a rationale for why it is reasonable to expect that those supports will enable teachers to improve their instruction, and thus their students' learning. On those occasions when system leaders detect a lack of improvement in students' learning, it is typically difficult for them to determine whether this disappointing outcome stems from inadequacies in their theory of improvement or from challenges in implementing the theory. However, a system of practical measures of the type that we envision would enable them to assess whether supports for teachers' learning were implemented adequately (measures of key aspects of professional development learning environments), and if they were, whether they enabled teachers to make the intended improvements in their instructional practices (measures of key aspects of classroom learning environments). As part of this analysis, systems leaders might also investigate variations in implementation across classrooms, grade levels, and schools, and might revise or elaborate their existing theory of improvement based on their findings.

We conclude this chapter by highlighting how use of the measures of the classroom learning environment can raise issues of equity that otherwise might go unnoticed. First, the three surveys assess the quality of instruction by soliciting students' perceptions of key aspects of the classroom learning environment, thereby giving students a voice in decisions about how their teachers might change their instructional practices to better support their learning. Second, all three student surveys assess aspects of instruction that are directly relevant to the equitable distribution of students' learning opportunities. For example, the decision to assess the quality of teachers' task introductions or launches was motivated by a prior investigation finding that in the majority of 1,700 video-recorded mathematics lessons, many of the students would likely not be able to begin working productively on the instructional tasks, particularly students from traditionally underserved groups.[57] Third, as we have discussed in this chapter, the use of the measures can reveal important issues regarding teachers' perspectives of their students' current capabilities, both in terms of students' responses to specific items (e.g., the item that assesses whether students perceive that the teacher valued their mathematical ideas), and in terms of how teachers engage in the analysis of the resulting data. This goes right to the heart of one of the most persistent and difficult equity issues in education today. Finally, the classroom measures enable system leaders to identify what Anthony Bryk and colleagues term "unwanted variation" in teachers' instructional practices. As Bryk and colleagues observe, reducing such variation is essential in redressing inequities in the performance of educational systems.[58]

ACKNOWLEDGMENTS

The work described and the writing of this manuscript was supported by the Spencer Foundation's Research-Practice Partnership Program and the National Science Foundation (Nos. DRL-1620851, DRL-1620863, DRL-1621238, DRL-1911492). The opinions expressed do not necessarily reflect the views of either foundation. We are grateful to our many collaborators, which include researchers, teachers, coaches, and district mathematics specialists. See a full list of our collaborators at https://www.pmr2.org/team.

4

The National Writing Project's Using Sources Tool

A Practical Measure for Informing Instruction and Building a Shared Vision of Argument and Student Capacity

Linda D. Friedrich
Rachel Bear

The National Writing Project (NWP) is a national network of over 170 local Writing Project sites. These Writing Project sites are housed at college campuses across the nation and partner with local school districts to provide professional development to teachers in their region. Every year since NWP was founded in 1974, Writing Project leaders have led programs that focus on developing teacher leadership capacities to advance the teaching of writing. In this chapter, we describe the role of practical measurement in one NWP improvement initiative: the College, Career, and Community Writers Program (C3WP), which aims to support teachers in teaching source-based argument writing. Three independent evaluations have found C3WP to be effective in supporting changes in teachers' practice and students' writing outcomes.

The first two cases in this volume describe practical measures that (1) operationalize a working theory of improvement; (2) are specific to the work processes that are the object of change; (3) have formative value in signaling subsequent actions that are useful to consider; (4) are framed in language that is meaningful to those engaged in the work; (5) produce data that are actionable and accessible in a timely manner; (6) are administered in a manner that minimizes burden and unwanted disruption to routines and processes; and (7) are embedded in social routines that secure the trust and openness necessary to sustain meaningful improvement efforts. Over the past eight years, the NWP has developed and expanded the use of one such practical measure as part of its C3WP: the Using Sources Tool (UST), which is designed to be used by teachers as part of C3WP professional development. The primary purpose of the UST is to provide teachers with a practical tool for analyzing their students' writing in ways that inform and support improvements in their teaching practices around source-based argument writing.

This chapter provides a brief background on C3WP, including a description of the UST and its development. It then outlines how C3WP's theory of improvement in action relies on collaborative professional learning to integrate this practical measure with a curated set of high-quality, teacher-developed instructional resources. The chapter concludes with an analysis of validity considerations for the UST and reflections on C3WP's potential contribution to the achievement of more equitable writing outcomes.

C3WP'S INITIAL IMPROVEMENT PROBLEM AND THEORY OF ACTION FOR IMPROVEMENT

In 2012, NWP launched the C3WP in response to the emphasis on argument writing of the Common Core Standards. Those standards identify the ability to craft arguments as a critical skill that young people need to develop for success in college and in their careers: "While all three text types, [argument, narrative, and informative/explanatory], are important, the Standards put particular emphasis on students' ability to write sound arguments on substantive topics and issues, as this ability is critical to college and career readiness."[1] It is important to note that the Common Core defines a sound argument as one that "convinces the audience because of the perceived merit and reasonableness of the claims and proofs offered rather than either the emotions the writing evokes in the audience or the character or credentials of the writer."[2] Throughout the Standards' Appendices and in the Standards themselves, there is a clear emphasis on students using evidence thoughtfully and purposefully to support their claims.

The Common Core's rigorous expectations for teaching argument writing entered a field in which there was generally little focus on teaching writing at all.[3] Teachers reported that their preparation programs left them underprepared to teach writing.[4] In 2016, a RAND Corporation panel of American teachers revealed that 41 percent believed that they would benefit from professional learning focused on "Engaging students in writing about complex topics in [their] subject area."[5]

NWP responded to this documented need as an improvement problem by mobilizing twelve local Writing Project sites across the nation to provide high-quality professional development that focused on teaching argument and that was facilitated by expert teachers of writing. Our initial theory of action for improvement (figure 4.1) emphasized key dimensions of professional learning associated with improvements in teachers' practices and students' learning: intensity, duration, a critical mass of

Figure 4.1 Initial theory of action for improving the writing of argument

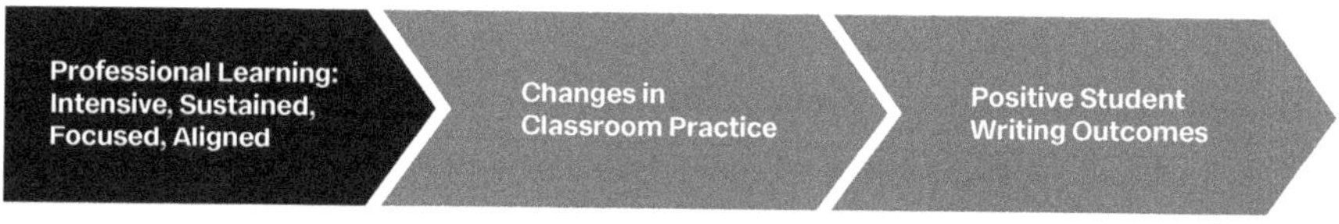

Professional Learning: Intensive, Sustained, Focused, Aligned → Changes in Classroom Practice → Positive Student Writing Outcomes

participation, clear content focus, and conscious effort to align professional learning goals with local priorities.[6] The Writing Project sites participating in the C3WP Networked Improvement Community offered 90+ hours of professional development (intensity) over two years (duration) to at least 80 percent of the seventh- to tenth-grade English language arts (ELA) teachers in each partner district (critical mass in the focus grades). Moreover, the local Writing Projects agreed to focus their professional development on argument writing (clear content focus) and to engage with districts in the ongoing coplanning and review of professional development implementation (alignment). C3WP professional development, which is locally adapted, includes the following elements: the introduction of C3WP instructional resources, professional reading and discussion about argument writing, analysis of students' argument writing, and coaching.

As the network hub, the NWP convened leaders from the participating local Writing Project sites and their partner districts to deepen knowledge about the teaching of argument writing, share expertise across the twelve Writing Project sites, and develop common agreements about the focus on and approach to professional development. NWP established a leadership team (comprised of experienced Writing Project teacher leaders and site directors) that co-led network convenings and served as thought partners to local Writing Project sites. The leadership team and the local Writing Project sites worked together as a networked improvement community to enact this initial theory of action for improvement. Very early, it became clear that efforts to implement this theory of action for improvement were not producing the expected shifts in teachers' instructional practices and students' learning. After the first semester of C3WP implementation, the independent evaluation team corroborated what the C3WP leadership team had already observed: that the C3WP network did not hold a common definition of argument, and only a few of the local Writing Project sites were focusing on argument in their professional development. Given these findings, it is not surprising that the evaluators also found little early evidence that teachers participating in C3WP professional learning were teaching argument.

BUILDING A SHARED VISION OF ARGUMENT AND REVISING OUR THEORY OF IMPROVEMENT: THE ROLE OF PRACTICAL MEASUREMENT

For students to learn to write high-quality arguments independently, the C3WP networked improvement community recognized that teachers would need to teach instructional cycles that have common key features, including the use of mentor texts (real-world examples of effective written arguments), integrated inquiry, close reading of nonfiction texts, and students making choices about what they write. Despite network-wide agreements that were established prior to the launch of professional learning, the early evaluation findings suggested that teachers were not making progress in learning to teach argument in this way. Therefore, the C3WP leadership team decided to create instructional resources that would exemplify a shared approach to teaching argument, as well as a formative assessment process that would engage local Writing Project sites and participating teachers in analyzing student writing in ways that were consistent with the goals of the program. These new tools were designed to be drivers of improvement and to become an integral part of professional learning. Adding these instructional resources and the formative assessment process expanded and refined the theory of improvement (figure 4.2).

C3WP's Approach to Teaching Argument Writing

C3WP's refined approach to argument writing focuses on engaging students in reading and learning from a variety of nonfiction texts that explore a range of perspectives as they form their own views of authentic, contemporary issues (e.g., widespread use of facial recognition technology, police use of force, social media). In many ways, Joseph Harris's *Rewriting: How to Do Things with Texts* provided a foundation for C3WP's definition of argument writing.[7] Harris frames academic writing as a conversation among sources, and thus between different perspectives. Rather than adopting a point-counterpoint view of argument, he emphasizes that varied sources often hold shades of agreement and difference. Harris makes

Figure 4.2 Refined theory of action for improving the writing of argument

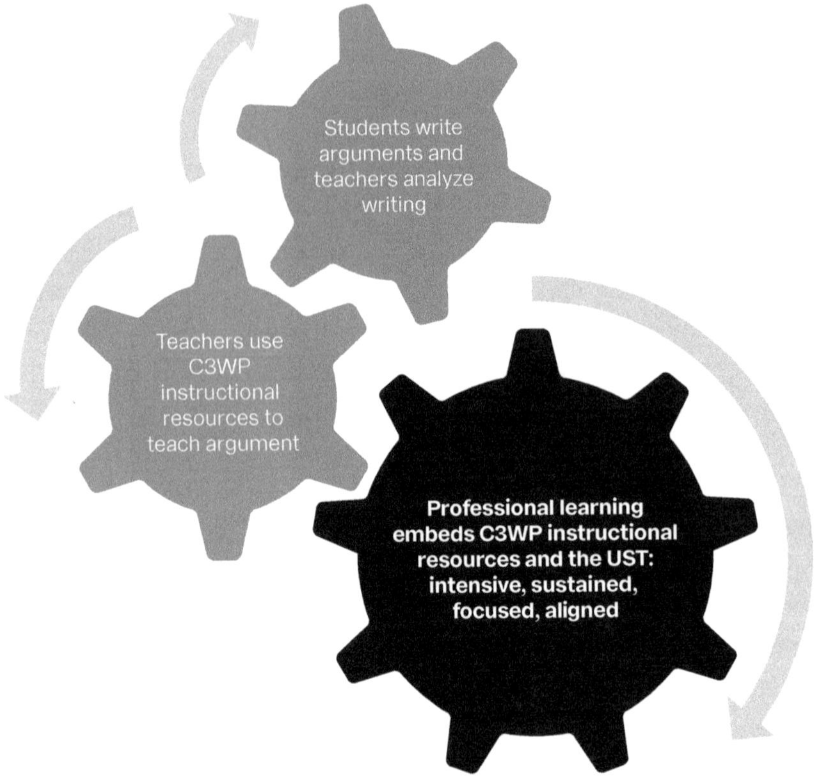

- Students write arguments and teachers analyze writing
- Teachers use C3WP instructional resources to teach argument
- Professional learning embeds C3WP instructional resources and the UST: intensive, sustained, focused, aligned

explicit the purposes for and the ways in which writers use other people's ideas and words as they form their own arguments. He refers to writers' engagement in doing this as "moves." The C3WP theory of improvement emphasizes students' careful selection, logical organization, and respectful commentary on source material in order to advance their own claims.

C3WP's approach to argument is unfamiliar to many teachers, given the rigid and formulaic view of argument that often dominates current practice. Traditional approaches to argument often involve students arguing for or against a claim or writing an essay by giving a claim, two paragraphs with supporting evidence, one paragraph that presents a counterargument, and a conclusion that repeats what has been said. In contrast,

C3WP emphasizes reading and learning about multiple perspectives on an issue before students form a claim, inviting students to recognize the nuances of arguments and to identify where there may be points of agreement among those who hold opposing views. C3WP further teaches students how to develop arguments that approximate the kinds of structures that exist in published arguments such as opinion and editorial pieces.

C3WP's Instructional Resources

Instructional resources developed by members of C3WP's leadership team figure prominently in the refined theory of improvement. These resources, the use of which is typically modeled during professional learning, offer concrete guidance to teachers about how they can teach argument writing in their classrooms. C3WP's instructional resources include the following:

- *Routine argument writing resources* that outline how teachers can provide students with regular, short (10–15 minutes) practice on specific skills (e.g., identifying an author's main point and best evidence) and emphasize brief, informal writing (e.g., writing a claim, practicing an argument move with a quote selected by a teacher).
- Resources that focus on *developing specific argument skills*, such as connecting evidence to claims, selecting and evaluating evidence, and coming to terms with opposing viewpoints. These resources typically take 3–10 instructional periods and allow students to fully develop an argument based on multiple sources.
- Resources that provide *opportunities for students to apply the argument skills* that they have learned independently, either while conducting independent research projects or during on-demand writing.

The resources outline instructional sequences that span multiple class periods and include the following components: becoming aware of both argument skills and the issue on which a resource focuses; becoming informed about an issue; joining the conversation (this is where students begin to develop their own position on an issue); making a plan for writing the argument; and drafting the argument. The resources also provide teachers with guidance about which skills students should have started to develop prior to engaging with the resources and which resources would help students revise their arguments. Each instructional resource includes one or more sets of texts (see figure 4.3 for an example) that support the skill being developed; each text set includes multiple nonfiction pieces that present a range of positions, information, and perspectives from which a student can draw to make and support a claim. For example, the texts in a unit on rating evidence present multiple types of evidence, including statistics, infographics, research studies, and individual opinions. The instructional resources describe how teachers should use the text sets to support students in developing their own arguments.

Figure 4.3 presents the core instructional sequence for the *Writing into the Day to Jumpstart Argument* instructional resource, along with one of the sample text sets from the resource. This resource is designed to support students in understanding C3WP's definition of argument as a conversation among sources and gives students the experience of joining that metaphorical conversation. While other C3WP instructional resources provide more elaborate instructions for teachers and additional scaffolding for note taking and writing, as well as emphasizing more challenging argument skills, this resource articulates the core principles of C3WP's approach to argument writing. Students are taught to read critically by identifying the author's main claim and strongest evidence (days 1 and 2) and are invited to think about what more they want or need to know about the issue. Students do not write about their own position on the focal issue until after reading (days 1 and 4). The texts provide a variety of perspectives on the focal issue of school start time and creating a graphic representation encourages students to think about the nuanced relationships among the perspectives, rather than merely developing a list of pros and cons (days 3 and 4).

The instructional processes and text set from the *Writing into the Day to Jumpstart Argument* resource (figure 4.3) illustrate how the resources support teachers in teaching writing while also exemplifying C3WP's values about argument writing. However, the instructional resources are also designed to be generative. As NWP developed and refined them over time, it articulated a set of design principles that allow teachers and local Writing Project sites to adapt the resources with integrity, thereby creating

Figure 4.3 Writing into the Day to Jumpstart Argument instructional sequence and sample text set

---

Sample Text Set: School Start Time
Three Shared Texts: These texts introduce the issue, relevant facts and data, and multiple perspectives that are part of the conversation.
- Text #1: News article that draws on research from the CDC and the American Academy of Pediatrics. Includes two infographics. Szabo, Liz. "Study: Most teens start school too early in morning to get enough sleep." *USA Today*. August 7, 2015.
- Text #2: News article that presents information from a recent study about the financial benefits of later start times and addresses counter arguments about the costs of changing. Includes a 2-minute video with highlights from the article. Ingraham, Christopher. "Letting teens sleep in would save the country roughly $9 billion a year." *The Washington Post*. September 1, 2017.
- Text #3: News article that acknowledges that later school start times are not always possible and offers some recommendations to help teens. Pannoni, Alexander. "How Teachers, Parents Can Help Sleepy Teens Stay Awake at School." *U.S. News and World Report*. September 28, 2015.

Becoming Aware
Day 1 (15 minutes):
During the normal "Writing into the Day" give students the following directions:
1. Instruct students to read Text #1 from your chosen text set.
2. Instruct students to underline or note in the margin the main claim of the article.
3. Ask students to highlight what they consider to be the writer's strongest evidence.
4. Prompt students to write informally about the topic for 5–7 minutes in their notebooks.
5. Ask students to write down what they want to know more about the topic.
6. Ask students to write about where they stand on this issue **today**.

Getting Informed & Joining the Conversation
Day 2 (15 minutes):
During the normal "Writing into the Day" repeat the process with the second article.
1. Instruct students to read Text #2 from your chosen text set.
2. Instruct students to underline or note in the margin the main claim of the article.
3. Ask students to highlight what they consider to be the writer's strongest evidence.
4. Prompt students to write informally about the topic for 5–7 minutes in their notebooks.

Day 3 (15 minutes):
During the normal "Writing into the Day" repeat the process with the third article.
1. Instruct students to read Text #3 from your chosen text set.
2. Instruct students to draw a simple graphic that represents the relationship among these three articles.
3. Prompt students to write a short explanation of their graphic in their notebook. Remind students to keep their graphic in their notebook for later.

Making a Plan & Writing an Argument
Day 4 (15 minutes):
On the fourth day, use the "Writing into the Day" timeslot and give the following instructions:
1. Ask students to take out the graphic and explanation that they composed yesterday and read it over. Ask students to mark on the graphic their own position in the conversation.
2. Prompt students to write a short argument that makes a claim and cities evidence from the three readings to support that argument.

---

their own resources of a character that would be coherent and consistent with those of the improvement community. Local Writing Project sites model the instructional resources during C3WP professional learning, and teachers then try using them in their classrooms and bring samples of the resultant student writing to the next professional learning session.

C3WP's instructional resources are also designed to support teachers in moving quickly from professional learning to classroom implementation. Inverness Research, an independent evaluator, explained the importance of the instructional resources in this way:

> The availability and accessibility of the C3WP resources, tools and strategies were instrumental in what teachers described as learning how to *teach* writing instead of just *assign* writing. They served an important dual educative function—as means for teaching teachers how to teach argument writing and as means for teaching students how to write argument. Embedded within these curricular resources were design features that reflected NWP values and pedagogical practices as well as a utilitarian function.[8]

There is clear evidence that the refined theory of improvement and the manner in which C3WP implemented it were effective. The effectiveness of C3WP has been assessed in three separate independent evaluations that included 228 diverse schools in twenty states, 78 percent of which were rural. In these studies, 65 percent of students were eligible for free or reduced-price lunch, and 39 percent were students of color. All three evaluations found positive and statistically significant effects on student achievement. According to an April 2021 research brief from SRI International (SRI), "the size, scale, rigor, and independence of these three studies provide a strong evidence base to support C3WP's effectiveness in improving students' secondary writing achievement at scale and in diverse contexts."[9]

The Using Sources Tool: C3WP's Approach to Practical Measurement

The refined theory of improvement includes not only the instructional resources described in this discussion, but also a formative assessment process designed to enable teachers to analyze student writing in ways consistent with C3WP's approach to argument writing. As teachers begin to use these instructional resources, students produce both more writing and writing that shows evidence of the kinds of argument moves that the program envisioned. Given that many teachers' prior approach to teaching writing included the ubiquitous practices of teaching grammar in isolation and assigning students to write the five-paragraph essay, we anticipated that they would need new language and tools for evaluating the quality of what is a novel form of writing for them.[10] Unless there were significant changes in what teachers looked for, the quality of students' writing would stagnate. The UST, the instructional resources, and the professional learning work together to communicate C3WP's vision for argument writing. While the instructional resources provide actionable steps for how to teach students, the UST, in the context of C3WP professional development, provides teachers with a clear picture of how to evaluate what students learned from that instruction.

The UST focuses on eight high-leverage argument skills, thereby distilling C3WP's definition of argument into a manageable set of questions that support teachers in understanding what high-quality arguments include and in analyzing the quality of students' moves in writing evidence-based arguments (figure 4.4). The UST deliberately focuses on a small set of high-leverage skills that enable teachers to see the difference that their teaching is making. Over time, this focus deepens teachers' understanding of the most important skills for argument writing, helps teachers focus on what comes next and how to teach it, and makes students' growth more visible in doing so.

The items on the UST were crafted based on C3WP's approach to teaching argument writing, which is described in the *American Educator* article "For the Sake of Argument":

> Teaching students to engage in public, civic, and civil arguments requires a focus on using legitimate nonfiction sources in their writing. Readers recognize a thoughtful argument when it is clear that the writer deeply understands the conversation around the issue, carefully engages a range of viewpoints, and skillfully handles the evidence with commentary that advances the claim.[11]

The UST's questions (figure 4.4) focus on key skills that contribute directly to this type of thoughtful, reasoned argument, with a clear

Figure 4.4 UST questions

1. Does the writing present a claim?			
The writing presents a claim that is nuanced, debatable, and defensible.	The writing presents a claim that is debatable and defensible.	The writing presents a summary statement about source material, but that statement is not debatable.	The writing does not present a claim.

2. Does the writing distinguish between the student's own ideas and the source material, including the use of clearly indicated paraphrasing, quotation marks, or signal phrases?

Not present	Developing	Competently	Effectively

3. Does the writing select and use evidence from sources to support the claim?

Not present	Developing	Competently	Effectively

4. Does the writing comment on source material in ways that connect the source material to the claim?

Not present	Developing	Competently	Effectively

5. Does the writing characterize the credibility of the source material or author?

Not present	Developing	Competently	Effectively

6. Overall, how would you describe the writing's use of source material? *Select an option that best describes the writing's overall use of source material.*

Skillfully integrates source material to fully support the paper's claim.	Uses source material to support a paper's claim.	Includes source material to somewhat support the paper's claim.	Summarizes source material, without connecting to a claim.	Does not use source material.	Primarily or exclusively copies source material.

7. Does the writing use source material for any of the following purposes? Check all that apply.

Illustrating | Using specific examples from the text to support a claim.
Authorizing | Refer to an "expert" to support a claim.
Extending | Put your own "spin" on terms or ideas you take from other texts.
Countering | "Push back" against the text in some way (e.g., disagree with it, challenge something it says, or interpret differently).

8. What do you see as next steps for this student?

---

emphasis on the use of evidence and commentary. Unpacking the language and organization of the UST items further illustrates how the tool can influence teachers' understanding of what to look for in student argument writing. For example, item 1 on the UST distinguishes between a claim that is "debatable and defensible" and one that is "nuanced, debatable, and defensible." A claim that is debatable and defensible is one that is open to discussion or argument and that can be defended with evidence. There is a good chance that teachers will have an understanding of the importance of debatable and defensible claims in an argument, but the UST proposes that the most effective claims are "nuanced," take into account multiple perspectives on a topic, and even anticipate possible counterarguments. The use of the term "nuanced" signals C3WP's approach to argument as conversation among multiple sources and voices. The language in each of the other items in the tool serves a similar signaling function.

Just as teachers might have limiting preconceptions about teaching argument writing in general, they often also have preconceptions about specific argument skills in action. The language in the UST provides teachers with clear definitions of what a specific skill might look like when it manifests in student writing. An example of this can be seen in UST item 2, which focuses on whether and to what extent students distinguish between their own ideas and ideas from source material, as indicated by "the use of clearly indicated paraphrasing, quotation marks, or signal phrases." A common belief that teachers have about the attribution of source material in argument writing is that it is accomplished through American Psychological Association (APA) or Modern Language Association (MLA) in-text citations. In contrast, the description of the ways in which students might indicate that they have used others' words in item 2 lists several options, including the use of "clearly indicated paraphrasing." These specific approaches to what this particular skill might look like are consistent with how this rhetorical move is handled in public arguments outside of academic publications. The language in this item was designed to signal these possibilities and to support teachers in developing an understanding of what this skill might look like in student writing.

The UST purposefully breaks down specific skills on which the C3WP resources focus into separate questions, in order to support teachers in identifying significant improvements in each of these high-leverage, teachable argument skills. This contrasts with summative assessments which typically prize parsimony and often integrate multiple related features of writing into a single summary score. For example, figure 4.5 shows how the Smarter Balanced Assessment Argumentative Rubric elegantly integrates the use of evidence, attribution of source material, and elaboration, along with vocabulary and style, into a single score. In contrast, the UST treats the first three of these as separate writing features and does not mention vocabulary and style at all. If the UST took an approach similar to the Smarter Balanced rubric, it would be difficult for teachers to see students' progress on the use of evidence if other components of their arguments were less developed. Similarly, by not highlighting dimensions of writing such as vocabulary and style, the UST focuses on difficult-to-teach and -learn skills. Each tool's design is appropriate to its purpose. Fundamentally, this illustrates what has been described as a distinction between the assessment *of* learning and the assessment *for* learning. Thought of in this way, practical assessment for improvement is more clearly aligned with assessment for learning or educative assessment.[12]

The UST went through several iterations to reach its current form as members of the NWP leadership team observed teachers using the UST, and based on feedback from both Local Writing Project teachers and teachers in the partner districts. Each revision of the UST focused on providing language that more effectively communicates C3WP's approach to argument writing. For example, the word "nuanced" in item 1 of the

Figure 4.5 Definition of score point 4 (evidence/elaboration) from the Smarter Balanced Assessment Argumentative Writing Rubric

---

The response provides thorough and convincing elaboration of the support/evidence for the claim and argument(s) including reasoned, in depth analysis and the effective use of source material. The response clearly and effectively develop ideas, using precise language:

- comprehensive evidence (facts and details) from the source material is integrated, relevant, and specific
- clear citations or attribution to source material
- effective use of a variety of elaborative techniques
- vocabulary is clearly appropriate for the audience and purpose
- effective, appropriate style enhances content

UST (figure 4.4) did not appear in the earliest versions of the UST but was added later to more clearly indicate how C3WP defines the most effective argument claims.

As illustrated in the refined theory of improvement, neither the instructional resources nor the UST are sufficient to support teachers in improving student performance when they are used in isolation or by individual teachers outside C3WP professional development. Even with the carefully crafted language of the UST, it is essential for Local Writing Project leaders to facilitate teachers' collaborative analysis of a sample of student writing with the UST to identify strengths and next opportunities for growth in students' writing. With support from Local Writing Project leaders, teachers individually and collectively select the next resources to use. The following section illustrates how our theory of improvement, now including the UST, plays out in practice.

FOCUSING ON THE UST'S ROLE IN THE LARGER THEORY OF ACTION

As we described earlier in this chapter, our refined theory of action for improvement included three components: professional learning, instructional resources, and analysis of student writing. The three components work together, but each individual element was designed to make unique contributions. The UST reinforces C3WP's definition of argument writing as it is presented in the instructional resources; that meaning is conveyed through the tool itself, exemplar papers, and related social processes. The tool also serves as a guide for making decisions about a focus for ongoing instruction and about which instructional resources to use in the classroom and in professional development. Further, the collaborative use of the UST supports teachers in building a shared vision of, and mutual accountability for, students' writing outcomes. Finally, and perhaps most notably, the UST emphasizes the importance of identifying strengths rather than deficits in students' writing, thereby promoting a vision of students as capable of writing high-quality arguments with appropriate instruction and support.

The UST Provides a Definition of Argument Writing

Once Writing Project facilitators have briefly introduced the overall vision for the UST, they take the first steps toward using the UST to develop a shared language around argument writing. Using hard copies of the UST (figure 4.4) and the scale-point definitions, facilitators engage teachers in a close reading of the UST and its scale during which they identify key words and phrases that contribute to their understanding. Facilitators then lead a discussion of those words and phrases, focusing on any that are unclear or that need further elaboration. For example, discussion of the first UST question (figure 4.4) often focuses on what it means for a claim to be "debatable and defensible" or what the key characteristics of a "nuanced" claim are. Jean Wolph, director of the Louisville Writing Project, noted, "In the initial sessions, our discoveries of teacher understanding of the moves and foundational aspects of argument writing came about because of the conversations in the room as we scored. We would be asked to 'arbitrate' as teachers discussed a piece of student work, for example, and couldn't come to agreement. Or we would be asked to explain [something like], 'so what really is a nuanced claim?'"

Similarly, a close examination of question 2 often prompts discussion of the various ways that authors signal that they are using others' words in writing. Question 2 is crafted to include definitions for the ways that writers signal the words of others by stating that this signaling might include "the use of clearly indicated paraphrasing, quotation marks, or signal phrases." Given that teachers often focus on this type of attribution as a means for avoiding plagiarism, including this range of possibilities often opens a conversation about the ways that students might distinguish their own words from the words of others, with a focus on their purposes as writers rather than on merely avoiding plagiarism. In this way, leaders support teachers in beginning to build a shared understanding of the key aspects of argument writing that the UST focuses on, what they mean, and how they are expressed in students writing.

Once teachers have been immersed in the language of the UST, facilitators model its application to student writing. Applying new and unfamiliar constructs to writing is not straightforward, so local Writing Project facilitators guide teachers through a student writing sample. First, without the UST in hand, teachers read along as they listen to the writing sample being read aloud and look for evidence of whether the student formulated a claim, employed logical reasoning, and used evidence and sources that are connected to the claim. Teachers share what they have noticed and then draw inferences about the impact of relevant teaching. This first round of engagement with student writing happens first as a whole group, and then in small groups with a second student sample. This descriptive process introduces the idea that the UST is designed to look for what is present in the writing rather than what is missing.

To strengthen the UST's signaling capacity, it is accompanied by annotated student writing samples (see an example in figure 4.6). In addition to signaling what C3WP values in argumentation, these samples indicate what is possible for student writers and how to describe rather than critique student writing.

Repeated use of the UST deepens teachers' understanding of which skills matter as they teach argument writing, and it also helps focus their

Figure 4.6 Annotated sample of student writing (excerpt)

	Student Writing	Annotation
5	Many people are against the idea of junk food being sold in schools. Though it seems a tad unreasonable considering most kids will still eat junk food outside of school, junk food is of no disturbance to the education of children, and the money junk food provides helps pay for school activities. (Schools should not ban junk food for these reasons.)	Claim is debatable and defensible.
10	Children are not always in school. They go home, they spend time with friends, and various other things outside of school. First lady, Michelle Obama, stated that, "We'll be eliminating advertisements for unhealthy food and beverages in our school because I think we can all agree that our classrooms should be healthy places where our kids are not bombarded with ads for junk food." Once again, children have lives outside	Commentary sets up evidence.

Evidence representing counterargument, introduced by name. |
| 15 | of school. The advertisements everywhere else will still stand, so removing them in schools will be incredibly useless. This is not the only reason that junk food in schools should not be banned. | Commentary provides reason why evidence for counterargument is limited. |
| 20 | In an excerpt from Chew on This: Everything You Don't Want to Know About Fast Food, authors Eric Schlosser and Charles Wilson said, "In 1906, most schools didn't serve lunch." I feel this is because a school's main purpose is to educate. I am not saying that schools should not serve food, but what they eat will not affect their education process. Furthermore, education is what we should be spending our money on since it will probably have a larger effect on children's futures. Junk food should not be banned in schools for these reasons. | Supporting evidence, introduced by names of authors and the title of the source.

Commentary names connection between claim and evidence and possible outcome or result. |

analysis and grading of student writing. Typical of many teachers who participate in C3WP, one teacher explained the connection between the UST's focus on specific writing moves and the development of argument skills:

> When I use the UST, it helps me to see where [students'] thinking is and be able to pull it out. . . . Instead of just going through and checking, I am not really focused on the grammar usage or anything like that, because I want the content. That's what's more important for me. What do they understand from the writing? What are they getting? What information are they gaining? Is it the right information? Does it fit? . . . [The UST] narrows down to have a focus, as opposed to before, we were looking for everything, which was hard to do, which took much longer and even then, it didn't help us be able to build on a skill.

This teacher's reflection contrasts with how she previously looked at writing ("grammar usage," "looking for everything") and what she looks for now ("What information are they gaining? Is it the right information? Does it fit?"). She emphasizes that this focus helps her build her students' skills. Such an understanding of what students are doing in turn allows for more in-depth planning and increased ownership of next instructional steps. Wolph describes shifts in teachers' use of the UST during her second year of working with them:

> Teachers now assumed ownership of the direction of professional learning. "We need PD [professional development] on commentary. We're not making progress on that," I remember one teacher announcing, as she quickly moved through her stack of papers. . . . Reinforced by the close examination of many dozens of student papers, they had internalized the meanings of these descriptors and, even better, had learned strategies to support students in reaching those higher levels.

The UST Supports Instructional Decision-Making

The UST can guide decisions about a focus for ongoing instruction and about which instructional resources to use in the classroom and in professional development. Use of the UST involves analyzing students' writing for all the key elements of argument, regardless of whether particular skills are taught in a given instructional resource. Analyzing student writing with all the tool's items, regardless of which skills teachers have taught, provides them with opportunities to see what prior experience students have with the skills that were not a focus of instruction. It also allows teachers to see whether students continue using previously taught skills as they learn new ones or whether instruction on particular skills needs to be reinforced.

Initially, the process of planning for next steps is directly supported by local Writing Project facilitators through individual coaching or demonstration of C3WP instructional resources. For example, in figure 4.7, site leaders might notice that after the first round of instruction, most students in the district are competently making claims in their writing. Although they will need to support students in writing nuanced claims in the future, this does not stand out as an immediate concern that needs to be addressed in coaching or in upcoming professional development. By

Figure 4.7 UST report for an entire district

1. Does the writing present a claim?

Value	Percent	Count
The writing presents a claim that is nuanced, debatable, and defensible.	20.0%	11
The writing presents a claim that is debatable and defensible.	70.9%	39
The writing presents a summary statement about source material, but that statement is not debatable.	5.5%	3
The writing does not present a claim.	3.6%	2
	Totals	55

3. Does the writing select and use evidence from sources to support the claim?

Value	Percent	Count
Effectively	1.8%	1
Competently	30.9%	17
Developing	61.8%	34
Not present	5.5%	3
	Totals	55

contrast, the data show that 60 percent of students are still developing the skill of selecting and using evidence to support a claim, which suggests that this is an area where teachers can build on an emerging strength.

Since Writing Project site leaders can immediately produce reports from the UST, they also use UST data to engage the teachers participating in a professional learning session in discussions about the patterns that they see across the data and their implications for instruction. For example, they can look at a report of all the "Next Steps" that teachers listed on item 8 of the UST (see figure 4.4) to discuss trends and identify the skills they might teach next and the resource(s) or strategies they might use. Figure 4.8 shows an excerpt from the "Next Steps" report for all the seventh- to twelfth-grade ELA teachers in one district. After discussing the report, teachers concluded that district students would benefit from additional instruction on selecting and commenting on evidence. The Writing Project site leaders pointed the group to C3WP's Instructional Resource Guide, which provides an overview of the argument skills addressed by each resource, and helped the group identify the resources that would be most helpful for their students.

Analyzing UST data also prompts individual teachers to reflect on their teaching and guides Local Writing Project site leaders to follow up

Figure 4.8 Sample of comments from "Next Steps" list

Analysis A

What do you see as next steps for this student?

670301A
Using commentary to connect their evidence to their claim.

670104A
Continue working on writing a nuanced claim, and finding relevant evidence to support a nuanced claim.

670201A
Establishing credibility.

670401A
Using the evidence to create a more nuanced claim.

670302A
Commenting on evidence consistently throughout the paper in order to connect it to the claim.

670109A
Needs to work on countering evidence, providing credibility of source material, and connecting the evidence to the claim.

on what individual teachers notice in their students' writing in subsequent coaching sessions and classroom demonstrations. In one-on-one coaching sessions, site leaders routinely ask teachers to reflect on what they noticed when analyzing student writing with the UST. Sherri Kinkopf, a site leader from Mississippi, shared an example of this from her work with a teacher:

> Terri and I spoke briefly after the Smith County teachers met at USM a couple of weeks ago. Based on [using the UST to analyze] her students' work, she expressed concern about the amount of time she had devoted to reading and coding texts rather than purposeful writing instruction. She explained that she wanted to go back and work on their introductions in particular before beginning a more intentional focus on the use of evidence and the Harris moves.

This example shows a teacher's emerging understanding of what she may need to do differently in supporting her students to be able to write high-quality arguments, as well as to read source texts. While this is just one example of how analyzing student writing with the UST led a teacher to reflect on her instruction, it illustrates how teachers often adjust their instructional practices in an individual coaching session with a Local Writing Project site leader.

As teachers become more experienced in using the UST, they are more likely to consult C3WP's Instructional Resource Guide independently as they ponder their next instructional steps. They also openly share their ideas about which next steps might be addressed through routine argument-writing resources, which require one class period or less to improve a single skill, and which require longer sequences of instruction. The UST's final open-ended question, "What do you see as the next steps for this student?" is especially important for prompting teachers to use their analysis of UST data to make decisions about their teaching of argument writing. Linda Denstaedt, a site leader from Michigan, reflected on how Pontiac teachers' use of the UST opened up new conversations about their practice: "We talked about strengths and next-step instruction as teaching from strength to introduce scaffolds to support growth." Denstaedt, along with other Writing Project facilitators, worked with teachers to see how analyzing student writing with the UST primed them to use the next instructional resource that she recommended. Two Pontiac teachers noted in a written reflection the connection between learning to understand what was present in a piece of writing and their teaching, "[The] UST was challenging because it requires a teacher to learn to describe what is in student writing, but it helped me understand how to identify and instruct for next-steps." In summary, the tool provides timely feedback that teachers can act upon immediately, either by reinforcing a particular skill through a routine argument lesson or by teaching new skills in a new cycle of instruction.

The UST Promotes Collective Responsibility for Teaching Argument Writing

The social use of the UST is central to C3WP's theory of improvement. Collaborative use of the tool builds mutual accountability for students' writing outcomes and promotes an understanding of how teaching affects students' writing performance. Analyzing students' writing together during professional learning fosters mutual accountability among teachers. In a professional development session that focuses on introducing the UST, teachers are typically asked to bring a set of ten to fifteen student papers written as a result of a C3WP resource. Seeing that all the other teachers in one's school or district have brought writing to the professional development session and are all wrestling with the same questions raises the stakes for each teacher to contribute. Sharing work across classrooms and grade levels contributes to more consistently held and applied expectations for students and can also raise teachers' expectations for what is possible. Over the years, several Writing Project leaders have shared anecdotes about high school teachers seeing examples of middle school students' arguments that were more fully developed than those that their own students were writing at the time. This often resulted in greater buy-in, renewed commitment, and raised expectations from teachers. This kind of mutual professional accountability is a common consequence of the introduction and use of practical measures for legitimate improvement purposes.

The UST Identifies Strengths in Students' Writing

The UST emphasizes the importance of identifying strengths rather than deficits in students' writing, thereby promoting a vision of students as capable of writing high-quality arguments about issues that matter to them, their communities, and the world, provided that they receive appropriate instruction and support. Identifying strengths in writing is essential to reinforcing and building upon those strengths. More important, students, especially those who are learning in communities that have long been disenfranchised and underserved, often do not have such opportunities to engage in interesting and challenging reading and writing.[13] These students and their teachers may be facing assessment data suggesting that previous attempts at reading, writing, and teaching may have failed. In introducing and using the UST, local Writing Project facilitators work to counter deficit thinking about students' capacities and teachers' ability to affect student learning.

During the introduction of the UST, local Writing Project leaders also share key points about it that set it apart from other, more summative assessments of student writing. Many checklists and rubrics use accomplished writing performance as the point of reference and then use language that contrasts less accomplished performance with that standard. This results in language that orients teachers to look for what students are *not* doing. One way in which the UST differs from typical assessments is its emphasis on *what is present in the writing* (figure 4.7). For example, the UST describes a developing piece of writing as follows: "The writing attempts the move (i.e., distinguishing student's and source's ideas, commenting on one or more sources, or characterizing credibility of a source), but may do so in a limited or underdeveloped way. If a move is attempted more than once, its use may be very uneven."

Use of the word *attempts* in the scale-point definition encourages teachers to look for the emerging use of a writing skill that otherwise might be missed when a teacher is looking only for genuinely effective use of the move. The UST supports a critical shift in teachers' perspective, with a focus on what the teacher can build on in a student's writing rather than how it fails to measure up when compared with accomplished performance.

After facilitators have immersed teachers in the language of the UST as described in figure 4.9, they support them in applying the tool to a common writing sample. Similar to the annotated student sample in figure 4.6, teachers engage in a guided process of highlighting key features of argument writing (e.g., pink = claim; yellow = evidence; green = commentary) and naming the argument moves that the student is making in their argument. The local Writing Project facilitator points to specific highlighted sections of the sample and engages the whole group in discussing which UST scale-point descriptors best fit the writing and highlighting features as appropriate. This process deepens teachers' understanding of the UST's language and of how it applies to student writing from classrooms similar to their own.

Unpacking the scale-point definitions by applying them to common exemplar papers is essential, as facilitators state how to determine the rating for each UST item and build a shared understanding of the development of students' argument writing (figure 4.9). For example, this conversation may focus on the distinction between a move being "purposeful, logical, and consistent" (effective writing) and "occasional lapses" (competent writing). This language conveys the point that within each rating, there is likely to be a range of writing quality, and having one missing element doesn't automatically warrant a lower rating. At first glance, the scale point "Not present" may appear to reinforce deficit thinking. However, in practice, facilitators support teachers in seeing and using this scale point as descriptive of developing argument writing. As students begin to write arguments, they often draft a claim without including evidence or they might draft a claim with information from sources, but do not yet explain how that evidence is connected to the claim. While there is no evidence of the move in a student's writing, discussion of the words and phrases used to define the scale simultaneously conveys C3WP's values about students as writers who might be at different levels of development but who all have potential to move to the next level with appropriate support.

In one sense, the NWP's systematic processes for introducing teachers to the language of the UST and to its application bear a strong familial resemblance to processes used for training scorers on summative writing

Figure 4.9 UST scale-point definitions

Scale-Point Definitions

FINAL

Effectively = The writing makes the move (i.e., distinguishing student's and a source's ideas, commenting on one or more sources, or characterizing credibility of a source) in a way that contributes to the overall development of the paper. When present, the move is purposeful, logical, and consistent.

Competently = The writing makes the move (i.e., distinguishing student's and a source's ideas, commenting on one or more sources, or characterizing credibility of a source). The move is generally controlled and satisfactory. There may be occasional lapses, if a move is attempted more than once.

Developing = The writing attempts the move (i.e., distinguishing student's and source's ideas, commenting on one or more sources, or characterizing credibility of a source), but may do so in a limited or underdeveloped way. If a move is attempted more than once, its use may be very uneven.

Not present = There is no evidence of a particular move in a paper (i.e., distinguishing student's and source's ideas, commenting on one or more sources, or characterizing credibility of a source). Alternatively, the writing cannot be evaluated for a particular move because it summarizes or copies without attribution or may be too brief to evaluate.

---

assessments. In both, teachers become immersed in the precise language of the assessment and, in both, teachers are supported to use the rubrics increasingly independently to assess students' writing. However and crucially, the social processes for working with the UST diverge from summative assessment systems. In summative assessments, which can have consequences for whether an individual student advances a grade, graduates, or gains admission to college, precise and consistent calibration is of critical importance. For the UST, surfacing patterns in students' writing that guide instruction matters more. UST professional development does not emphasize calibration in a technical sense; instead, it focuses on teachers developing a shared perspective on quality. Having teachers work in pairs to analyze each piece of writing helps to develop this sense of consistency.

As the results of external evaluations indicate, teachers' routine use of the UST and C3WP resources result in greater student success in writing arguments. One professional development facilitator noticed that teachers' expectations for their students' performance rose over the course of their two-year professional development work. She described teachers' reactions to their new seventh graders' arguments during the first meeting of the second year. The teachers were concerned that the arguments did not include nuanced claims, let alone evidence or commentary. Crucially, these students' sixth-grade teachers were not part of C3WP. To help the teachers see how their expectations had increased, the facilitator showed the teachers their UST analysis from the previous year. During the first year in which the teachers implemented C3WP in their classrooms, students had difficulty writing claims. In the second year, not only were students writing claims, but their claims were nuanced. The facilitator reflected, "The only thing that had changed was [the teachers]. Their expectations were much higher the second year. They knew these kids could do it and they were making them do it."

ISSUES OF VALIDITY FOR THE UST

The UST represents one component of C3WP's larger professional learning system. While the description of the UST in this chapter has focused primarily on how teachers use the tool, as we turn to the validity argument, it is important to make explicit that the UST was designed with two audiences in mind: the teachers and the Writing Project site leaders who facilitate C3WP, including teachers' use of the UST. To understand the validity of the UST, we have focused on three areas. First, we have analyzed evidence about whether the tool supports both teachers' and professional development leaders' understanding of the quality of students' writing and of whether performance has changed over time. Second, we have analyzed evidence from site reports and from site leaders' reflections on the how teachers' use of the UST has influenced both their instructional vision and practice of instruction. Finally, we have analyzed the relationship between the UST and an independent measure of students' writing outcomes to establish the tool's concurrent validity.

The UST Supports Teachers and Site Leaders in Understanding Writing Quality

We developed the UST to support both teachers and Writing Project site leaders in understanding the quality of their students' argument writing and to be able to see improvement in students' arguments when it occurred. To understand whether the tool was operating as intended, during the first two years of its use, we regularly asked Writing Project site leaders to address the question: "Based on your analysis of student work this month, what are teachers and students taking up from C3WP professional development?"[14] At least half of the site leaders' comments focused on the patterns that they observed in students' writing (e.g., use of evidence, the presence of the argument moves that Harris identified). This suggests that the UST helped site leaders understand the argument moves that their students were making in their writing.

One additional theme that emerged is that many teachers could see improvement in their students' writing based on using the UST (between 5 percent and 20 percent of site leaders made comments related to this theme each month). While some observations were very general, others pointed to the kinds of growth that teachers could see in their students' writing:

> Teachers have been excited this year to observe their students' progress and to see evidence of their instruction in nonfiction argument writing (February 2015).
>
> Middle school teachers, especially, were pleased with their students' writing. They commented on how effectively their students developed a claim and supported it with textual evidence (February 2016).[15]

The Writing Project site leaders who shared these observations and reflections worked with teachers, in person, at least once a month and often spent time in teachers' classrooms coteaching or providing coaching. This evidence suggests that, as intended, the UST supports teachers in understanding what is present in students' writing and in seeing growth.

In addition to noting that the UST revealed students' growth in writing arguments to their teachers, four of the twenty site leaders noted that they had observed teachers raising their expectations for what students could do. For example, one site leader reflected, "We were pleased to see somewhat of a shift away from deficit thinking when teachers used the tool with student work. We heard lots of teachers focusing on how students HAD taken up the instruction they provided" (March 2015). Over the six years that C3WP has included use of the UST, we have consistently heard similar observations about increasing expectations from Writing Project site leaders. Wolph, who worked monthly with several Kentucky districts over two years, offered a more nuanced description of how the UST helped to raise teachers' expectations for their students: "Teachers' expectations of their students increased as well, perhaps in part because they had come to clearer understandings of the differences between 'developing,' 'competently,' and 'effectively.' Reinforced by the close examination of many dozens of student papers, they had internalized the meanings of these descriptors and, even better, had learned strategies to support students in reaching those higher levels."

The UST helped these teachers see their own students' growth, and they therefore raised their expectations for future students. While a fraction of site leaders made comments like this, changing teachers' expectations is critical if they are to provide more ambitious learning opportunities for their students. Based on observations from multiple site leaders over time, we also have confidence that the UST supports teachers in detecting improvement in their students' writing.

The UST Shapes Instructional Practice

As illustrated in this chapter, in addition to supporting teachers in applying scale points consistently, Writing Project leaders use the UST for "developing and refining a shared sense of values," leading to changes in practice. Validity for practical measures requires an additional step: to provide information that can guide action. Since the UST's inception, teachers have analyzed 86,377 samples of student writing, and 85.9 percent of the UST records include comments about the next instructional steps.

In the previous section, which focused on the UST's role in the larger theory of action, we demonstrated that with consistent and repeated use, teachers were able to understand how they can use what they learned about students' emerging argument writing to shape their teaching. In answering the question, "Based on your analysis of student work this month, what are teachers and students taking up from C3WP professional development?" nearly all site leaders noted that as a consequence of using the UST, teachers were able to identify where students needed additional support and began making instructional decisions that would help students strengthen their writing. The following observation by a site leader is representative in this regard: "The analysis of student writing has been very useful. Teachers were clearly able to see that students needed to work on authorizing what they say. Teachers have noticed a trend and are constructing mini-lessons on *quote sandwiches*." Similarly, another site leader noted, "This analysis had teachers returning to the importance of practice in developing claims that are debatable and defensible."[16]

An especially strong and nuanced example of teachers improving their practice based in part on what they learned from the UST comes from Pontiac, Michigan. Denstaedt observed that not only did the UST inform teachers' planning for instruction, it also shaped what they did in the classroom. She worked with the Pontiac teachers on a weekly basis. During each visit, she spent at least one class period in each teacher's room, taking careful notes of what students were saying, asking, and doing in their writing. Denstaedt would occasionally participate in the teaching, and she would always ask several students for samples of their work. During the teachers' planning meetings, she shared her observations and engaged the teachers in collaboratively analyzing students' work and planning next steps. Like other site leaders and teachers, Denstaedt emphasized how the UST provided a focus for teachers, saying, "The UST was the short list of source-based skills that was a new way of thinking about teaching argument." In Denstaedt's estimation, this list served as a springboard for classroom action on the part of both teachers and students. In a written reflection, she identified improvements in teachers' micromoves in the classroom that emerged from their use of the UST and her coaching:

- Modeling increased when teachers understand what skills look like, sound like, and are developed in student thinking.
- Working the room changed to noticing and naming what a student is doing or listening to students name what they were doing and how it was impacting their thinking. This was seeable/hearable in the language uptake and use in daily teacher/student, student/student, and metacognitive exit slips. The UST language was shared in purpose and meaning.

"Modeling" involves a teacher demonstrating what a specific skill looks like. For example, a teacher might demonstrate how to write commentary that connects a piece of statistical evidence to the overall claim or how to transform a simple claim into a nuanced claim. "Working the room" means that the teacher moves around the room while students are working individually, in pairs, or small groups; watches or listens to what they are doing; and gathers qualitative information to inform instruction. For example, a teacher might listen for students correctly using the language of claims and evidence as they discuss drafts of each other's writing.

This case illustrates that the UST can play an important role, along with the use of instructional resources during professional development and coaching, in shaping what teachers modeled for students and what they noticed in students' conversation, as well as in their writing. Multiple site leaders' reports of the impact of the UST on teachers' instructional decision-making and classroom practice, coupled with more nuanced observation, suggest that the UST is valid as a practical measure the use of which shapes teachers' instruction.

The UST Serves as a Leading Indicator of Positive Impact on Students' Argument Writing

While we have not formally tested whether the UST has predictive validity, its results appear to serve as a *leading indicator* for positive impacts on student writing. As leaders for C3WP, we sought to understand the relationship between the UST and the Analytic Writing Continuum for Source-Based Argument Writing (AWC-SBA), which was used as the outcome measure for SRI's independent evaluations of C3WP.[17] We wanted to understand whether the UST might bear a relationship to the findings of the impact evaluations regarding the quality of student argument writing. To explore these questions, we first determined that the components of writing measured by the UST most closely align with the AWC-SBA's Content attribute, which emphasizes reasoning, selecting and using evidence, providing commentary, addressing alternative or opposing perspectives, and showing that material was taken from sources. We then analyzed the correlation between the AWC-SBA's content attribute and the sixth item on the UST, "Overall, how would you describe the writing's use of source material?" We found that the two measures are moderately correlated: r = 0.57 for middle school writing and r = 0.58 for high school writing.[18] This analysis provides moderately strong evidence of concurrent validity between the UST and the AWC-SBA.

As noted, all three independently conducted randomized controlled trials consistently have demonstrated statistically significant, positive impacts on students' source-based argument writing as measured by the AWC-SBA. Prior to the collection of outcome measures in each of these studies, we observed substantial increases in the number and percentage of arguments rated as using evidence to support a claim or integrating evidence to fully support a claim on the UST. In the most recent independent evaluation, for example, SRI found that students in C3WP classrooms outscored students in business-as-usual classrooms on the quality of the content (including the quality of reasoning and use of evidence).[19] Prior to the collection of outcome data for this study, the NWP leadership team observed substantial shifts in teachers' ratings of the overall use of source material. While only 4 percent of writing samples were rated as skillfully integrating source material at the first use of the UST, 19.2 percent of samples received this rating at the last use. Based on the patterns observed in all three studies, we can infer that when we observe group-level improvements in writing measured by the UST, we can expect to see positive impacts on students' writing performance on the AWC-SBA as well. The concurrent validity of the UST and AWC-SBA, along with the pattern of positive UST results preceding positive outcomes on independent evaluations, suggest that the UST is measuring important dimensions of the quality of argument writing and teachers are able to apply the UST in ways that accurately reflect the quality of their students' writing.

REFLECTIONS ON EQUITY AND THE UST

In 2018, The New Teacher Project (TNTP) conducted a landscape analysis of teaching and learning conditions in five districts and identified four conditions that prepare students for success beyond high school: consistent opportunities to work on grade-appropriate tasks; strong instruction in which students do most of the thinking; deep engagement in learning; and teachers' belief that students are capable of grade-level work. TNTP found that these conditions were generally in short supply, and they were virtually nonexistent in classrooms that serve students who have been least well served, specifically "students of color, from low-income families, new English speakers, or those with mild to moderate disabilities."[20]

One way in which C3WP advances equity aims is by providing access to the kinds of challenging learning opportunities identified by TNTP. C3WP addresses the first three conditions primarily through its instructional resources and professional development that supports teachers in enacting these resources. The UST squarely addresses the fourth condition: teachers' expectations. Because of the tool's focus on identifying and developing evidence of even the most sophisticated argument moves (e.g., characterizing the credibility of the source material or author), it encourages teachers to plan instruction for *all* students to use the moves in their writing. Further, since the use of the tool focuses on naming what is present in the writing rather than what is missing, teachers are much more likely to focus on where students might be attempting a move that they have not yet mastered, but that they could use effectively in future writing with some targeted instructional support. The annotated writing samples that accompany the UST, which are drawn from schools serving large numbers of minority or low-income students, also contribute to raising teachers' expectations for all their students' argument writing. These samples signal to teachers that they can expect higher-quality writing from their own students, when they explicitly teach these skills.

The vast majority of schools that participated in the three C3WP evaluation studies serve a high proportion of students who are eligible for free or reduced-price lunch (65 percent) and are rural, which means that they have often had limited access to the kinds of support for instructional reform that suburban and many urban districts have. While overall, C3WP districts served 61 percent white students and 39 percent students of color, each district had a unique demographic makeup, and our sample included several rural districts in which 90 percent or more of the students are Black. We found that teachers and their students have not experienced high levels of student success with ELA outcomes, including (and perhaps especially with) writing. Across all three C3WP evaluation projects, teachers' entering expectations about students' capacity for reading and writing were low, similar to those reported by TNTP.

In 2015, the Education Trust West analyzed over 1,000 assignments from middle school classrooms. They found that only 4 percent of ELA assignments both required high levels of cognitive demand and were linked to writing extended pieces.[21] All of C3WP's resources include readings with high levels of cognitive demand, and, aside from routine argument writing resources, engage students in writing extended pieces. Through our independent evaluations, we know that teachers in C3WP engaged students in these rigorous tasks. One SRI study showed that in contrast to control classrooms in which teachers were not using the UST and C3WP resources, students in C3WP classrooms were far more likely to write for the purpose of making an argument (64 percent versus 18 percent of class periods) and to use more than one source to develop their arguments (76 percent versus 28 percent).[22] As evidenced throughout this chapter, teachers' use of the UST supported them in identifying how their instruction affected students' writing and in seeing where students needed additional instructional support; and, for many, it also raised their expectations for their students. C3WP's integrated approach of professional learning and instructional resources with rigorous reading and writing tasks and repeated, systematic analysis of students' writing began to shift these expectations. As noted previously, these three elements work together and define C3WP as a whole, with each element essential to the success of the program in these contexts.

C3WP also addresses equity through its focus on teachers shifting from a deficit perspective to a developmental perspective on students' capabilities. Rather than using a lower rating to describe a piece of writing if something is missing, the UST invites teachers to consider the preponderance of evidence and focus their ratings of student writing on the presence of critical attributes, be they characterized as effective, competent, or developing. Denstaedt recalled her early experience of introducing the UST to teachers in Pontiac, Michigan. Teachers there had previously used a district checklist that included a "deficit description of missing and wrong." Denstaedt worked with the teachers to help them reframe their understanding of how to assess writing by modeling the process of looking for a preponderance of evidence of being confident, giving "competent to a student who was just over the edge and competent to a student that was almost effective."

The UST's scale-point definitions also push teachers to look closely for and detect even the earliest evidence of a developing argument move. A student who might otherwise be identified as unable to demonstrate an argument move, or even identified as "failing" at a move, becomes someone who sees the value of using the move in their writing, even though they can't yet use it consistently and effectively. In this way, the UST aims to shift teachers' perspectives from focusing on what a student can't do to focusing on what the student has that the teacher can build on. We carefully crafted the language of the UST to provide teachers with the kind of language that identifies *all* students as writers who can (and should) have opportunities to engage in C3WP's approach to argument writing. Further, the information produced provides teachers with data that can be used to plan for adjustments in instruction for individual students, smaller groups of students, and the class as a whole, ensuring that teachers can plan instruction that serves the needs of each student in their classroom.

The UST's emphasis on evidence of learning and noticing what is there reinforces C3WP's vision of students as capable of learning to write arguments if they receive appropriate instruction and support. It also sets the stage for the identification of those attributes of writing that may need to be encouraged and reinforced to greatly strengthen students' writing. By analyzing student writing with the UST, teachers focus on evidence of their students' learning and evidence of their own teaching. These points subtly emphasize NWP's belief that all students, especially those who have traditionally been underserved or experienced low expectations, are capable.

CONCLUSION

Repeatedly, and across three separate and independent evaluations, teachers, schools, and districts that are able to consistently learn from and use C3WP instructional resources and monitor their impact with the UST experience a clear shift in teachers' instructional practices and ownership of responsibility for teaching argument writing. As Barbara Heenan and her Inverness Research colleagues found in their qualitative analysis of C3WP's first iteration:

> After the C3WP, teachers reported that they realized that teaching involved handing over responsibility to students, that they needn't stand center stage. They explained that with the changing nature of their relationship with students their classrooms became more "alive." They also noted that by actively teaching specific argument writing skills, they were able to give their students more responsibility and autonomy to think for themselves. In response teachers described structuring their classrooms differently, in ways that promoted independent student thinking.[23]

Engaging with the UST plays a central role in providing teachers with the shared language, understanding of key argument skills, relevant data, and tools for moving students forward with their writing that make this goal possible. In this way, it serves as a practical measure that has the potential to advance more equitable outcomes for students who are the furthest from opportunity.

5

Using the Freshman Ontrack Indicator to Improve High Schools in Chicago

Elaine Allensworth

This is a story of success.[1] In the decade of the 2000s, low graduation rates seemed like an insurmountable problem in Chicago's high schools. Half of all students who started high school in the Chicago Public Schools (CPS) did not get a diploma. Four-year graduation rates had risen from 42 percent to 51 percent during the first half of the decade and then stayed at around 50 percent in the second half. Five-year graduation rates were not much better, at 55 percent. Then something changed. Beginning in the 2010s, four-year graduation rates started improving, increasing every year and reaching 78 percent in 2019.[2] In less than one decade, there was a 27-percentage point increase in four-year graduation rates in the city. All groups of students by race, ethnicity, and gender showed improvement, and the largest increases were among Black and Latino young men, students living in neighborhoods with the most families below the poverty line, and students with diagnosed learning disabilities. CPS awarded thousands more diplomas every year by 2019 than in the 2000s, even though the number of students entering high schools remained fairly constant.

When people hear these numbers, they are immediately suspicious. Did the district hide nongraduates by recording more students as transfers? Did the composition of students in the district undergo a dramatic change? Did academic standards decline? Transfer rates did increase in the 2000s but declined during the first part of the 2010s, and they never rose as high as among cohorts graduating in the late 2000s. Dropout rates declined even more rapidly than graduation rates rose—nongraduates were increasingly students who were still in school or had left with a General Education Diploma (GED) instead of a regular diploma, rather than students who left school altogether or disappeared.[3] The composition of high school classes also changed over time, but those changes could not have led to a change in graduation rates of more than a couple of percentage points.[4] In the 1990s, both researchers and practitioners predicted that achievement would go down if high schools succeeded in keeping more students in school. But the opposite happened—compared to students who graduated in the 2000s, graduates in the 2010s had taken many more Advanced Placement (AP) courses, had higher AP exam pass rates, higher average ACT scores, and higher college enrollment rates.[5] The combination of more high school graduates and higher college enrollment rates resulted in about 3,000 more CPS graduates entering four-year colleges each year, increasing from 6,876 in 2010 to 9,798 in 2018 (with immediate college enrollment rates among high school graduates increasing from 35 percent to 42 percent, and college enrollment rates of their ninth-grade cohorts increasing from 23 percent to 34 percent).[6] Changes in student achievement happened quickly once it started, but it was based on years of a research partnership and reciprocal learning among school practitioners, central office staff, researchers, and staff in school support organizations.

How did this all come about? In the 2000s, there were no good answers for questions about how to increase graduation rates, or even how to identify who was at risk of not graduating. Research had shown that whether students graduated from high school or dropped out was related to a multitude of factors that were either outside school or occurred well before students entered high school—family background, neighborhood, peers, elementary school experiences, health, and mobility, among others.[7] It also indicated that it was hard to accurately predict who would drop out.[8] The danger with having no answers is that it leads to tacit acceptance—the feeling that low graduation rates might be inevitable. At one meeting with school principals, I presented graduation rates for high schools serving students with similar backgrounds and showed that there were sometimes considerable differences between schools.[9] Several of the principals questioned the implication that school practices accounted for the differences.

Addressing dropout rates was also treated as a distraction from the goal of preparing students for college and careers. I remember talking with school leaders in Chicago and elsewhere in the country about improving graduation rates and hearing concerns that by working to keep more students in school, standards would drop and test scores would go down. I also remember meeting with city and district officials in the late 1990s about improving graduation rates, and noting that conversations often turned to special groups—students returning from incarceration, or pregnant and parenting students. Strategies proposed to address graduation rates often focused on special programs and classes for students who were at risk by virtue of clearly identifiable conditions, such as those who had failed half their courses or were rarely attending school. But in a district with a 50 percent graduation rate, typical students were at risk of not graduating, not just special populations. Subsequent research showed that students failing half their classes had a probability of graduating of about 3 percent.[10] Even a program that doubled students' chances of graduating would fail to have most of its participants graduate.

Nobody knew how to improve graduation rates in the 1990s. The answer did not come from the design of a successful program or from a planned research study. Instead, beginning in the 1990s, the answer slowly developed over time through an iterative process involving research, policy, and practice. The University of Chicago Consortium on School Research had been founded in 1990 as a collaboration among researchers, CPS, and stakeholders from various sectors of the education community. Its mission was to provide rigorous evidence to inform decision-making about

Chicago's schools—not to make policy recommendations, but rather to provide data that promote a common understanding of issues so policy discussions would be based on facts rather than hearsay. As city and district officials tried to develop strategies to improve graduation rates, they asked researchers at the Consortium to do research on questions that developed. Over the course of fifteen years, an empirically grounded theory of improvement and associated data systems were developed that transformed the ways in which educators support students' successful completion of high school. It required a number of conceptual shifts, a system of practical measurement that identified students who were just beginning to fall off track for graduation, and processes for using data to continually improve the ways that schools supported students to graduate eventually.

The system ultimately included a number of different data elements, and systems for using data. These included (1) the end-of-year freshman ontrack indicator, which signals that a student is likely to graduate and is used for goal-setting and accountability; (2) real-time practical data reports (Freshman Success Reports) used by school staff to monitor and support ninth-grade students throughout their freshman year so they end up on track at the end of the year; (3) school diagnostic data reports that show patterns of grades and attendance by student backgrounds, as well as changes over time, for school improvement planning; (4) research reports about what matters for high school graduation that provide the evidence behind the data tools; and (5) supports for school staff to use the practical data reports to keep students on track during their first year of high school.

AN ITERATIVE PROCESS OF RESEARCH AND PRACTICE LED TO A DIFFERENT WAY OF THINKING

Developing a data system to support student success in high school was not an overnight process. It began in the late 1990s, when one study suggested that schools should focus more attention on students' first year of high school. This finding went against the grain, as there was little guidance at that time about what should happen in ninth grade. The ninth-grade year was sometimes seen as being of little consequence because adults often assumed that students had plenty of time to catch up if they fell behind. This study, by Melissa Roderick and Eric Camburn, showed that a large proportion of students failed courses in their very first year of high school, that most of those students never recovered the credits, and then they failed more classes in the following years.[11] Roderick and Camburn interviewed a group of students in their eighth-grade year and then again in ninth grade, gathered their academic records, and asked those students' teachers in both years to give an appraisal of their academic performance. Most of the students were doing fine in their eighth-grade classes, but when they got to high school, many started to fail courses for the first time. Something about high school suddenly put them at risk of failing. This study suggested the transition to high school was a critical time for many students.

Practitioners in the middle grades recognized the relevance of these findings for their work. Staff with the federal GEAR UP program in Chicago worked with students in the middle grades to help get them ready for college. If even students who seemed to be prepared for high school in the middle grades ended up failing when they got to high school, how could they know if their efforts were successful? There was no information available to middle schools, or to anyone in the district in fact, about whether students were succeeding during their first year of high school. GEAR UP program managers asked the Consortium to provide summary reports showing how the eighth-grade graduates from each of the middle schools had performed in their ninth-grade year. That led researchers to develop a new metric showing whether students had made sufficient progress in ninth grade: the freshman ontrack indicator.

The indicator was simple. A student had to have enough credits at the end of the ninth-grade year to be promoted to tenth grade, and no more than one semester course failure in a core academic course (mathematics, English, science, social science). Shazia Miller led the work to develop the freshman ontrack indicator, and along with other Consortium researchers produced a report for every school in the district serving eighth graders, and every school in the district serving ninth graders. For schools serving eighth graders, the reports showed the freshman on-track rates for their eighth-grade graduates over the last several years, regardless of which high school they attended. For high schools, the reports showed the freshman on-track rates for each cohort of ninth grade students that had started at the school over the last several years.[12] For cohorts that started ninth grade four years or more earlier, the reports also showed whether students in the cohort obtained a diploma within four years of starting high school. As researchers at the Consortium looked through the reports for the different schools, they noticed a pattern. Eighth-grade graduates from some middle schools had low freshman on-track rates, while those from other schools had high rates; across schools, the high school graduation rate for those same students four years later was pretty much the same as the on-track rates in ninth grade. It looked as though one could predict high school graduation rates very accurately just by knowing how many students were on track when they were freshmen. Miller and I first noted the strong correlation between being on track in ninth grade and eventually graduating in a book chapter on school performance in CPS.[13]

District leaders, including CPS chief executive officer (CEO) Arne Duncan, were the ones who recognized the relevance of the freshman ontrack indicator for their work. They wanted a metric of how students were doing early in high school, and they incorporated the freshman ontrack indicator into the district accountability policy for schools for the first time in the 2002–2003 school year. That year, the freshman on-track rate went up from 59 to 62 percent. The next year, it dropped to 57 percent, and then it remained between 57 and 59 percent for the next three years. Neither the existence of the indicator nor the incentive to improve end-of-year freshman on-track rates through an accountability policy were enough to bring positive change on their own.

The initial validation of the indicator had been done quickly. Now that it was used for accountability purposes, the stakes around the indicator were high and called for a thorough validation. John Easton, the director of the Consortium at the time, realized that researchers had to do more work before they could feel confident about the metric, and he and I developed a more thorough validation plan. Was the indicator equally predictive of graduation in all schools, and for all subgroups of students? Was it predictive of graduation simply because it was related to test scores and student backgrounds, or was it providing new information about who would graduate? In 2005, we summarized our findings in a report that not only validated the indicator, but also challenged preexisting beliefs about why some students succeeded in school and others did not. Not only did we find that the relationship between success in ninth grade and eventual graduation held for all groups of students at all schools, but the ontrack indicator was much more predictive than students' test scores and background characteristics combined.[14] In fact, test scores and background characteristics provided little additional information about who would graduate once a student's freshman on-track status was known. Many students with high middle-grade test scores failed courses in the ninth grade, and those course failures put them at higher risk of not graduating than students with low test scores who passed courses in ninth grade. Graduation was not determined as much by students' backgrounds and prior test scores as it was by whether they passed their classes in the ninth-grade year. We realized that the influence of factors external to and prior to high school on graduation were mediated by students' freshman-year performances. This had practical implications; school staff did not need to measure and track every aspect of students' lives to know who needed additional support to graduate. They needed to pay close attention to students' grades in the ninth-grade year. The freshman ontrack indicator was both simple and intuitive, and yet it captured a complex array of information—the culmination of the effects of myriad factors on students' engagement and performance in their ninth-grade classes.

THE DISTRICT DEVELOPED EARLY-WARNING DATA TOOLS WITH PRACTICAL MEASURES TO HELP SCHOOL STAFF SUPPORT NINTH-GRADE SUCCESS

There was increasing recognition that ninth grade was important, but this insight alone was not enough to help school practitioners better support students. It was frustrating to have yet another metric that came at the end of the school year, when it was too late to make a difference. While the ontrack indicator was a strong leading indicator of eventual graduation, it was not a practical measure that could be used effectively for improvement. School and district leaders asked whether information available earlier in the ninth-grade year could be provided to identify students who were falling off track. That led us to conduct a study in 2007 that became the building block for an Early-Warning Indicator (EWI) system. The central components of the system consisted of tools that used practical data based on student grades and attendance.[15] These data were embedded in teachers' regular work and collected frequently, with direct links to being on track and graduating—qualities that align well with the definition of practical measures and measures for improvement.

The 2007 study showed that ninth-grade course grades were strong indicators of eventual high school graduation, and absenteeism was the main driver of being off track. Even missing small amounts of school could have a large impact. Missing five days of class in one semester in ninth grade, no matter what the reason, was associated with a 20-percentage-point drop in the probability of graduating four years later. Missing school occasionally seemed to matter much more than anyone would have believed. Five days a semester was about one day per month, and many students were missing this much school without adults even realizing it. This study countered perceptions that it was fine for students to miss school now and then. It also countered perceptions that students failed in high school mostly because they lacked the academic skills.

The CPS Department of Graduation Pathways responded quickly to these findings and began promoting them at meetings of school principals and support staff. They invited researchers to talk with school leaders and their teams at these meetings. Consortium staff developed flyers for parents and teachers that the district sent to the family of every incoming ninth grader. Most important, the district rolled out three types of data reports in the 2008–2009 school year that schools could use to identify students who were falling off track early in ninth grade. One was designed to identify incoming high school students who would likely need support based on their middle-grade academic performance. Another was designed for early intervention during ninth grade, flagging students with low grades or attendance so school staff could reach out early enough to prevent them from failing. The third was designed for recovery—to get students back on track after they failed courses.[16] All three types of reports helped schools organize their efforts to support ninth graders, but the second type of report—which alerted school personnel to how students were doing in the ninth-grade year—was the key resource for changing students' experience in high school so they eventually graduated.

This Freshmen Success Report simply listed all first-time ninth graders, with their current grades and attendance in each core course, with color-coded flags if a student had high absences or low course grades (i.e., Ds or Fs). Updated every five weeks, the Freshmen Success Report allowed immediate interventions with students who missed class or whose midterm or semester grades were low. Counselors could easily identify students who were failing or close to failing their classes throughout the year, and they could develop targeted intervention strategies based on how many courses a student was failing. Teachers could get together and see if any of their students were falling behind and then develop coordinated plans for helping individual students.

The tools were easy to understand, as they were reports of data that teachers worked with every day (grades and attendance). But the reports organized the data in a way that school staff had not seen before. Seeing students' grades in all their courses together showed teachers that some students who were struggling in some class were doing fine in other classes—suggesting that there may be something about a particular class that was problematic for these students, or that one teacher figured out how to support students in a way that others had not. Other students were struggling across all their classes—there was something interfering in their education that went beyond one individual class. Without seeing the data together, teachers had no way of differentiating among their students who were struggling. In contrast, knowing that a student who was failing in one class was doing fine in another could lead to conversations about what was different for that student in the class that was the problem. Or seeing that a student was struggling in all her or his classes might lead teachers to recognize that the student needed broader supports than any one teacher could provide.

The flags highlighted students who needed help, even if they appeared to be doing OK relative to students with multiple failures or extremely high absences rates. The 2007 study had shown that even one F, or a D grade point average, or several days of course absence in a term were strong signals that a student would end the ninth-grade year off track and eventually not graduate. The reports signaled clearly that the student needed help. Instead of ignoring something because it did not seem like a problem, teachers received a signal that they needed to reach out and provide support.

The focus on grades and attendance meant that teachers were talking about factors that they could influence—not factors happening outside of school. The summary data in the Freshman Success Reports came from individual pieces of data that they input on a daily basis. As educators started using the data more frequently, it also provided incentives for them to keep better records, for teachers to keep up with grading and to record attendance accurately. Those actions in themselves resulted in better support for students. In a qualitative study of the freshman transition, we found that some students failed classes without even realizing it because teachers had not kept up with grading. Teachers said they used grades to motivate students, but students did not always know how well they were doing in class, which undermined any potential effects on motivation—whether they are the pride that students might feel from getting a good grade, satisfaction that their grade was improving, concern from seeing their grade drop, or alarm that they were likely to fail a course. And parents often did not realize how much school or coursework their children were missing until they had already fallen far behind.

SUPPORT FOR USING DATA TOOLS SPURRED INNOVATION

While the data reports were simple, there were initially no guides on how to use them. When district leaders rolled out the reports, they provided six high schools (out of about one hundred in the district) with two new staff members each for two years. These new positions were to support school staff in using the new reports to help students. These ontrack lab coordinators were encouraged to experiment; the coordinators in different schools approached their jobs in different ways and met regularly to share and learn from each other. In the end, the district wrote a guide for schools based on the coordinators' experiences.[17] Consortium researchers, including myself, conducted qualitative interviews with ninth graders at some of the schools with ontrack coordinators, as well as other schools without ontrack coordinators. Students in all the schools talked about how they needed to stay "on track," echoing the messaging that was coming from the district that year. In addition, students from schools with ontrack coordinators mentioned specific ways that the coordinators helped them to stay on track. For example, one student described receiving a first-quarter F and being called into a conference with her ontrack coordinator, teacher, and parent. That student subsequently stopped skipping that class and raised her grade as a result. Another student talked about how her ontrack coordinator would be "on her" if she were absent and continued to recognize how much that coordinator cared about her success. The interviews showed that the coordinators took a direct role in supporting students and also organized school staff around broader school efforts to improve attendance and course grades. For example, the ontrack coordinators at some schools facilitated freshman teacher teams, or teams of teachers and staff members, who met to discuss the Freshman Success Reports.[18]

Also, in the first year that the data reports were released, a group of high school principals approached a Consortium researcher, Melissa Roderick, with a request to provide support to their school leadership teams. This developed into the Network for College Success (NCS), a group that brought together leadership teams from multiple diverse types of high schools to look at each school's data with the teams from other schools, researchers, and facilitators. Looking at data from other schools helped school leadership teams develop insights into their own data—things that might have been invisible to them otherwise. For example, a school team might see that students with high test scores had a higher attendance rate than students with low test scores in their school—that would not be surprising. But by sharing data across schools, they might see that their students with high test scores had substantially lower attendance than students with similar test scores at another school. Suddenly, they would have questions about why their academically strong students were coming to school less.[19]

Requests for the researchers to do more analysis and to present the data in different ways came out of those conversations. School leadership teams wanted information that would help them diagnose the problems at their schools in a systemic way, and they had concrete ideas about what they wanted to see, including breakdowns by race, gender, and prior test scores. In response, the researchers developed school-by-school diagnostic data reports that showed patterns in ninth-grade performance data over time, broken down by subgroups of students.[20] This allowed school teams to ask the essential improvement questions, as advanced by Bryk and colleagues: What works? For whom? And under what conditions?[21] The reports could be used to determine whether particular groups of students were struggling, such as male students or those with low test scores, and whether those groups of students had responded to previous efforts to support them. The reports also showed students' responses to surveys about issues such as school safety and teacher support—elements of the school climate that Consortium researchers found to be related to student attendance and engagement in school. Looking at data from other schools helped school leaders gain insight into what was needed in their own school, and it provided a community for sharing successful practices.[22] In the end, the schools that were part of NCS showed some of the most dramatic improvements in student performance in the district, and many of those school leadership team members subsequently became leaders in changing practices districtwide.[23]

It was when the district introduced the Freshman Success Reports and provided several schools with on-track coordinators, and the NCS was initiated, that freshman on-track rates started going up in a sustained and continuous way. In the three years prior to the 2007–2008 school year, between 57 and 59 percent of freshmen in the district passed enough classes in their ninth-grade year to be on track to graduate each year. There was a slight rise in the 2007–2008 year, to 60 percent, which was the year after the 2007 research report was released. During this year, we presented our findings on the importance of attendance and grades in ninth grade at meetings for high school principals and district staff, and we also met with district leaders a number of times to talk about the implications of the research. Only three high schools (out of 117) showed substantial improvements in freshman on-track rates that year. During the 2008–2009 school year, the first year in which the Freshman Success Reports were produced and the first year of the on-track coordinators and NCS, the percentage of ontrack ninth graders increased to 64 percent. The three schools that showed improvement previously continued to improve, while seventeen additional schools showed improvements in on-track rates. In the 2009–2010 school year, freshman on-track rates rose again, to 69 percent. The twenty schools that showed improvement in the prior two years continued to improve their freshman on-track rates, while additional schools showed improvement for the first time in each of the subsequent years. By 2013, seventy-six high schools had freshman on-track rates above 70 percent, compared to just twenty-two schools in 2005.[24] By the 2018–2019 school year, 89 percent of ninth graders were on track to graduate. As those freshman cohorts moved through high school, the improvements paralleled this freshman on-track trajectory as graduation rates rose by about the same number of percentage points four years later.

FRESHMAN ONTRACK WAS THE ORGANIZING CONCEPT BEHIND IMPROVING GRADUATION RATES; PRACTICAL DATA REPORTS ON GRADES AND ATTENDANCE WERE THE KEY DRIVERS OF IMPROVEMENT

It is important to note is that there was no "freshman on-track program" per se, and use of the indicator itself did not result in higher graduation rates. Being on track in ninth grade is a goal, while freshman ontrack is an indicator. The freshman ontrack indicator gets calculated at the end of the year and serves as a goal toward which schools should strive. Meeting that goal is important because being on track at the end of ninth grade is highly predictive of high school graduation, which matters considerably for students' long-term health, employment, and other life outcomes. While the freshman ontrack indicator is seen as a leading indicator of high school graduation because it is available years before students graduate, it is obviously too late to change students' freshman on-track status once it is calculated. The key to improving graduation rates is to keep students from being off track during ninth grade through the use of the practical data collected by teachers, organized in a strategic way. Freshman Success Reports that were pushed out by the district every five weeks were the initial tools used to organize practical data on grades and attendance; these eventually evolved into data reports that could be downloaded by schools at any time during the academic year.

The ninth-grade transition year is critical because it is when students are developing their habits for "doing" high school, as well as their mindsets about whether they belong and if they can succeed. Research has shown that mindsets are strongly related to motivation, just as motivation is related to effort and effort to success. Negative mindsets undermine work effort and positive mindsets are crucial for perseverance.[25] Failing a class, especially early, can lead students to wonder whether they can succeed in high school, whether they belong, and whether they will fail again. Thus, the key to improving graduation rates is making sure that students develop the strategies, habits, and mindsets in the ninth grade that will allow them to succeed. To do this, schools need to use data that are available from the beginning of the ninth-grade year to monitor whether students are succeeding in their classes.

It is through data based on attendance and grades—data that are available throughout the year—that school administrators, teachers, and school support staff develop strategies to prevent students from falling off track in ninth grade. Through frequent monitoring, they can identify students who are beginning to struggle. They also can quickly see whether their strategies for supporting individual students and structures to support groups of students are having the intended impact. Often, interventions and changes in strategy do not work, and those things that do work can be difficult to sustain unless there is evidence that they work. It is critical to have quick turnarounds of information on the impact of improvement efforts in order to make corrections and keep successful efforts going.

The specific ways that school staff use the practical data reports, reach out to students, design schoolwide and individual support structures, evaluate their impacts, modify plans, and so on, differ across schools. The focus is on the problem—keeping students on track—and the practical data show how the school is doing and how individual students are faring. The district sets goals for on-track rates, emphasizing their importance by incorporating the end-of-year freshman ontrack indicator in accountability systems, and provides ongoing practical data reports on grades and attendance that school staff can use for reaching those goals. For their part, school staff are responsible for figuring out local uses of those practical data, which are available throughout the school year. School staff learn by doing, monitoring the results of their efforts and sharing strategies across networks of schools. While there is not one way of using the practical data, there are particular structures that schools can develop that support the productive use of those data.

THE NCS MODEL INCLUDES SCHOOL STRUCTURES THAT SUPPORT THE USE OF DATA FOR CONTINUOUS IMPROVEMENT

The leadership and staff of the NCS have continued to refine and develop their methods for supporting high school teams to work together around data. They now work with school teams in cities outside Chicago, while continuing to provide targeted support to specific schools in Chicago, and at times they have provided professional development for all high schools in CPS. The model that they have developed has five elements: engaging in research, developing teams, distributing leadership, using data for improvement, and learning through networks.[26]

The first element of their model is to engage in the research. This is a necessary step if schools are to address assumptions that are counterproductive to improving student outcomes. For example, the belief that failing a class teaches students to work harder makes sense from one perspective. Some students have undoubtedly worked harder after failing. But for most students, failure leads to embarrassment, lower self-efficacy, and questioning of whether they belong in an academic environment—mindsets that tend to lead students to withdraw effort.[27] Teachers may believe that by reaching out to find out why students are struggling, they are undermining their independence and resiliency. It is a very different perspective to see that their job is to teach students how to be resilient and to help them develop strategies to deal with whatever is preventing them from succeeding. They also don't realize that by not reaching out, they are sending the messages that missing class or missing assignments does not matter, or that they simply do not care. Myths about why students succeed or fail, and what educators can do about it, are pervasive. Even today, NCS and district administrators have to keep bringing people back to the evidence for them to focus on what really matters. Understanding the research is critical for educators to have buy-in to using the data systems and making them work so they have shared understandings that can guide their interpretation and use of those data.

The second and third elements of the NCS model are to develop teams and to distribute leadership. Consistent with the improvement science idea of adaptive implementation, schools start with ideas about changing practices—developed on their own or learned from other schools—that they want to test to see if they can be effective in their contexts. Developing solutions themselves, they can ensure that their strategies fit their school context and there is buy-in from the team. NCS staff believe that sustainable improvements in freshman success require a dedicated team of ninth-grade teachers. The work takes coordination to design systems that enable teachers to help each other to support students, such as regular meetings where teachers share data reports on the grades and attendance of students and discuss strategies for supporting students who are struggling. Our research on school leadership has likewise shown that at schools making the largest gains in student achievement (measured through test scores and grades), principals engaged teachers in shared leadership around student-centered goals (including improving grades, college outcomes, and test scores).[28] There was active teacher leadership, and it was not left to students to seek support when they needed it, or to teachers to offer support only if they chose to do so. Systems of support were opt-out instead of opt-in, with students automatically receiving help when they fell behind and all teachers developing support strategies together.

Principal leadership and support for the use of the practical data reports are critical. I have seen schools go through periods of substantial improvement, as well as substantial decline in the use of practical data reports on grades and attendance when principal leadership changes. For example, I recall a principal who immediately organized her school to use its own data around attendance and grades after the 2007 research report came out, and she subsequently used the Freshman Success Reports extensively in her school. I visited the school several times over the years and was amazed by how systematically they used data to better support students, as well as by the rapid improvement that the school made. Then the principal left, and the new principal faced pushback from teachers who did not want to keep up the work of meeting to discuss student data. They let go of some of their structures around data use, leaving it up to teachers to monitor their own students' grades and attendance, and their on-track rates went down dramatically the next year. After a couple of years, the school administration decided to go back to the way that they used to do things, and on-track rates went back up.

NCS has found that teacher teams need support for facilitating meetings about student data. Improving practices often requires difficult conversations and reflections on how individuals and the school could do things better. For example, we identified one school where ninth-grade failure rates were much higher in English classes than in algebra classes; something about the way English was being taught led the exact same students to be more likely to fail than in their math classes. NCS has developed protocols for helping structure difficult conversations at team meetings, and they spend time coaching members of school leader teams how to do this work with their grade-level teams.

Another approach using the practical data reports, complementary to the NCS model, is to have support staff—counselors and on-track coordinators—monitor the practical data reports and to draw in students, parents, school administrators, and teachers to figure out how to support students when they show signs of struggling. A downside to this approach is that when used in isolation, it may not lead teachers to recognize how their own practices in the classroom affect student success, or to change their ways of interacting with students to be more supportive. Often, school teams will begin the process of using practical data reports in a way that focuses on individual students. But NCS staff have described a change that occurs over time, wherein teachers recognize the need to change their own behavior or to work together to provide broader support for students in the school so change goes beyond student-by-student interventions. At the same time, having staff that focus primarily on ninth-grade student support can amplify other school efforts and provide other supportive adults in the school for students who may have difficult relationships with their teachers. Some schools with both dedicated staff members and teacher teams have made considerable progress because dedicated staff keep the work going and organized.[29]

The fourth element in the NCS model is to use data for improvement. This is a critical component and will be discussed further in the section of this chapter on that topic. School practitioners drove the changes that led to improvements in student outcomes, but having the right data made that work possible.

The final component in the NCS model is networked learning. Through NCS, and also through district efforts to network schools and develop cross-school learning, school practitioners have been able to talk to peers and share lessons about what worked for them. While NCS did not intentionally start as a networked improvement community, it shares many of the same design characteristics: focused on a well-specified common aim (keeping ninth graders on track); guided by a deep understanding of the problem and the system that produces it (continually bringing people back to the research and underlying theory); allowing adaptive innovation as schools tried different strategies in an iterative way; and diffusing innovation through networks of school leadership teams.[30] NCS coaches supported innovation at the school level and hosted meetings where school leadership teams would report on what they had tried and hear about the efforts of teams at other schools in the network. Over time, NCS staff developed their own understanding of what seemed to work best in schools by hearing from school teams and the experiences of coaches in the schools. Thus, the processes for using the data in schools, in coaching, and the district as a whole have continually evolved over time.

NOT ALL DATA ARE EQUALLY USEFUL FOR IMPROVEMENT; ATTENDANCE AND GRADES ARE IDEAL

Data that are useful for improvement are not necessarily the same data that schools regularly have access to, which are data for accountability, compliance assurance, or simple record keeping. Putting a focus on the right indicators is critical; otherwise, school staff could expend considerable effort trying to restructure their school or help individual students, and then never see any gains. The data elements in the freshman ontrack EWI system—including the end-of-year freshman ontrack indicator and the practical data reports on attendance and grades available throughout the year—met a number of important criteria that made that work manageable and rewarding. They were predictive and reliable, had a direct causal linkage to attainment, were clearly understandable, and were available in real time and actionable—meaning that it was within educators' locus of control to produce change.[31]

Predictiveness and Reliability

The end-of-year freshman ontrack indicator has a strong relationship with eventual graduation. By itself, it produces an 80 percent correct classification rate when used to predict who will graduate.[32] Ninth-grade grade point averages and course failure rates are slightly more predictive than freshman on-track status, while ninth-grade attendance is slightly less predictive. A comparison of metrics used across the country found that the only indicators with higher correct identification rate/lower false positive rate are indicators taken at the end of high school instead of the beginning.[33] In comparison, students' eighth-grade test scores, race, gender, and neighborhood poverty data, combined correctly, produce a 65 percent classification rate.[34] A strongly predictive indicator allows practitioners to be sure that students identified as at risk of not attaining a diploma/degree really do need support. When practitioners use indicators that are not strongly predictive of educational attainment, they risk missing students who need support, wasting limited resources, and misestimating the impact of their practices on students' educational attainment.[35] There are so many pieces of data that seem important that teachers and principals could potentially use to try to improve student outcomes, and it is overwhelming to try to improve everything simultaneously. Sarah Duncan, one of the directors of NCS, told me that one of the important aspects of the ontrack work was that it took things off the table that were less important, focusing attention on what mattered most.

To be predictive, an indicator has to be reliable, representing the same likelihood of graduating in different schools and across time. Perceptions that grades are subjective or have different meanings in different schools can lead people to be hesitant to use indicators based on them. The early research on the reliability of the end-of-year ontrack indicator showed it to be a highly reliable indicator of high school graduation. Its relationship with high school graduation was the same across very different high schools. In fact, in the original validation study, only one high school showed a significantly different relationship between students' end-of-year freshman on-track status and whether they graduated, and that difference was modest in size.[36] Even though grades are perceived to be subjective and unreliable, that is not the case when they are averaged over multiple classes and aggregated into a student's grade point average that is then used to determine ontrack status. They are highly reliable indicators of later performance in high school and in college, showing stronger and more consistent relationships than standardized test scores.[37]

Direct Causal Linkage to Educational Attainment

Even if a measured indicator of achievement, like freshman on-track status or scores on standardized tests, is related to later educational attainment, it does not necessarily follow that educational attainment will change later if the early indicator of achievement changes. The relationship might be spurious (caused by a third factor) or too indirect (requiring some other factor to change, as well). For example, in the early days of the freshmen on-track work, researchers did not know if there were factors outside of school that might lead students to fail courses in ninth grade, and then also influence graduation directly, such as negative peer influences or insufficient family economic resources. If this were the case, educators might help students succeed in ninth grade but still not improve graduation rates. It also could have been that improvements in ninth grade were insufficient without similar efforts in tenth and eleventh grade—maybe improving ninth-grade course performance would just delay failure until later years of high school without additional supports in those years. However, improvements in ninth-grade grades and attendance were followed by improvements in course performance and attendance in tenth and eleventh grades. There was almost a one-to-one improvement in graduation rates with improvements in ontrack rates, suggesting a direct relationship between ninth-grade course performance, subsequent course performance, and high school graduation.[38] Even more striking, the relationship between freshman on-track status and high school graduation has remained the same over time, even as many more students are on track than in the initial days of the validation study.[39] If the relationship were spurious, caused by factors external to the school, the relationship should have weakened as more students became on track.

Usability and Clarity

The early-warning data elements—end-of-year freshman on-track status and the practical data on grades and attendance during the year—were easy to understand and had direct implications for practice. Researchers often want to develop complex indicators with sophisticated methods that combine many different data elements. That leaves practitioners dependent on researchers to create the metrics, and then they wonder what actually has an impact on the metrics. In contrast, the early-warning system developed by CPS was simple, focusing attention on a small number of indicators. Often, people will try to put as much information as possible into an indicator system. To the extent that indicator systems contain many data elements, there is the risk that people will focus on those elements that are easiest to track and manipulate or that correspond with their preexisting assumptions about what matters, even if those data elements have less potential leverage for improving educational attainment than other indicators in the system. Educators may benefit from supplemental information that can inform intervention efforts.[40] But the primary focus of the indicator system that CPS developed was on those elements that were most important, which kept conversations and strategies focused on those factors that were most important for eventual graduation—grades and attendance. It is essential that indicators are easy to use and have clear meaning if practitioners are to engage with the data in a productive way. Data should provide insight into practices that make it easier for people to do their work, not that increase their cognitive load.

Real-Time/Right-Time Availability

Grades and attendance data are available year round, and data reports can be continuously updated. Data that are available in real time can be used for continuous improvement, providing information about whether the strategies that school staff are currently using to support students are working. This allows practitioners to change course, make adjustments, or double down on what they are doing that seems to be successful.[41]

Actionability

Indicators that are causally linked to students' educational attainment can be targeted in an effort to improve their attainment, but if educators cannot change them or do not know how to change them, then they may not be useful as key components of the indicator system. There is evidence that both grades and attendance are strongly influenced by the school and classroom contexts. For example, we found that unexcused absences quadrupled when Chicago students moved from eighth to ninth grade in 2009, and course grade point averages declined by 0.4 points.[42] The change in context from the middle grades to high school led students to be absent more often. Students' grades and attendance are also influenced by characteristics of their classrooms (e.g., which teacher they have, their classroom peers, the class size and content).[43] Because teachers do not generally observe students' behaviors in other classes, they do not know how their students' attendance and grades would be different in other contexts. It can seem, therefore, as though student behavior is not something that they can influence. It is critical that educators understand how their practices influence students' behaviors and experiences in school.[44] Otherwise, the temptation is to blame students and their families for low attendance and work effort, and to focus on the students who seem to care more about education, simply because they face fewer barriers to engaging fully in the demands of the school.[45]

The practical data reports, as well as the freshman ontrack indicator, also brought attention to students who were just starting to fall off track—those failing just one class, getting Ds, or missing a number of days of school. These were students for whom modest interventions could be highly effective because they were still mostly engaged in school. School staff could actually see improvements in their data reports and feel excited about the students' progress.

PUSHBACK AND CRITICISMS TO PROMOTING FRESHMAN ONTRACK RATES

The organization of data around ninth-grade attendance and grades, as well as the supports for using the data productively, allowed schools to make progress on a problem that previously seemed intractable. But that did not happen without pushback and criticism. District leadership changed every year or two after Arne Duncan left in 2008 to become the US secretary of education. Some of the new district leaders had never heard of the freshman ontrack indicator, or of EWI systems. One district leader made moves to stop providing schools with the Freshman Success Reports and changed priorities from keeping ninth graders on track. School and network leaders responded by using their own school data and bringing in Consortium researchers to show how graduations rates had improved because of the freshman on-track work. The district ended up keeping the supports in place, and freshman ontrack and graduation rates continued to rise under their tenure.

There have also been ongoing concerns about the use of the end-of-year freshman ontrack indicator for accountability purposes and the comparisons that arise as teachers collaboratively look at the grades that each of them has given to the same students with the practical data reports. In talking with teachers, some have questioned whether their colleagues might be giving out Ds instead of Fs or otherwise lowering their standards so more students receive passing grades. My colleagues looked into those concerns and found no evidence that the improvements in on-track rates were driven by turning Fs into Ds, moving students just above the margins of failing or being off track.[46] Moreover, the relationship between the ontrack indicator and high school graduation remained consistent over time, when we would expect it to diminish if the ontrack indicator were compromised. We also found that achievement as measured by standardized test scores, taking of AP courses and scores on exams, and college outcomes has been going up in CPS high schools over time; grading standards have not declined based on other measures of achievement.[47] There are pros and cons of including any indicator for accountability purposes, as doing so fosters concerns about manipulation and can lead to mistrust of the data. At the same time, this signals to schools where they should direct their efforts. It is not clear that schools would have continued to focus as intently on improving freshman on-track rates had the end-of-year metric not been included in accountability. And teacher discussions of grades based on the practical data reports were central to improving student outcomes.

Teachers and administrators also continue to raise questions about whether grades can be trusted as a metric to track and try to improve student performance. There is a need to continually direct people to the research and address these concerns, particularly as school staff turn over.

And there should be regular examination of the data to be sure that these concerns are not borne out since conditions do change over time.

EQUITY IMPROVED AS SCHOOL STAFF WORKED TO KEEP ALL STUDENTS ON TRACK

The percentage of off-track students has declined precipitously, and yet the relationship between on-track status and graduation is the same as it was in the 2005 validation study. The relationship that has changed is the relationship between students' background characteristics and high school graduation. While there continue to be large differences in graduation rates by students' economic background, race, ethnicity, gender, and identified learning disabilities, the relationships of students' background characteristics with graduation have grown weaker over time.[48] Students' background characteristics, factors outside of school, and students' prior academic histories in school all influence high school graduation, but they do so because of the ways that they affect students' engagement in their courses in ninth grade. If problems are not addressed in ninth grade, they continue to influence students' engagement throughout high school. Educators cannot change factors outside of school, but they can design their schools so that factors like family income and the effects of structural and interpersonal racism have less influence on students' engagement. Schools must change how they operate so external inequities are counteracted through schooling rather than reinforced by it.

In interviews with students during a study on the transition to high school, my colleagues and I asked why students sometimes missed school or fell behind on schoolwork. There were myriad reasons in addition to medical or health causes; for instance, one student was taking care of a parent with cancer, and there was no one else who could provide care; another student was suffering from depression after losing a friend to gun violence; another student could not wash his one school uniform because his family had no money for soap; another student thought that her first-period teacher was rude and skipped class to avoid him; another was afraid of being involved in a fight at school; and another had problems with unreliable buses. Many of these are problems that more affluent parents minimize with financial resources—better health support, paying caretakers, engaging in therapy, buying laundry soap, and getting rides to school. Getting to school every day and being ready to engage in challenging work require resources that many families do not have. These issues were often invisible to students' teachers—we interviewed their teachers as well, and while some teachers were aware of students' struggles, many were not. They only knew whether students had shown up and done their work. As a consequence, teachers' perceptions have the potential to align with overt or subconscious biases, such as that students who are low-income, Black, Latinx, or male do not care about good grades or their parents do not care if they get low grades.

Teacher beliefs that attendance and grades are about students and their families, and not about structures and teacher/administrator decisions, are pervasive. It can be difficult to recognize that schools are typically set up to require families to have sufficient economic resources to enable participation. Teachers also sometimes express concerns that too much support could hurt students by making them less self-reliant. Yet there is little concern that middle- and upper-income families harm their children by arranging for transportation, hiring tutors, and making sure that family members obtain health and mental health services when they need them. Some of the challenges are easy to fix with a little help, while others require deeper and more sustained problem solving with others in the school community. If nobody reaches out when a student begins to struggle, the student is likely to fall further and further behind. As teachers and school staff reach out to students to help them get caught up on their work and address the challenges that they face by getting them the support they need, they show that they care about their students as learners and change their own perceptions about what they can do as educators. By systematically using the practical data reports on ninth-grade attendance and grades, teachers and staff are induced to reach out to all students who need support, including students whom teachers might not otherwise have recognized as in need of support and students whom they might have assumed simply did not care about education.

CONCLUSION: LARGE GAINS WERE MADE BY WORKING ON AN INTRACTABLE PROBLEM THROUGH PRACTICAL MEASUREMENT

Policy makers are forever searching for a singular policy or program that will be a game changer. In Chicago, graduation rates did not improve because somebody developed the right dropout prevention program that schools then implemented, but because over time, practitioners innovated, researchers responded, innovations were tested and refined, and the resulting insights initiated the next round of inquiry. Eventually, key insights developed in this manner led to innovations in high school practice. The centerpiece of the effort was the use of practical data for setting goals and monitoring change, along with strategies for using those data productively. Grades and attendance were already collected as part of routine practices, but they had to be organized so they could be used for continuous improvement purposes. Eventually, as teachers in some schools started focusing more and more on why students were failing or missing school, they shifted how they saw their job and their role in supporting student success. By reaching out to students, they developed relationships that promoted stronger engagement. By working together—both within and across schools—they saw patterns that otherwise would have eluded them. By analyzing those patterns in data, they began to see how the ways that their schools were organized and the ways that classes were taught could influence whether students were successful. Improvements were not the result of somebody developing the right dropout prevention program; they were achieved incrementally as practitioners, researchers, and policy makers together innovated and had insights that fueled iterative rounds of improvement. Eventually, key insights led to innovations producing dramatically different practices, and levels of accomplishment in high schools.

6

Designing an Instructionally Focused Practical Measurement System Centered on Equity

Adrian Larbi-Cherif
Anna Premo
Christian Schunn
Jennifer Lin Russell

In this chapter, we present and illustrate a set of practical measures that are being used to guide instructional improvement efforts in a network of fourteen middle and high schools in a large urban district in the South.[1] The network's goal is to improve ninth-grade literacy outcomes for Latinx students, Black students, and Emergent Multilingual Learners (EMLs) in schools that have historically had low achievement for these groups on state English and language arts (ELA) assessments. Coaches from an intermediary organization that coordinates the network introduced teachers to new approaches to literacy instruction that center students in the learning process, and in so doing aim to create more equitable learning opportunities. As teachers worked with coaches to learn and implement new teaching practices, the network's data analysts developed practical measures designed to help teachers and coaches better understand students' experiences with changes in instruction. These practical measures are student-facing "exit tickets," or mini-surveys that ask students to share their experiences with student-centered literacy instruction.

Our experience designing student-facing exit tickets inspired our articulation of a set of design principles for instructionally focused practical measures that can inform other networked improvement efforts aimed at producing more equitable teaching and learning opportunities. In this chapter, we outline the nature of the instructional changes pursued in the network, present a vignette illustrating how a teacher experimented with these teaching changes with support from practical measure data, and elaborate four design principles that informed our development of exit tickets as practical measures that support improvement. We believe the design principles can support other educators developing instructionally focused practical measures in the context of collaborative, data-based, and disciplined instructional improvement initiatives.

A NETWORKED APPROACH TO INSTRUCTIONAL IMPROVEMENT: STUDENT-CENTERED LITERACY INSTRUCTION AND TASK SHEETS

Student demographics and patterns of achievement in our network schools underscored the need to develop student-centered, equitable instruction that would lead to improved postsecondary outcomes. Most of the students in our network's schools are economically disadvantaged, and 90 percent identify as Latinx or Black. In addition, more than one-third of the students are classified as EMLs, with Spanish being the predominant language outside of English. These historically minoritized student groups often have not had access to rich literacy learning opportunities, which has contributed to persistent gaps in achievement compared to the performance of their more advantaged peers locally, statewide, and nationally.

Initial efforts to understand the root causes contributing to these students' low achievement in ELA indicated that instruction was typically teacher-centered, had relatively low rigor, and did not attend to developing text comprehension.[2] Text comprehension is a critical and yet often-neglected component of secondary ELA instruction, and it is essential for developing the reading and analytic writing skills necessary for career and college readiness. Furthermore, interviews conducted with students and teachers suggested that they felt that instruction was rarely culturally responsive, which led to teachers and students feeling disconnected from each other and from the curriculum being taught. Classroom observations revealed that teacher-centered instruction and outdated instructional materials resulted in suboptimal student engagement in literacy learning activities.

Coaches from the Institute for Learning (IFL), data analysts from the Learning Research and Development Center, and equity scholars at the Center for Urban Education, all of whom were affiliated with the University of Pittsburgh, collaborated to support teachers in using instructional materials and routines that are comprehension based, student centered, and culturally responsive. The aim of these pedagogical changes was to develop students' analytical writing skills and their capacity to analyze texts that focus on contemporary issues relevant to their families, neighborhoods, and cultures.

To support instructional improvement and greater student engagement in classroom literacy activities, IFL coaches introduced comprehension task sheets as a key support for student-centered literacy instruction. Comprehension task sheets provide guidance to students on how to analyze texts as they complete a sequence of learning activities. They are organized around complex texts that are grade-appropriate representations of a genre or subject matter. Such texts put significant demands on the reader as they include domain-specific or academic language, incorporate complex structures, use more implicit meaning in literary texts, and often require readers to analyze information from multiple sources and perspectives. The task sheets support students in critically analyzing the content of the text while also reflecting on how their prior knowledge, ideas, and experience relate to the text.

Figure 6.1 provides an example of a sequence of student-centered activities that comprise a comprehension task-sheet lesson. Students first

Figure 6.1 Sample task sheet

Step 1: Read "Friendship in the Age of Economics." As you read, please do two things:
- Mark places in the margin with a check-mark that help you understand the author's ideas about friendship.
- Mark places in the margin that you don't understand with a plus sign.

Step 2: After you have finished reading and you have marked passages, please compose a quickwrite in response to the prompt below:

- Explain the author's big ideas about friendship—the kind of friendship he values—to someone who hasn't read the essay. Draw on and refer to those moments that you marked, citing them as you can, to make your case for the kind of friendship that you think the author values.

Step 3: Take five minutes to share your quickwrite with a partner. As you share, notice where you agree and where you disagree with each other about the kind of friendship that the author values.

Create a chart of your ideas on a sheet of paper. Be sure to list both the things you agree and disagree on. Post your chart on the wall.

Step 4: Once everyone has posted their chart, move around the room and read the charts. Please take notes on the ideas that are similar to and different from yours. The process of viewing the charts is called a gallery walk.

Step 5: After the gallery walk, please sit in a circle in preparation for a whole group discussion of the following questions:

- How would you describe the kind of friendship that the author, Todd May, values?
- Why would you say he values it over other kinds of friendships?

During our discussion, you should refer to your notes and what others have said on their charts as well as to your own ideas. Keep the essay with your marks in front of you. I'll ask you to back up your ideas with references to the text.

Step 6: After our whole group discussion, please complete a quickwrite to reflect on your thinking using the following question:

- How was your thinking about the kind of friendship that the author values changed or confirmed after completing the gallery walk and whole group discussion? What did you hear or see from your classmates that confirmed or changed your thinking?

---

read a complex text and make annotations, such as indicating which portions of the text they understand and which they do not (step 1). Students then use these annotations to produce a quickwrite—a five-minute writing activity in which they record their initial thoughts on the main ideas of a text (step 2). Quickwrites are intended to function as scaffolds that help students develop text comprehension through writing about the text. Students then engage in small-group and/or whole-class discussions to further substantiate, modify, or transform their initial understandings of the text (steps 3–5). Comprehension task-sheet lessons then conclude with students revising their quickwrites to produce a more detailed, formal written product such as an essay (step 6). The arc of task-sheet lessons is designed to foster active student engagement with the text and the classroom community, and in the process provide students with multiple opportunities to revise and deepen their initial understandings of the main ideas of the text.

In addition to supporting students' learning, comprehension task sheets scaffold teachers' learning to sequence student-centered activities to help them develop students' analytical writing skills. Over time, IFL coaches encouraged teachers to use the general sequence of student-centered activities illustrated in figure 6.1 to design and enact their own task sheets for other complex texts. IFL coaches also encouraged teachers to analyze how specific features of task sheets supported improvements in students' text comprehension. Although not the topic of this chapter, participating teachers were also introduced to task-sheet models that focused on synthesizing and on analyzing texts, both of which are central to the development of academic writing skills.

IFL coaches designed and introduced the initial comprehension task-sheet model and subsequent adaptations of this model as "change ideas" that teachers could incorporate into their regular lessons and experiment with to enhance their student engagement and literacy learning. Change ideas included ways to present the task sheet (i.e., electronically or on paper) and ways to enhance specific student-centered activities embedded in the task sheet, such as teachers modeling for students how to do a quickwrite. IFL coaches introduced the latter change ideas in response to the challenges that teachers encountered when they used comprehension task sheets in their classrooms. Hence, change ideas were designed partly in response to what teachers and students experienced in student-centered ELA instruction.[3]

To further support teachers' uptake of new instructional practices and promote their engagement in testing the new practices, IFL coaches and data analysts collaborated to design and introduce a set of practical measures that could inform instructional improvement through an exit ticket routine. Later in this chapter, we will detail and illustrate the design principles that informed the development of these practical measures.

First, however, we should clarify that these exit tickets were administered at the end of lessons and took the form of mini-surveys that probed specific instructional change ideas, such as the Comprehension Task Sheet change idea. Teachers would enact a specific change idea and then have students complete the corresponding exit ticket at the end of the lesson. Teachers would then receive a feedback report that summarized students' exit ticket responses within and across their classes. They then worked with an IFL coach to analyze the data to determine their next steps in improving their instruction. Analysis of student responses helped teachers and coaches determine if the change idea was effective in supporting student engagement in literacy learning and should be adopted and integrated into day-to-day instruction, if the change idea should be adapted and then tested further, or if repeated testing without the desired outcomes suggests that the change idea should be abandoned. One key advantage of using the exit ticket as a modality for collecting practical measure data was that teachers could use the same data collection routine (i.e., exit tickets) to collect data on different change ideas.

In the next section, we use a vignette to illustrate a teacher's experience in using and learning from practical measures to guide her efforts to improve her instruction. After the vignette, we step back to unpack the design principles that informed the development of our practical measures and that can orient the design of other practical measures for instructional improvement. We then conclude with considerations on the validity of the practical measures described in this chapter and offer closing remarks.

An Illustration of Teacher Learning in and from the Use of Practical Measures

Pearl Green is a middle school teacher who recently learned how to design comprehension task sheets for students.[4] Figure 6.2 displays the journey map for Ms. Green as she progressed from implementing the

DESIGNING PRACTICAL MEASUREMENT CENTERED ON EQUITY 163

Figure 6.2 Journey map for Pearl Green

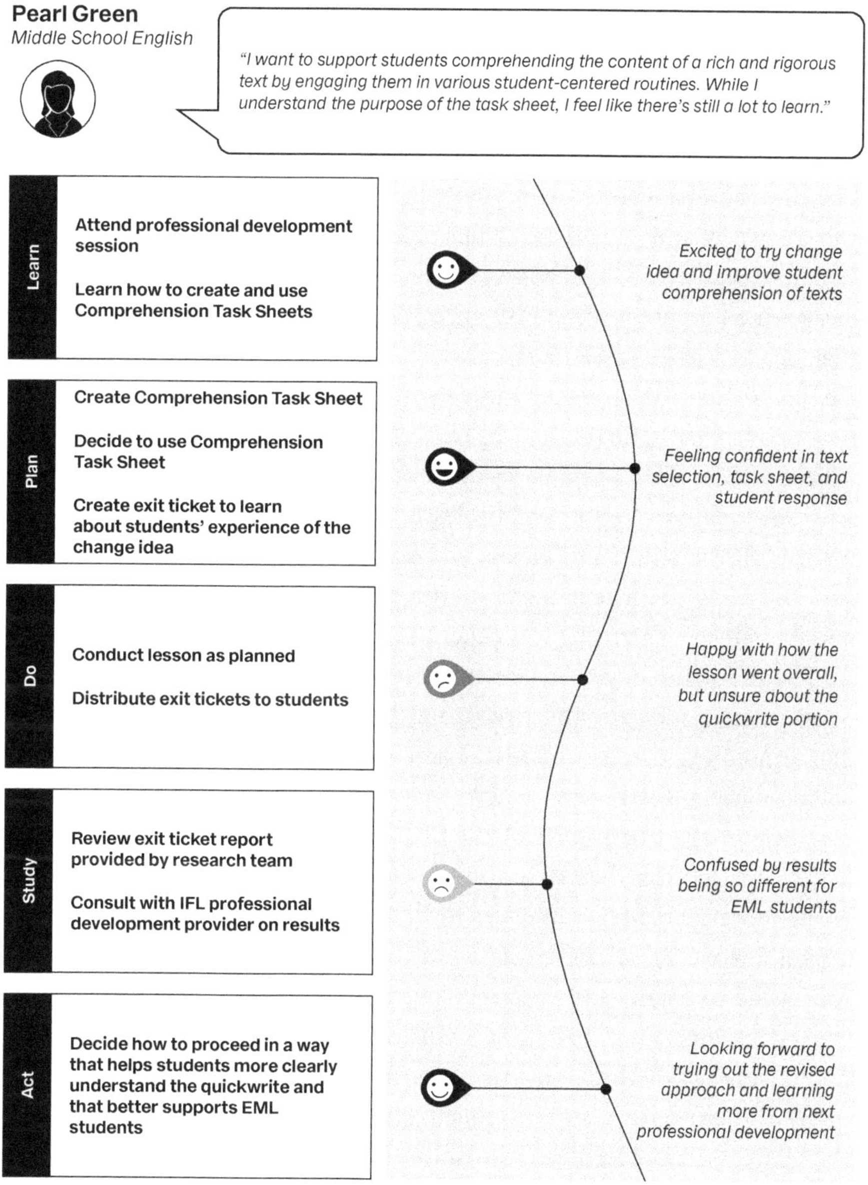

Pearl Green
Middle School English

"I want to support students comprehending the content of a rich and rigorous text by engaging them in various student-centered routines. While I understand the purpose of the task sheet, I feel like there's still a lot to learn."

Learn
- Attend professional development session
- Learn how to create and use Comprehension Task Sheets

Excited to try change idea and improve student comprehension of texts

Plan
- Create Comprehension Task Sheet
- Decide to use Comprehension Task Sheet
- Create exit ticket to learn about students' experience of the change idea

Feeling confident in text selection, task sheet, and student response

Do
- Conduct lesson as planned
- Distribute exit tickets to students

Happy with how the lesson went overall, but unsure about the quickwrite portion

Study
- Review exit ticket report provided by research team
- Consult with IFL professional development provider on results

Confused by results being so different for EML students

Act
- Decide how to proceed in a way that helps students more clearly understand the quickwrite and that better supports EML students

Looking forward to trying out the revised approach and learning more from next professional development

Comprehension Task Sheet change idea to implementing the Modeling the Quickwrite change idea with the support of an IFL coach. Both these change ideas were central to the improvement work in this network.

Ms. Green believed in the underlying instructional vision of the task sheet: to support students in comprehending a rich and challenging text by engaging them in a sequence of student-centered instructional activities (Learn). She also felt confident that the text that she planned to use was rigorous and would push her students' thinking as they grappled with its main ideas (Plan). However, as this was the first time that she had designed a comprehension task sheet, she wanted to learn how to ensure that her task sheet and its implementation would provide an appropriate intellectual challenge for students, while also helping them to struggle productively with the main ideas of the text. Ms. Green read the exit ticket (figure 6.3) for the Comprehension Task Sheet change idea. She noted that it asked students to report on how lesson activities supported their engagement with the text. In addition, she noticed that it focused on students' experiences with the text, particularly as they related to their backgrounds and daily lives, which she was eager to learn more about.

The following day, Ms. Green implemented the Comprehension Task Sheet change idea for the first time (Do). Students started by reading and annotating the lesson's text. Then Ms. Green instructed the students to complete a quickwrite, where they jotted down their initial understanding of the main ideas of the text for five minutes. This was where Ms. Green felt that her lesson might have faltered. Only a few students wrote more than a few sentences for their quickwrite, with many writing only a few words or not engaging with the routine at all. As the lesson proceeded to small- and then whole-group discussions, she realized that the discussions were not as rich with ideas as she had hoped. This led her to wonder whether students' struggles with the quickwrite resulted in many of them generating incomplete understandings of the main ideas of the text. Students completed the online exit ticket for the Comprehension Task Sheet change idea on their laptops at the end of the lesson. Data analysts at the University of Pittsburgh were notified about the incoming data

Figure 6.3 Comprehension Task Sheet exit ticket

Comprehension Task Sheet exit ticket
Ticket de salida de la hoja de tareas de comprensión

The text we worked with today... (check all that apply)
El texto con el que trabajamos hoy... (Marque todos los que correspondan)
- ☐ was boring (era aburrida/o)
- ☐ was relevant to my background (fue relevante para mi experiencia)
- ☐ was relevant to my daily life (era pertinente para mi vida diaria)
- ☐ made me want to read (me dio ganas de leer)
- ☐ was worth my time (valió la pena mi tiempo)
- ☐ was worth talking about (valió la pena hablar del texto)
- ☐ had interesting ideas (tenía ideas interesantes)
- ☐ was hard to understand (fue difícil de entender)
- ☐ None of these! (¡Ninguno de esos!)

The task sheet today... (check all that apply)
La hoja de tareas de hoy... (Marque todas las que correspondan)
- ☐ helped me understand the text (me ayudó a entender el texto)
- ☐ was easy to follow (fue fácil de seguir)
- ☐ made sense (tuvo sentido)
- ☐ had enough information (tenía suficiente información)
- ☐ included all the steps to complete the tasks (incluyó todos los pasos para completar las tareas)
- ☐ None of these! (¡Ninguno de esos!)

Was any part of the task sheet confusing?
¿Alguna parte de la hoja de tareas fue confusa?
- ○ Yes (Sí)
- ○ No

What was confusing?
¿Qué fue confuso?

_____

_____

Only displayed for students who selected "Yes (Sí)" in the previous question

I answered this exit ticket primarily based on the
Respondí este boleto de salida basado principalmente en el
- ○ Questions in English
- ○ Preguntas en Español
- ○ Questions in both English and Spanish (Preguntas en Inglés y Español)

and generated a feedback report for Ms. Green summarizing her students' experiences with this change idea.[5]

At the end of the following school day, Ms. Green received her feedback report for the Comprehension Task Sheet change idea (see figure 6.4). She analyzed her students' open-ended responses and learned that many of them had difficulty comprehending the text, particularly the students who responded in Spanish (Study). Some students reported that they had difficulties understanding the text's main ideas. Ms. Green reviewed the quickwrites from the lesson and noticed that very few students had written initial thoughts on the main idea of the text. Because the quickwrite can help students begin to make sense of a text, she wondered if students' general lack of engagement with this routine contributed to their struggles

Figure 6.4 Exit ticket report for Comprehension Task Sheet change idea

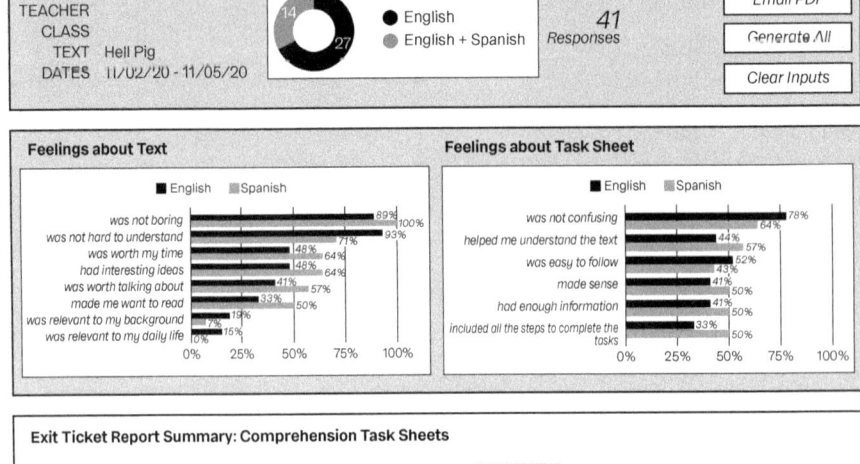

with comprehension. She was also concerned that most students did not find the text relevant to their backgrounds or daily lives, with the students who responded in Spanish finding the text less relevant than those who responded in English. This observation led her to conjecture that the students would have been more engaged if they read a text that they found more culturally relevant.

Ms. Green set up a session with an IFL coach to discuss her report for the Comprehension Task Sheet change idea. After analyzing the report and students' quickwrites with Ms. Green, the coach agreed that the quickwrite was likely the best instructional routine to focus on to improve text comprehension. The IFL coach noted that many teachers across the network had reported that their students were struggling with the quickwrite portion of the comprehension task sheet. The coach also shared that other teachers in the network had found that students produced richer quickwrites when they implemented a second change idea: Modeling the Quickwrite. Ms. Green was convinced and committed to trying this new change idea. She also indicated that it might be helpful to select a culturally relevant text for her Latinx and EML students, as the practical measure data indicated that most students from these groups did not find the prior text relevant to their backgrounds or daily lives.

They spent the rest of the coaching session rehearsing this change idea, discussing strategies for selecting culturally responsive texts, and reviewing the exit ticket that Ms. Green planned to use to learn about student experiences with the Modeling the Quickwrite change idea (shown in figure 6.5). Ms. Green was confident that the exit ticket would help her evaluate the efficacy of this subsequent change idea because it asked students to reflect on whether the teacher's modeling helped them understand how to get their initial thoughts about a text down on paper. Ms. Green and the IFL coach wrapped up the session by reviewing the text that she had selected, her task sheet, the change idea, and its attendant practical measure. Ms. Green had now planned the implementation of two change ideas, with the analysis of practical measure data from the first change idea informing her decision to implement the second change idea (Act). These practices of iterative implementation and disposition toward

Figure 6.5 Exit ticket aligned with the specifics of the Modeling Quickwrite change idea

1. After seeing the teacher model a quickwrite, I now feel _____ about quick writes. (Select your strongest feeling)
   ○ stressed
   ○ comfortable
   ○ interested
   ○ bored
   ○ confused

   Measuring Student Sensemaking of the Change Idea

2. After seeing the teacher model a quickwrite, I still have questions about

   _____

   _____

3. The quickwrite helped me stay focused on the text.
   ○ YES!
   ○ yes
   ○ no
   ○ NO!

   Measuring Immediate Outcomes of the Change Idea

4. The quickwrite helped me understand the text.
   ○ YES!
   ○ yes
   ○ no
   ○ NO!

---

analysis and reflection are foundational to the effective use of practical measures for improvement.

Stepping back from the details of this vignette, it is important to note that prior research indicates that practitioners' interpretation and use of data depend on both a focus on problems of practice central to their work and on their capacity to use and make sense of data.[6] Without support for interpreting and using practical measures, it is possible that the data may be interpreted with a deficit framing or used for purposes counter to improvement (e.g., teacher evaluation). Therefore, it is vital to support practitioners in developing the capacity to understand and use practical measures for improvement purposes. Our network provided teachers with professional learning opportunities focused on doing so. Teachers were first introduced to practical measures and feedback reports, like those displayed in figure 6.4, in network events prior to the implementation of change ideas. These events supported teachers in becoming familiar with the practical measures and how to assess the impact of a change idea. Teachers were also provided with coaching following implementation of change ideas, as illustrated in the vignette, to support the interpretation and use of practical measure data to inform subsequent change ideas.

DESIGN PRINCIPLES INFORMING THE DEVELOPMENT AND USES OF PRACTICAL MEASURES FOR INSTRUCTIONAL IMPROVEMENT

Now we present four design principles that guided the development of our practical measures for instructional improvement.[7] We posit that these principles can also support the design of other robust, instructionally focused practical measures:

- Design Principle 1: Focus on students' experiences of the instructional change
- Design Principle 2: Embed practical measures in existing instructional routines
- Design Principle 3: Produce data that identifies inequities
- Design Principle 4: Provide timely feedback

These design principles were informed by prior research, the demands of our improvement context, and our own learning about which approaches to improvement were more effective in that context. Prior research on the development and use of practical measures highlights the importance of designing measures that address relevant problems of practice while also affording timely feedback (Design Principles 1 and 4).[8] Design Principle 2 stemmed from the challenges of collecting practical measure data without disrupting the flow of instruction or overburdening teachers who were developing new, complex practices. More specifically, we prioritized embedding practical measures in exit tickets to allow teachers to focus primarily on implementing change ideas and developing new instructional practices. Design Principle 3 was informed by equity issues that students encountered in our context, such as minoritized students often having few opportunities to engage meaningfully with rigorous, culturally relevant texts. We therefore found it essential to identify differences in how specific groups of students experience change ideas.

In addition, experience in implementing change ideas and analyzing practical measure data further contributed to these design principles. In our context, we increasingly focused on how EMLs experienced change ideas, as initial practical measurement data often indicated that they were less engaged than students who were fluent in English. This led to further inquiry into why EMLs were experiencing change ideas differently. Consequently, we paid more attention to how instruction could be adjusted to better support EMLs. It also led us to reflect on how we could design practical measures and present feedback reports to identify and then present potentially inequitable learning opportunities more effectively.

Part of our motivation in presenting the design principles is that they oriented our improvement work in a network comprising multiple organizations. That is, it took some time and consideration to develop design principles that could orient the efforts of classroom teachers, improvement science scholars, equity scholars, and ELA teacher educators to address agreed-upon problems of practice through practical measurement. The design principles are the product of our efforts to distill some key lessons from our experience to help practitioners and other researchers adapt the practical measures to their own contexts. In what follows, we define each principle and provide a justification for its inclusion. We also illustrate how we applied these principles to the design and use of our practical measures.

Design Principle 1: Focus on Students' Experiences of the Instructional Change

This design principle is founded on understanding students' experience of the change idea. Students are both the targets of the educational process and the group that usually has the least power in the educational system. However, it is essential to attend to their perspective when determining whether the changes introduced constitute improvements. Too often, students' perspectives on schooling in general and instructional processes in particular are not considered by teachers. Prior research has demonstrated that incorporating student voice into the improvement processes involving curricula and instruction can increase students' sense of agency, belonging, and ultimately learning, particularly when efforts solicit student input on how to increase their engagement.[9] In addition, equity scholars have long posited that it is crucial to include students' perspectives on the educational process to help teachers reflect on and confront implicit biases and deficit-based perspectives.[10] As a consequence of attending to students' experiences with change ideas, network teachers would receive the very type of feedback that they indicated was lacking in typical day-to-day practice—how students experienced instructional support and change ideas.

To ensure that student voices are used to guide the instructional improvement process, we designed practical measures for specific instructional change ideas to measure *student sensemaking of those change ideas*. We also acknowledged the importance of students being able to complete focal tasks successfully and to realize the specific learning outcomes by designing practical measures for the *immediate outcomes of the change idea*.

In targeting student-sensemaking of the change idea, we focus on whether the change idea helped students make sense of the learning activity at hand. If the change idea is a model or tool, do students perceive it to be confusing or incomplete? If the change idea is an activity, do students feel that they were adequately prepared to engage in it? The measure's items focus on likely ways in which the specific tool could fail (e.g., whether Ms. Green's students felt confused by the teacher's model of a quickwrite). Qualitative feedback from students can indicate what specifically was problematic with the change idea (e.g., what was confusing?), which then can further guide the improvement process.

The exit ticket in figure 6.5 includes two questions that focus on students' sensemaking of the change idea. These questions ask students how they felt after the teacher modeled the quickwrite and if they still had questions about the quickwrite. Data from these questions can help teachers understand how students responded to their modeling of the quickwrite and whether the modeling helped them engage with the quickwrite itself.

We found it essential to understand students' sensemaking of the change idea because sensemaking of lesson activities profoundly influences whether they can complete those activities successfully. Teachers are already very familiar with analyzing student work to assess students' mastery of learning objectives. Here, we contend that teachers can enhance what they learn from student artifacts by understanding whether instruction itself helped students engage with lesson activities or tasks. Thus, we viewed understanding students' experience of the change idea as an important supplement to the work in which teachers already engage. Teachers are then positioned to use evidence of student learning (as revealed in the student work) and evidence of how students perceived the task (derived from practical measures) to inform their decisions about this and subsequent change ideas.

We also designed practical measures to gauge the *immediate outcomes of the change idea* to understand if students were able to successfully complete the task that the change idea targeted. For example, if students were previously struggling with a particular lesson activity, like using a quickwrite to generate ideas about the text, the practical measure probed whether the change idea resolved these struggles. Focusing on the immediate outcomes of the change idea gives teachers direct feedback on the implementation of the change idea and whether it produced the desired improvement in learning. Thus, the items in the practical measure also focus on what a successful version of that learning activity involves (e.g., generating ideas, noticing differences in ideas, organizing ideas, clarifying ideas, resolving confusions, developing a plan). By designing practical measures that attend to both students' sensemaking of a change idea and the immediate outcomes of the change idea, teachers are positioned to analyze whether students understood lesson activities and if they were able to successfully complete these activities.

Designing practical measures that center on student experiences requires the integration of four kinds of expertise: (1) instructional expertise, which reflects deep knowledge of the content, instructional practice, and how the change idea is likely to succeed or fail in implementation; (2) measurement expertise on developing items that are meaningful to users (e.g., teachers) and parsimoniously measure the success of change idea implementation; (3) improvement expertise in understanding how to design and enact routines that support improvement through the analysis and use of practical measures (which also will be addressed in Design Principle 4); and (4) practical expertise, which subsumes knowledge of the context, the structures and policies of the school system, and how the environment and the school system interact to mediate instruction and related improvement work.

We assert that all these forms of expertise are required to ensure that the use of practical measures for improvement actually drives improvement, not only in our context but in others as well. First, it takes considerable time and effort to integrate the first two forms of expertise with each other. In our work, IFL coaches provided the instructional expertise and our analysts provided the measurement expertise; however, we had to develop routines to bridge these perspectives and ensure that the important features of a given change idea were captured by a parsimonious set of practical measures that accurately and efficiently assessed both students' sensemaking and the immediate outcome of the change idea.

Integrating both instructional expertise and measurement expertise underscored the challenge of capturing the nuances of complex instructional activities with a discrete set of measures that can provide fruitful feedback to teachers. Often, we had to make compromises about how many practical measures were generated for each change idea, as well as about the focus of these measures to capture important aspects of the change idea while not overwhelming teachers with feedback. One key takeaway from this work is that it is essential for improvers to develop routines to ensure that the use of practical measures involves the effective integration of content and measurement expertise. In our context, it was essential that we achieved this integration to ensure that practical measures were student-centered and effectively captured key aspects of student sensemaking and learning. As is the case with many processes in improvement science, our team found the integration of different forms of expertise to be an iterative process that was refined while developing and enacting multiple change ideas.

Design Principle 2: Embed Practical Measures in Existing Instructional Routines

Fundamental questions to consider when designing practical measures is how to collect practical measure data that will drive improvement efforts in ways that are minimally burdensome to the practitioners collecting the data, unobtrusive to the flow of classroom instruction, and temporally proximate to the changes introduced to produce valid data. Prior research has found that it is effective when practical measures are embedded within experiences that are familiar to teachers and students (e.g., common instructional routines), as well as minimally disruptive of routine school practice.[11] For example, the Carnegie Foundation's Community College Pathways Project collected practical measure data via short student surveys that required no longer than three minutes to administer. Collecting practical measures in ways that were minimally burdensome, unobtrusive, and temporally proximate to change ideas allowed our research project to collect information close to the change ideas being implemented, while not taking away too much classroom time or overburdening teachers with complex data-collection procedures.

By "minimally burdensome," we are underscoring the importance of designing routines for collecting practical measure data that require both minimal teacher learning and minimal reorganization of current practices. By "unobtrusive," we are highlighting the importance of collecting practical measure data in ways that do not disrupt the flow of classroom instruction. In our project, we initially designed tools that teachers could implement throughout their lessons to collect data. However, classrooms are complex environments in which teachers manage a multitude of demands while facilitating student learning. We therefore decided to change course after early adopters indicated that it would be too demanding to collect data during lessons while teaching. We then developed practical measures in the form of student surveys that teachers could implement within an existing routine (i.e., exit tickets). Doing so reduced the burden on teachers and enabled them to focus on implementing change ideas without also having to systematically record students' responses to the change idea.

As illustrated in the earlier vignette involving Ms. Green, our network used exit tickets as a method for collecting practical measure data on change ideas. Most teachers in this context were already familiar with using exit tickets and regularly used the routine to conclude lessons. Teachers' familiarity with the exit ticket routine also allowed our network to use the same method to collect practical measure data for different change ideas. This required that we develop different practical measures for each change idea of interest; however, the data-collection process could remain unchanged. Consequently, teachers could implement a different exit ticket to generate practical measure data for the change idea that they were currently testing. This is demonstrated in the vignette as Ms. Green used different exit tickets for the Comprehension Task Sheet and the Modeling Quickwrite change ideas.

In addition, embedding practical measures in familiar routines allowed our network to allocate most of the professional development time to pedagogy. This was crucial in our context because the majority of the teachers were still learning how to design and implement the student-centered activities embedded in the task sheets. Thus, IFL coaches were able to spend more time unpacking the change ideas and how to implement them rather than training teachers on how to collect practical measure data.

Although our network chose the exit ticket as a high-leverage routine for collecting practical measure data, various other routines can be used as well. Aspects of the school and district context influence which routines might be used to collect practical measures. For example, if teachers are using digital technologies to collect formative assessment data, they could embed practical measures in such assessments. Fundamental to Design Principle 2 is that the practical measures align with the change ideas being tested and teachers can readily collect the practical measure data without taking on additional tasks in the classroom.

Design Principle 3: Produce Data That Identifies Inequities

A key consideration when designing practical measures for educational improvement is the degree to which the measures can produce data that can guide the pursuit of more equitable processes and outcomes.[12] Here, we mean designing practical measures that make it possible to identify how different groups of students responded to change ideas, and thus have better predictive analytics to address these disparities. This consideration is critical because it is a moral and social imperative for educational systems to find ways to ensure that all students have adequate opportunities to learn in school, and thus to be adequately prepared for postsecondary education and careers. This is especially true for students who are members of marginalized groups.[13] Prior research on culturally responsive instruction has extensively documented how students who are members of minoritized groups can disengage when tasks and texts are rarely culturally aligned or when texts portray nondominant cultures negatively.[14] We therefore designed practical measures to capture whether students perceived instruction as culturally responsive and engaging.

Pursuing equity of outcomes requires that measures enable improvers to detect and address *systemic* inequities. Although centering measures on student experiences is important for achieving equitable outcomes, we do not think that it is sufficient. Equity-focused practical measures should also illuminate the students' experiences by affording the disaggregation of the resulting data, thereby making it possible to understand the experiences of particular groups of students, especially those previously found to have unequal outcomes in the local context (e.g., by race/ethnicity, language, or gender). Analysis of these data can then help identify particular inequities and inform the development of change ideas that are responsive to those inequities.

A recurrent source of inequity in instruction is the failure to attend to the learning needs of students whose native language is not English. Given this common source of inequity, it is important to design practical measures that capture the experiences of students with different native languages. Students whose native language is not English often find themselves immersed in classrooms that do not employ their native language resources to support their learning. EMLs are then likely to have different experiences with instruction conducted in English than do native English-speaking students, which then contributes to inequitable learning opportunities and outcomes. Thus, it is important to design practical measures such that analyses of the resulting data can identify differences in students' experiences of a change idea by native language. The findings of such analyses can then inform the adjustment of change ideas to address the identified inequities.

Figure 6.6 presents an exit ticket designed for our Comprehension Task Sheet change idea, which illustrates how practical measures can be designed to understand potential sources of inequity. Here, we highlight four components of the practical measure's design that afforded attention

Figure 6.6 Culturally responsive text measure

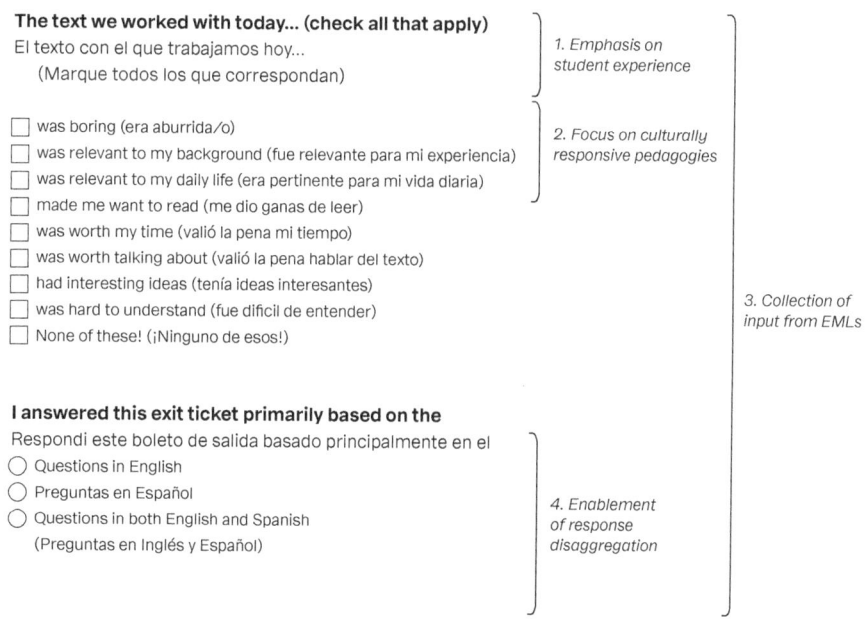

to equity issues in subsequent analyses. These aspects were also noted by Ms. Green in the vignette. First, the exit ticket emphasizes student experiences rather than just capturing student or teacher activities, as discussed in Design Principle 1. Second, it captures aspects of students' experience that are common sources of inequity, such as differences in the relevance of and personal interest in the source text that are aligned with language status, race, ethnicity, or gender.[15] Although the text was not itself the change idea, it serves as a potentially inequitable foundation for the change idea if texts rarely reflect students' cultural backgrounds or if they portray nondominant cultures in negative terms. Third, it addresses the challenge of collecting input from EMLs in English-only surveys by adding Spanish translations. Fourth, it asks how students completed the survey to permit the disaggregation of responses without requiring students to disclose personal information. Taken together, these four aspects of the design enabled us tap into students' perceptions of cultural relevance, as well as the experiences of students who are members of historically minoritized groups, in order to better understand if change ideas differentially shaped student learning.

It is important to consider which data might be challenging to collect in a particular research context, as soliciting information about students' race, gender, or native language may be sensitive or controversial. Ideally, our network would have designed practical measures to learn more deeply about the experiences of different student groups who have been historically minoritized, such as Black students. However, various stakeholders in our network found this issue to be politically sensitive. Through ongoing conversations and negotiations, we were able to pilot student exit tickets asking for students to identify their race at the current time. We recommend that improvement enterprises weigh potential political considerations against the benefits of collecting more fine-grained data to understand the experiences of different student groups.

Along these lines, it is also important to consider whether seeking fine-grained information may identify individual students. The degree to which students' responses are authentic may be jeopardized if they feel that they can be identified. If students are part of the processes that generate practical measures, such as through completing exit tickets, it is essential that their input is not individually identifiable and they trust that their feedback will not come back to haunt them. Consequently, collecting more fine-grained data may not necessarily yield more useful data. Hence, it is important for improvers to consider what data are useful, minimally burdensome, and maintains benefits to students. Doing so can ensure that the use of practical measures avoids common pitfalls of bias, such as using data to reinforce implicit biases or singling out students who are perceived to be "difficult."

Design Principle 4: Provide Timely Feedback

Given the fast-paced and action-oriented nature of schools, providing timely feedback for different audiences is essential if practical measures are to be useful. Timely feedback provides various practitioners involved in improvement processes with feedback soon after the implementation of change ideas.[16] That is, practitioners are provided with actionable feedback that fits within timelines for effective reflection on the implementation of change ideas and for the timely testing of new change ideas based on these reflections. This requires that routines are established to quickly process practical measure data and produce data representations that are easily interpreted by different audiences (e.g., the feedback report in figure 6.4). The crux of timely feedback, though, is that various users can analyze practical measure data to make informed choices that are consequential for improvement processes.

The provision of timely feedback to individual teachers shortly after they have implemented a change idea can support them in learning how students experienced the change idea and thus whether it needs to be adjusted.[17] In addition, it is important that feedback addresses salient issues and feedback reports are intuitively understandable.

With regard to the former, IFL coaches were able to develop an understanding of what feedback teachers desired through ongoing interactions with them in network professional development and coaching settings. With regard to the latter, analysts designed feedback reports that provided both visual and numerical representations of the data to enable multiple access points for teachers. We also limited feedback reports to one page to ensure that teachers could process the data in the reports quickly and see all relevant data elements in proximity to each other. Furthermore, teachers were introduced to change ideas and examples of feedback reports concurrently in network professional development sessions. This ensured that teachers had opportunities to understand both change ideas and the practical measures embedded in exit tickets before they implemented the change ideas and received the corresponding feedback reports. The feedback reports themselves underwent iterative refinement that was driven by our developing understanding of the aspects of instruction on which teachers needed feedback. Understanding what teachers struggled with led our team to design feedback reports that were our best bet on essential practical measures that could support instructional improvement. Thus, even the design of feedback reports themselves was part of the network's improvement process.

Analysts provided teachers with feedback reports within one school day of students submitting their exit tickets. This provided teachers with timely access to results, and thus with opportunities to reflect on their implementation of a change idea. The feedback reports supported teachers in considering whether the instructional change that they had made led to improved student learning soon after a lesson was implemented, or whether further adaptations of instructional practice would be necessary to improve student learning. These determinations could then be used to inform the next inquiry cycle, as was demonstrated in the vignette when Ms. Green reflected on her feedback report for the Comprehension Task Sheet change idea. Her analyses of the report led her to conclude that students had difficulties comprehending the text used in the lesson, which in turn led her to question whether students understood the purpose of the quickwrite, a routine intended to support text comprehension. After discussing her hypothesis further with her coach, she decided to focus on improving the quickwrite routine and investigated whether implementing the Modeling the Quickwrite change idea would result in improved student comprehension.

The provision of timely feedback can also support the work of improvement team members (i.e., coaches) who work directly with teachers by informing them of the outcomes of change idea implementation soon after it has occurred. Coaches can use this feedback to inform their work with individual teachers, as well as to stimulate reflection on broader trends that they have observed throughout the network. In our case, IFL coaches received feedback reports at the same time as teachers. IFL coaches analyzed these reports to plan follow-up sessions with individual teachers, similar to the session described in the vignette. Coaches often learned in these sessions about the challenges that teachers encountered in implementing change ideas. This point is illustrated in the vignette when Ms. Green and her IFL coach reflected on her implementation of the Comprehension Task Sheet change idea and hypothesized that improving the implementation of the quickwrite routine could improve student comprehension. In this example, the IFL coach anticipated this challenge, as he had observed it throughout the network.

The IFL coaches also analyzed practical measure data that was aggregated at the grade, school, and network levels. Quick processing of practical measure data allowed IFL coaches and analysts to understand which change ideas had been implemented, by which teachers, in which schools, and with what degree of success. The coaches analyzed data at these levels in concert with their coaching sessions with teachers to reflect more systematically on trends observed across the network. Consequently, our network could investigate variation in implementation and in student outcomes at multiple levels (i.e., teacher, grade band, school, network). We could then assess which change ideas were (or were not) successful, where they were (or were not) successful, and why they were (or were not) successful. This was consequential because it helped our improvement team determine whether variation in outcomes was confined to specific contexts or was reflective of patterns that could be observed across the network. As a result, the subsequent support provided to teachers was responsive and informed by practical measure data.

The development and implementation of the Comprehension Task Sheet provide an illustration of how timely feedback led to better support for teachers networkwide. IFL coaches' observations and the practical measure data indicated that the majority of teachers needed additional support with the Comprehension Task Sheet change idea. One common sticking point for teachers was using the quickwrite to support student comprehension, as was the case for Ms. Green. IFL deduced from the practical measure data that teachers were not scaffolding student engagement with the quickwrite, which resulted in students being largely disengaged. This led our network to provide teachers with additional training on the design and implementation of comprehension task sheets, as well as to develop change ideas specific to the quickwrite routine, such as the Modeling the Quickwrite change idea. Hence, timely feedback not only supported teachers and coaches, but it also guided the entire improvement effort as new change ideas emerged in response to teachers' current practices.

One critical consequence of developing a system of practical measures that provided timely feedback was that our network could readily demonstrate to district leaders the impact of the improvement work. We found this to be essential, as district leaders required evidence that new improvement initiatives were impacting student learning in ways that could improve student performance on state assessments. Being able to demonstrate to district leaders that the use of practical measures supported improvements in teaching and students' learning gave our network legitimacy and ensured that it would be given space to operate, thereby signaling to other stakeholders in the district and throughout the network that district leaders valued the improvement work. This was crucial, as it ensured that efforts to use practical measures for improvement were not crowded out by the myriad of other reforms and demands that teachers had to contend with day in, day out. Thus, being able to provide timely feedback not only supported teacher learning and how analysts and IFL coaches guided improvement efforts, but also enabled us to demonstrate to district leaders that engagement with rigorous improvement methods that use practical measures could positively affect student achievement.

VALIDITY CONSIDERATIONS

Validity is an important concern in all forms of measurement, but somewhat different challenges need to be addressed in practical measurement than in evaluative assessment or in measurement for research purposes.

The primary concern here is whether the use of practical measures supports the improvement process. A robust measurement system for improvement will likely have a mixture of student artifacts, teachers' subjective experiences within the classroom, and occasional expert input. Here, we have focused on exit tickets as providing an important kind of data that gives feedback on students' experience with a change idea. Given the primary goals of a practical measure for improvement, our focus in validating the exit tickets as a practical measure has been on the meaning-making of teachers and teacher teams, as well as the consequences of their use. What kinds of decisions does the measure inform? What kinds of actions does the measure enable? Here, we argue that our practical measures have met an important validity criterion if (1) teachers seek the data (i.e., see it as relevant); (2) it is appropriately interpretable with relatively little expert support; (3) it supports making rapid and effective instructional changes that address problems of practice; and (4) the accumulation of such instructional changes results in improved student outcomes (and especially equity in such outcomes). The first three criteria are about making sure that the measures have consequential validity for the users and interpreters of the measures; the fourth criterion is about making sure that the measures have consequential validity for their students.

All four of our principles for designing practical measures play an important role in supporting practitioners' efforts to address problems of practice central to their day-to-day work. Design Principle 1 emphasizes that practical measures should focus on students' experiences. The resulting measures provide feedback to practitioners about exactly where they have indicated to us that there is a significant gap: how students experienced instructional support and change ideas. To address this need, we designed exit tickets with embedded practical measures on how students experienced change ideas.

Design Principle 1 also focuses on change idea outcomes, which support teachers in making connections between their implementations of a change idea and practical measure data, reducing the need for experts to help them make connections between data and action. Furthermore, Design Principle 2 supported teachers in making connections between change idea implementation and student learning by embedding practical measures in routines that teachers could reliably implement. This design principle afforded teachers the opportunity to focus on change idea implementation rather than also having to contend with complex data-collection routines.

But peering into the minds of students, particularly those who have been historically marginalized, is where teachers also have sought input. Design Principle 3 emphasizes the importance of differentiating that feedback along accessible student demographic dimensions (rather than more abstract characteristics of students, such as prior performance levels). This principle increases the consequential validity of the measures for minoritized students by ensuring that their experiences (1) are not hidden in aggregated reports and (2) become the focus of subsequent change ideas and improvement activities.

Design Principle 4 contributes to the consequential validity of practical measures by providing timely feedback to teachers and coaches to inform actions that have the potential to improve instruction and student outcomes. The other design principles reduce the likelihood of teachers needing help to interpret the problems of practice, but understanding problems does not necessarily suggest actions that are likely to produce further improvements. Teachers could confer with coaches after receiving feedback reports to design and enact change ideas that are principled and focused. Consequently, not only were practical measures actionable in this context, they were also part of a social learning system in which teachers, content coaches, and data analysts collaborated to solve problems of practice. As illustrated in the vignette, Ms. Green learned from the feedback report and a check-in with the coach that her implementation of a quickwrite was problematic, so she decided to implement a more fine-grained Modeling the Quickwrite change idea. The system of practical measurements presented here integrated these design principles to help teachers learn quickly to make adjustments that had the potential to improve instructional practices and student learning.

Directly linking the use of exit tickets to student outcomes is a complex analytic challenge that is well beyond the scope of this chapter. However, as indirect evidence, analysis of student growth related to the depth of engagement with our approach that teachers have (e.g., number of change ideas implemented, frequency of attendance at network events) has some encouraging findings. When teachers more regularly implemented change ideas and task sheets, their students were more likely to make significant gains during the school year in their reading scores as measured by the Northwest Evaluation Association's MAP assessment—an interim assessment administered multiple times throughout the school year. Not only did every demographic subgroup show this pattern of positive results associated with testing and refinement of practice through practical measurement, but larger impacts were found for historically underachieving groups of students (e.g., Black students, male students, and students with special needs). Of course, the pedagogical practices and small tests of change within those practices were the primary drivers of student learning, rather than the exit tickets themselves. But association with more equitable results when teachers more consistently implemented these practices potentially indicates that teachers were making productive adaptations to address the student needs indicated by practical measure data. With this acknowledged, teachers who used practical measures regularly found that using them was relevant to their practices and supported the improvements of those practices, and these teachers produced more equitable outcomes.

CLOSING REFLECTIONS

In this chapter, we presented four design principles that guided our development of a practical measurement system to support instructional improvement. In so doing, we argue for the value of designing practical measures that align with specific change ideas; focus on student experiences with these change ideas; support the disaggregation of data to understand the experiences of specific student groups; embed measures in familiar instructional routines; and enable system learning through timely feedback for multiple role groups. In our context, we used the exit ticket routine as a practical measure to collect data for instructional improvement because many teachers were already familiar with that routine. We maintain that the exit ticket routine could also be used to collect practical measure data for other improvement aims, such as fostering learning environments that encourage student collaboration or coming to a consensus when solving classroom tasks. Here, it is important for readers to consider the improvement aims of their contexts and whether the exit ticket routine could be an effective vehicle for collecting relevant practical measures.

Based on our experiences with exit tickets, we offer a few recommendations for others engaged in formal improvement work and considering their use. First, the development of practical measures can be approached as an improvement undertaking in itself—one that requires iterative testing and refinement before full implementation. Along these lines, we encourage improvers to start with a few early adopters when testing some practical measure. By starting small, the early adopters provide key information about the obstacles that they encounter when using these practical measures that can guide design improvements before implementing this routine at scale. In our project, some teachers encountered implementation issues and did not have time to execute the change idea and implement exit tickets within the same lesson. This experience led to the IFL coaches providing teachers with practical guidance on time management to ensure that they could implement the change idea and collect practical measures within the course of the same lesson. Furthermore, initially testing the exit ticket data collection routine with a few teachers can provide a validity check to ensure that the practical measures as designed provide useful information that can inform the improvement process. It is common for improvers to find that measures that sound good on paper may not provide useful data when practitioners actually use them. Hence, starting with a few early adopters can serve as a strategy to improve the design of practical measures more generally.

Finally, and based on prior research and our experiences in our partner district, we propose that our four design principles can also provide guidance when designing practical measures other than exit tickets to inform instructional improvement. For example, in contexts where classroom observation is common, improvers could design "Look For" protocols to collect practical measure data on a specific change idea. Here, Design Principle 2 would be expanded to include observational routines. Classroom observers might then ask students about their experiences with change ideas, in addition to recording observations to learn more deeply about the impact of change ideas (Design Principle 1). In addition, observers could discreetly note the experiences of specific students, as they will likely have relationships with these students and have an understanding of their learning needs that reaches beyond what can be captured on a survey (Design Principle 3). Looking beyond this illustration, it is essential that improvers think through how they will collect, process, analyze, and use practical measure data to ensure that it can be generated in a timely manner and can inform the practice of various stakeholders (Design Principle 4). Adhering to a set of design principles is a way to keep the focus and desired function of practical measures front and center during the design, development, and implementation processes.

7

Validity and Technical Quality of Practical Measures

Thomas M. Smith

How do you know if a change is an improvement? For practical measurement to answer this question, we first must ensure that the surveys, rubrics, assessments, observation protocols, and other tools designed to measure processes, influencing factors, and outcomes in an improvement project are measuring what they are intended to measure; and that their users' interpretations of the resulting data are aligned with that intent.[1] In other words, establishing the validity of practical measures requires us to consider both what they are designed to measure and how they are actually used.[2]

Practical measures are used to refine improvement goals, assess progress toward those goals, determine the efficacy of factors in the theory of improvement, and assess whether specific changes introduced to attain those goals are, in fact, leading to improvement.[3] As the chapters in this book illustrate, improvement is an iterative, data-driven process. To measure whether a change is an improvement, measures are typically selected or developed to help those involved in improvement work track whether the changes that they are testing have the intended impact on outcomes. As Takahashi and Norman note in chapter 2, practical measures are "practical" in that they can be collected, analyzed, and used within the daily work lives of practitioners. If the users of a practical measure interpret the resulting data in ways that differ from the intent of the developers of the measure, its usefulness for improvement work is compromised.

This chapter aims to clarify the technical qualities of effective practical measures, which I will call *validity-for-use*. I then introduce the notion of *validity-in-use*, which focuses on whether the use of a measure is appropriate given the school, district, or user context. I draw on the five cases detailed in chapters 2 through 6 to highlight examples of validity-for-use and validity-in-use. I then conclude by outlining a framework for thinking about the critical technical and contextual attributes of practical measures. Along the way, I offer practical advice about realizing the desired attributes of practical measures and knowing if we have done so. Before getting into validity-for-use, however, I review the five criteria for practical measures presented by Takahashi and Norman in chapter 2 and detailed by Bryk and colleagues in *Leaning to Improve,* as they have implications for understanding the importance and challenges of developing a validity argument that attends to users' interpretations and use.[4]

HOW DO THE CHARACTERISTICS OF PRACTICAL MEASURES RELATE TO VALIDITY?

First, practical measures should operationalize a theory of improvement, linking processes, practices, and outcomes that will improve if change ideas are successful. They are a "way to see into the black box" of a system and to detect changes in what you intend to measure (chapter 2). These measures of system linkages can be derived from theory (e.g., lack of financial resources negatively affects college attendance), from prior research (e.g., students who complete the Free Application for Federal Student Aid (FAFSA) are more likely to go to college), or from the experience of practitioners (e.g., many families say that they would like their children to go to college but they just can't afford it). The FAFSA completion indicator (chapter 2) directly measures that component of the Carpe College Access Network's theory of change—namely, whether a student has completed the FAFSA, which is one factor that affects the ultimate aim of improving college attendance and persistence. This yes/no measure tracks the percentage of students who have completed the FAFSA. The data can then be disaggregated by subgroups to highlight submission rates for students who have historically been underrepresented in college. While it is important to recognize that FAFSA completion is part of a suite of measures linked by theory and research to college attendance, each measure relates to a different element of that theory, and therefore the validity of each measure must be assessed separately. As improvement at the scale of a school, district, or larger network is likely to rely on designing, testing, analyzing, and implementing multiple changes (i.e., the running of multiple Plan, Do, Study, Act (PDSA) cycles on different change ideas), it is essential to design, test, and analyze the validity of each measure separately to test whether each change idea needs to be modified, abandoned, or can be implemented.[5]

Second, practical measures must be actionable, in that the information that they provide should inform whether a change idea should be implemented, modified, or abandoned after testing. The Carpe Network (chapter 2) assessed the effectiveness of different change ideas (e.g., reaching out to parents to invite them to FAFSA workshops) by examining changes in the percentage of students completing the FAFSA. Coaches in districts working to improve mathematics instruction used student responses on the Practical Measures, Routines, and Representations (PMRR) student surveys (chapter 3) to assess where teachers might need support to improve their practices (e.g., in the lesson launch, small-group work, or whole-class discussion). Then, data from the PMRR surveys could be used to determine if an instructional change (i.e., a change idea) leads to improvements in students' perceptions of aspects of the classroom learning environment that prior research indicates influence their learning. The Using Sources Tool (UST; chapter 4) helps teachers analyze their students' writing by focusing on eight high-leverage argumentation skills. The tool also provides data that can help teachers engaged with the National Writing Project's (NWP) College, Career, and Community Writers Program (C3WP) to determine if the instructional changes that they have made improve their students' source-based argument writing, and thus to identify their next instructional steps. The Freshman Success Report (chapter 5) is produced for each public high school in Chicago. It lists every first-time ninth grader's current grades and attendance in each core course and identifies students who need immediate help by flagging those with a high number of absences or low course grades (Ds or Fs). The Comprehensive Task Sheet exit ticket (chapter 6) was designed to provide teachers with feedback on their students' understanding of and reactions to the implemented literacy task sheet. This measure provides teachers with information about how students experienced a literacy lesson in which they are trying an instructional change. Each of these five cases illustrates the importance of validity-for-use in practical measures. For a measure to be actionable, it must measure what it is intended to measure and be sensitive enough to detect changes reliably.

Third, practical measures should be meaningful and informative to those engaged in improvement work. If improvers do not think that a measure adequately assesses the processes that they are trying to improve, then it is unlikely that they will make a sufficient effort to collect the data that goes into the measure or use the data derived from it to improve practice or processes. In developing practical measures for improving mathematics instruction, the PMRR team (chapter 3) included district mathematics specialists, coaches, and teachers in designing and testing the launch, small-group, and whole-class measures. This helped to ensure that the language used in the survey questions had common meaning across developers, users, and students, and the questions reflected high-leverage aspects of classroom instruction. Getting input from teachers on how to best represent the data also increased the likelihood that the information will be understood by users. C3WP (chapter 4) had feedback from both Local Writing Project teachers and teachers in partner districts, with each revision of the UST providing language that more effectively communicated the intended source-based approach to argument writing. Focusing improvement efforts on areas where practitioners see a need for improvement can help the entire process be more meaningful to them. Codesigning practical measures with practitioners, or at least involving them in an authentic, in-depth review of measures already designed, can also help ensure that the measures are meaningful to them. At a minimum, the improvement team should describe to users how the measures were designed by mapping individual items to research, showing their link to desired outcomes, and explaining how practitioners participated in their development.

Fourth, the measures should be minimally burdensome. As noted by Takahashi and Norman, "Measures that require burdensome data collection, such as lengthy surveys or extensive training for data collection, will be less likely to be taken up and sustained than measures that can be quickly administered, with limited disruption to routine practices" (chapter 2, p. 30). Using data that already exists (e.g., FAFSA completion in the Carpe Network; student absenteeism and course grades in the Freshman Early-Warning Indicator (EWI) system; chapter 5) or adding data collection to existing instructional routines, such as short student surveys at the end of lessons in both PMRR and the University of Pittsburgh (Pitt) cases (chapters 3 and 6), make the data collection burden more manageable for educators. The C3WP practical measure (UST; chapter 4), differs from these latter measures in that the data are not directly collected from students. Instead, the UST is a rubric for assessing students' work, enabling teachers to give students individual feedback on a source-based argument-writing activity and to identify which of the eight high-leverage argument skills their students are struggling with. Constructing the UST as a rubric that teachers use in their instruction likely makes their grading of written assignments better without adding to the burden. Tightly linking measures to users' current routines and practices can enhance their validity-in-use. If teachers find that collecting practical measures data is a burden, they could unintentionally impact the validity of the measure by not giving students enough time to complete it or by providing instructions that could lead students to abbreviate answers to questions in ways that invalidate them for their intended purpose.

Fifth, practical measures should provide timely feedback. In the context of improvement research, "timely" is meant in two senses. First, it means timed to provide data when it can be useful to improve practice. It also means that the data are provided to users quickly so it can be acted upon when it can support improvement. The end-of-year freshman ontrack indicator, which signals whether a student is likely to graduate and is used for goal setting and accountability, is not available until after the time when intervening with students could prevent failure. The real-time Freshman Success Reports, published every five weeks, allow teachers, counselors, and other school staff time to intervene with students who are failing courses or missing classes while there is still time to have an impact during the school year. Interpreting data for events that occurred weeks (or sometimes even days) in the past makes it less likely that a teacher or another user can connect the students' responses to particular actions that they took during a particular lesson or activity. Both PMRR and the University of Pittsburgh worked to provide teachers with feedback within twenty-four hours of the teaching events wherein the student surveys were collected. In addition, the improvement teams working to improve FAFSA completion (chapter 2), mathematics instruction (chapter 3), high school completion (chapter 5), and literacy tasks (chapter 6) all made the information derived from practical measures available to users through a dashboard or similar online tool. Instead of sending teachers their data back in a spreadsheet, data were presented in aggregated forms that were highly accessible to users, such as bar graphs or trend lines. By making user-friendly representations available to teachers and other users, the developers made it more likely that the data would be interpreted as intended and, as a result, would support improvement.

Creating improvement measures that are practical, in the sense of both deriving from and contributing to practice, does not mean that we should be any less concerned about their technical rigor and quality or how they are used. In the next section, I review four types of validity-for-use and describe how they are addressed in the five cases in this book. I then discuss validity-in-use, which presupposes validity-for-use and focuses on the conditions of use that need to be satisfied for practical measures to be valid.[6]

VALIDITY-FOR-USE

In the context of improvement work, validity-for-use focuses on whether a practical measure (e.g., survey questions, observation protocol, routinely collected administrative information) measures what it was designed to measure.[7] Validity is not a binary attribute, such that a measure is determined to be either valid or not. Rather, it is a continuum that refers to how well an instrument or tool actually measures what it is intended to measure. A practical measure should have enough signaling power to allow users to determine whether a change (e.g., an increase from two to three on a rubric measuring instructional quality) corresponds to a commensurate change in the desired outcome (e.g., specific improvement in students' argument writing).[8] Five types of validity are often examined to make claims about how valid the information produced by a measurement instrument is: face, content, construct, concurrent, and predictive validity.[9] I define each type of validity and review how the practical measure development processes for each case in chapters 2–6 attended to it.

A measure is considered to have *face validity* if it looks appropriate to potential users for its designed purpose. If a formative assessment developed by a district to administer at the end of each quarter does not assess what teachers in the district see as the critical content that they have taught over that period, the assessment would not have face validity to some of its key users. Routinely collected administrative data (e.g., absences, suspensions, expulsions, quarterly grades) may have face validity for district administrators when included in accountability systems, but it may not have face validity for teachers if they feel that they are not able to influence it. For administrative measures such as the FAFSA (chapter 2) and the real-time Freshman Success Reports (chapter 5), face validity relies on whether users (primarily students, teachers, and administrators) believe that the measure assesses what it is supposed to measure. For example, measures of absenteeism used as part of student or school accountability systems are unlikely to have face validity if the process for identifying whether students were absent from classes throughout the school day is known to be error-prone or haphazardly followed.

Improvement teams can establish face validity by including users' voices in the design or review process. For example, in PMRR, the lesson launch, small-group work, and whole-class discussion surveys were reviewed by coaches and teachers during the development process. Face validity was further enhanced by involving students in cognitive interviews that focused on the survey items and then modifying items if students understood them differently than intended.[10] By attending to the language that teachers and students associate with important aspects of classroom teaching, the PMRR team was able to enhance the face validity of its measures for future users. However, including the language of users in the practical measure does not necessarily mean that a measure will have face validity for others who were not represented in the design process. For example, teachers who were not directly involved in the development of the real-time Freshman Success Reports sometimes questioned their validity (chapter 5). Unless they receive professional development on the subject, most teachers might not believe that even a small number of days absent or getting a D or F in the freshman year is so predictive of failing to graduate from high school. In addition, reading a Freshman Success Report on its own would not necessarily help a teacher, counselor, or principal know what to do with the data. Professional development on what influences whether ninth graders stay on track was needed for some teachers to see the "on track" data as valid. Improvement teams can improve the face validity of practical measures by involving practitioners and users in their development and, as noted previously, by orienting new users on the process of developing the measures and how the measures were designed (e.g., by mapping individual items to research, showing their link to desired outcomes, and explaining how practitioners participated in their development).

A measure is considered to have good *content validity* if it adequately covers the domain that it is designed to measure. For example, an algebra end-of-course exam would not be considered to have good content validity unless it includes questions covering the depth and breadth of the relevant mathematics curricula or standards. For practical measures, content validity is often established by mapping measures to high-leverage processes that prior research or expert knowledge links to the desired outcomes. For example, the questions that comprise the PMRR surveys (chapter 3) were mapped directly to research linking a practice (e.g., using tasks that can be solved in multiple ways) to increases in students' conceptual understanding. This mapping is publicly available on the PMRR website, helping to enhance the content validity of the measures among potential users.

The designers of the UST (chapter 4) also drew on the research literature, in this case on argument writing, when they developed it. The tool was mapped directly to C3WP's framework for teaching argument writing. Ensuring that the tool matched the content and language used in C3WP professional development helped give participating teachers more confidence in the validity of the tool. The Comprehensive Task Sheet exit tickets (chapter 6) were designed to identify how students experienced specific instructional changes that teachers were attempting to make, directly tying the exit tickets to the content of the reading lesson that the developers wanted teachers to attend to. By mapping the content domain (e.g., argument writing, mathematics instruction, or reading instruction) to the items in a practical measure, the improvement team can more readily demonstrate the content validity of measures.

For a measure to have *construct* validity, it must adequately represent the concept or construct that it is intended to measure. Constructs are abstract ideas (e.g., early literacy, instructional quality) that are not directly observed but can be inferred from observable indicators (e.g., a literacy assessment or certain high-quality instructional practices indicated by an observation protocol). For example, while an experienced mathematics or literacy coach can usually identify aspects of instruction that affect students' learning, the challenge is to turn that knowledge into a practical measure that can be reliably used by less expert observers. The goal is to design a set of indicators (e.g., teachers' actions, classroom interactions, student work) that, as a collection, align with what research evidence and practitioner expertise indicate are high-quality instructional practices. To have construct validity, an instructional quality measure would need to assess enough aspects of high-quality teaching and learning that research and practitioner experts would see it as adequately covering the important aspects of instructional practice. Multiple items are often needed to sufficiently represent the construct being measured (especially complex ones), whether the construct is the quality of the lesson launch in PMRR or high-quality written arguments indicated by the eight high-leverage argument skills on which the UST focuses. In the context of practical measurement, there sometimes has to be a trade-off between maximizing construct coverage and minimizing user burden. A strategy for addressing this is to attend to the components of the construct that prior research suggests have the highest leverage for improving the intended outcome when designing the measure.

Another way to assess validity-for-use is to examine whether the data produced by a measure is correlated with the data from a different measurement instrument that was designed to measure a similar construct (*concurrent validity*) or predict desired future outcomes (*predictive validity*). For the freshman ontrack system (chapter 5) and FAFSA (chapter 2) measures, prior research links these indicators to the desired outcomes: high school graduation and college attendance and persistence, respectively. The data elements in the Freshman Ontrack Early Warning Indicator system—including the end-of-year freshman ontrack indicator and the practical data reports on attendance and grades that are available throughout students' ninth-grade year—demonstrate considerable predictive validity by showing a correlation to high school graduation. The PMRR measures of instruction are linked to increased student learning opportunities in the mathematics research literature and were validated against expert observations of the same lessons (concurrent validity). C3WP analyzed the relationship between the UST and an independent measure of students' writing outcomes administered later to establish the tool's predictive validity, finding a moderate correlation at both the middle and high school levels. When developing practical measures, improvement teams should turn to the research literature to identify constructs that have been previously linked to the outcomes specified in their theory of improvement (thereby making an argument for predictive validity). When possible, the improvement team should also test the designed measure against a previously validated measure or process to establish concurrent validity. This is where a measure that is too disruptive for improvement purposes (e.g., a classroom observation protocol, a lengthy survey or assessment, or a clinical diagnostic process) can aid in assessing the concurrent validity of a much less intrusive practical measure.

When applied to practical measures, these five components of validity-for-use address the issue of technical rigor. Validity-for-use is often attained for research or accountability measures by including more test items, survey questions, or "Look Fors" on observational protocols. Since an abstract construct like teaching quality can rarely be captured by a single item, multiple items that relate to the same construct are often created, with an indicator or scale generated by aggregating across items through the application of appropriate statistical techniques, like simple addition or averaging or principal component or factor analyses. These types of measures usually take considerable time to administer, and the data that they provide are highly abstracted from the point of measurement (e.g., a relational trust scale based on five to seven survey items). In contrast, a key characteristic of practical measures is that they fit with practitioners' current work practices and thus must be minimally intrusive on practice, minimally burdensome to administer and score, and actionable. They must also be accepted as meaningful and transparent to users, which can be an issue for individuals who were not directly involved in their development or testing. Minimally intrusive and minimally burdensome mean "short" in the case of survey measures, a characteristic that has to be balanced against having enough items to achieve construct validity. Both the PMRR (chapter 3) and Pitt (chapter 6) surveys were designed to take less than three minutes for students to complete. The PMRR team tested the concurrent validity of the measures by comparing the data to classroom observations. Correlation between the survey results and the classroom observations contributed to an argument that the measures are valid. In other words, when we say that a measure is valid, we are making a claim, and that claim must be supported by evidence. As detailed in this discussion, the design and testing of practical measures should aim to substantiate arguments that they meet validity criteria that are adequate to their purpose.

VALIDITY-IN-USE

While validity-for-use focuses on whether practical measures actually measure what they are designed to measure, validity-in-use focuses on the practical implications of using the measures, including the social consequences.[11] The question of whether a measure of instructional practice has validity-in-use can be addressed by examining whether the data produced by that measure stimulate and inform a productive dialogue about appropriate changes to the practice or process. For this to happen, users of the data should share a common understanding of what the data mean and arrive at a shared sense of how to act appropriately based on it. Such a measure can be said to have validity-in-use for traditionally marginalized groups if users can act on the data derived from the measure in a way that benefits students in those groups. Thus, the Carpe Network used its FAFSA completion indicators to identify groups for which their current improvement strategies were not working, targeted the groups of students they were not serving well, and worked harder to identify the root causes of the problem (chapter 2). It is important to attend to both validity-for-use and validity-in-use when designing, testing, and implementing practical measures and when interpreting and acting on the resulting data. As noted by Jackson and colleagues in chapter 3, "a practical measure can be used appropriately for some purposes but not others, in some contexts but not others, and by some users but not others" (p. 85). Next, I explore how the validity-in-use of practical measures for improvement can be addressed by examining the purposes for which they are used, the school and district contexts in which they are used, and user perspectives that influence how they are used.

Appropriate Purposes

The purposes of practical measures are to support individuals engaged in improvement work to determine whether a change is an improvement, to inform modifications to improvement strategies based on what has been learned, and to assess whether the working theory of improvement needs to be revised to reflect what has been learned. As noted by Jackson and colleagues in chapter 3 and Larbi-Cherif and colleagues in chapter 6, using practical measures for accountability purposes can undermine their usefulness and threaten their validity. Campbell's law suggests that "the more any quantitative social indicator is used for social decision-making, the more subject it will be to corruption pressures and the more apt it will be to distort and corrupt the social processes it is intended to monitor."[12] As an example, Donald Campbell highlighted that when test scores become the primary goal of teaching, they lose their value as indicators of learning or educational status. Instead, they distort the educational process, leading to practices like "teaching to the test" or actions that make the data generated by the tests invalid. In other words, the higher the stakes attached to a measure, the greater the incentive for users to take actions that corrupt its usefulness.

In chapter 3, Jackson and colleagues describe how a teacher might coach their students to fill out a survey in a particular way if the results were going to be used for accountability purposes rather than solely for improvement. However, Allensworth argues in chapter 5 that the use of the freshman ontrack indicator by Chicago Public Schools (CPS) as an accountability measure may have made it more likely that principals attended to freshman-year grades and attendance. She found no evidence that teachers manipulated data (e.g., gave higher grades) because their schools were held accountable for this measure. Allensworth, aware of the possibility that using the ontrack indicator as an accountability measure might compromise its validity, wisely conducted an analysis to probe this very question. In doing so, she contributes to the argument in support of its validity-in-use. Generally, though, if the stakes are high enough, users will have an incentive to engage in activities that will return more favorable ratings—in many cases, ratings that will not lead to valid inferences.

School and District Contexts

Aspects of schools' and districts' contexts can influence how practical measures are interpreted and used. Validity concerns can arise when measures are used in schools and districts beyond those where they were initially developed and tested. For example, the PMRR classroom measures were designed to be used in districts that were attempting to implement inquiry-oriented instructional practices and had the resources (e.g., curricula, coaching, professional development) to help teachers develop these instructional practices. For teachers to use the data derived from these measures in ways that could help them improve their instruction, the data needed to make sense to them and point to aspects of their instructional practice that they might want to work on. Having access to someone with expertise in the instructional practices that they are trying to improve (e.g., a coach or professional development facilitator) makes it more likely that their interpretation of the data will lead to changes in practice that improve student learning. Teachers who do not work in this kind of supportive context might interpret the information from the student surveys in ways that run counter to the development of inquiry-oriented instructional practices. For example, a teacher might interpret data indicating that her students used only one way to solve tasks in a lesson as feedback that their instructions were clear and that she had effectively scaffolded their learning. While this interpretation would be at odds with the intent of the PMRR developers, it would be understandable in a district that was not supporting teachers' implementation of tasks that can be solved in multiple ways. Similar issues arise in the C3WP and Pitt cases (chapters 4 and 6), where it is not clear that teachers using the practical measures would interpret the resulting data as intended by the developers unless they were participating in improvement efforts with goals and supports aligned to the underlying theory of improvement. These cases suggest that challenges to validity-in-use arise if the interpretation of the data or how it is used in practice does not align with the intent of the developers of the measures. This challenge is likely to apply to instructionally focused improvement projects more generally.

The instructionally focused improvement cases included in this book also suggest that it may not be enough for users' visions of high-quality instruction to be aligned with the corresponding visions of the measure developers and of their districts and schools. Even if the information generated from practical measures meets the validity-for-use criteria described here, it may be difficult for users to understand what to do with the resulting information in a way that advances the improvement effort. The PMRR, C3WP, and Pitt projects addressed this challenge in two ways—first, by developing routines for when and how to interpret the data after they are collected, and second, by recommending that the data be analyzed in a professional learning context (coaching, professional development, common planning time led by an expert facilitator). A coach can help teachers or other data users interpret the data and help them plan changes to their practices that can lead to an improvement in students' learning. Across all three instructional improvement projects (chapters 3, 4, and 6), the practical measures were designed to first provide baseline data, and then to assess whether a particular instructional change was an improvement. Coaches who were part of the improvement team could analyze the data from the measures with teachers and guide them in making instructional changes or identifying new instructional changes, such as helping students understand the goals of a quickwrite in the Pitt case. In PMRR, the practical measures were designed to help schools and districts provide teachers with the support that they required to improve their instructional practices. The development of routines and tools for data interpretations (e.g., dashboards in the PMRR and Pitt cases) and guidance from an "analytic partner," such as a coach, is a way to improve the validity-in-use of practical measures.

Users' Perspectives

Another element that could affect the validity-in-use of practical measures relates to whether users' views are consistent with the theory of improvement that guided the development of a practical measure. For example, if users have detrimental beliefs about students and their families (e.g., the belief that parents of English learners don't fill out the FAFSA because they do not care whether their children go to college, or that students who are a grade level behind will not benefit from inquiry-oriented instruction), then it is unlikely that the data produced by practical measures will be used as intended by their developers (e.g., call parents to see if they need assistance in filling out the FAFSA or try an instructional practice that research has shown reduces inequities in students' learning opportunities).

In the freshman on track indicators case, Allensworth (chapter 5) details how it was important for users to understand why students were absent or failing courses for the data to be useful in helping them get back on track for graduation. Contrary to the findings of research conducted by the "on track" team, some teachers felt that students did not care about coming to school, or they thought that giving an F would motivate students to do better. Both these assumptions run counter to prior research and to practices that were proving effective in getting students back on track. Teachers had to be exposed to and accept what prior research suggested about why students were absent or failing for them to respond to the on-track reports in ways that are consistent with the theory of improvement.

In the FAFSA case, Takahashi and Norman (chapter 2) noted that it was important for the users to have an asset-based rather than deficit-based interpretation of why families were not filling out the financial aid forms for the data to be useful in helping increase completion rates. Similarly, the PMRR team (chapter 3) found that if teachers' perspectives on their students' current mathematical capabilities were negative (e.g., teachers felt that low-income students, students of color, or English learners were not capable of learning from inquiry-oriented instruction), they were more likely to interpret data from the practical measures as indicating the limitations of students or their families rather than limitations in their current instruction. These examples highlight the importance of the alignment between the theory of improvement that guided the development of the practical measures and the user's perspective on which students would benefit from change ideas aligned with that theory.

If the use, context, and users' perspectives matter so much to validity-in-use, does every improvement project need to develop its own practical measures? That would not be very practical. When preparing to use measures for a new purpose or in a new setting, potential users need to assess how the measures align with their own theory of improvement. If aligned, small-scale testing of the measure can help provide confidence that it is measuring what it was designed to measure (validity-for-use). Getting feedback from users through focus groups or cognitive interviews can help identify where the language used in the measures needs to be adapted to maintain validity in a new context.

A FRAMEWORK FOR EXAMINING THE VALIDITY OF IMPROVEMENT MEASURES

Building on the characteristics of practical measurement detailed by Takahashi and Norman in chapter 2 and their implications for validity-for-use and validity-in-use described previously, I propose a framework for addressing the validity-for-use and validity-in-use of measures designed to inform improvement efforts. The framework sets out three criteria for designing, testing, and using practical measures and illustrates how to address validity issues within each by drawing on examples from the case chapters. The three criteria are elaborated in the remainder of this chapter.

Ensure Practicality and Coherence in the Design of Tools and Routines for Use

As noted previously, practical measures should operationalize a theory of improvement, linking processes, practices, and outcomes that should improve if organizational or instructional changes are successful. To know whether a change is an improvement, a measure must meet the validity-of-use and validity-in-use criteria detailed above. Balancing validity with practicality is one of the biggest challenges for developing practical measures.

To be practical, we want measures to be minimally burdensome for educators and their students. They should also return data in a timely manner to inform ongoing improvement efforts. This often implies that surveys or other measurement tools, whether administered to students, teachers, counselors, or school leaders, need to be short, while at the same time addressing content, construct, concurrent, and predictive validity. Content validity can be enhanced by carefully reviewing the research literature relevant to an improvement project's aim and involving practitioners in the development of measures. In addition, root cause analyses (e.g., the five whys, fishbone diagrams) and visualizations of the high-leverage components of the theory of improvement (e.g., driver diagrams) are all tools that can be used to confirm that the critical components are addressed.[13]

To ensure construct validity, developers need to assess enough aspects of the construct being measured (e.g., quality of whole-group discussion, essential components of an argument, student experiences of instructional changes in literacy instruction) to cover it adequately in the judgment of academic and practitioner experts. In the case of survey measures, multiple items may be needed to adequately represent the construct being measured. But this must be balanced against the need for instruments to be short and fit into current work routines. Furthermore, if the time provided to complete a measure is inadequate, then rushed or incomplete responses will restrict the measure's signaling capacity and negatively affect validity.

Validity-for-use can be improved by capitalizing on item language that has been used successfully in survey measures from prior research and improvement efforts with the same or similar aims. For example, the Math Practical Measurement Repository maintained by WestEd includes practical measures developed across multiple improvement projects that focus on a range of issues, including student socioemotional learning, teacher mindsets, and the rigor of mathematical tasks.[14] Starting with previously validated measures can help improvement teams design their own measures that balance burden with validity-for-use.

Sharing drafts of items with professionals with content, research, practice, and measurement expertise can also improve validity-for-use. These experts can help improvement teams determine if their measures adequately cover a content domain and focus on what research and practice suggest are high-leverage practices. Conducting cognitive interviews to assess whether users understand survey items in ways intended by developers is also an effective method for enhancing validity-for-use, as language can be interpreted differently by different groups (e.g., students versus teachers, teachers versus researchers).

Testing the concurrent and predictive validity of practical measures is also necessary for establishing validity-for-use. While concurrent validity can be assessed when measures are being "pretested" prior to the start of a study, testing predictive validity often must wait until the outcomes for an improvement study become available. Comparing the results of a practical measure (e.g., the PMRR student survey of whole-class discussions) to another measure with data collected in the same context at the same time (e.g., expert observations of the same lesson) can help establish concurrent validity prior to the testing of improvement ideas. Predictive validity is tested by correlating the data from a practical measure (e.g., PMRR, ontrack, FAFSA) with longer-term outcomes, such as end-of-course assessments, graduation rates, and college-going rates. If a practical measure does not have predictive validity, then it cannot be used to assess whether an associated change will likely lead to improvement in the intended outcome. Starting with measures that have demonstrated predictive validity in the past can confer at least provisional status to the evidence until it can be assessed more directly.

The validity of practical measures can also be enhanced by ensuring that there are systematic routines for data collection, analysis, and interpretation. By standardizing these processes, practitioners are more likely to interpret and use the data in ways that align with the developers' intent. In addition, turning data around quickly and presenting it through easily interpretable visual representations increase the likelihood of validity-in-use. The Carpe Network (FAFSA; chapter 2), PMRR (classroom instructional measures; chapter 3), C3WP (UST; chapter 4), CCSR (Freshman Success Reports; chapter 4), and Pitt (Comprehensive Task Sheet exit ticket), all established routines that are likely to increase the validity-for-use and validity-in-use of data produced by practical measures.

Analyzing the data in a professional learning context (coaching, professional development, common planning time led by an expert facilitator) can also improve the validity of inferences made from practical measures. A coach can help teachers or other data users interpret the data and plan changes to their practices that can lead to improvement. Supports for interpreting practical measures data were provided in all five improvement cases reviewed in this book.

Design Measures with Adequate Sensitivity

The data generated from practical measures are intended to help users identify when a change is an improvement and act on that information. For practical measures to fulfill this purpose, they must have adequate signaling capacity; that is, the measure must be sensitive enough to detect a change that will likely make a difference when one has occurred. The sensitivity of a measure can be assessed during the design process by comparing data collected using the measure across users or contexts that designers reasonably expect would yield different student learning outcomes (e.g., high-quality, procedurally oriented instruction versus high-quality, inquiry-oriented instruction, and low-quality versus high-quality, inquiry-oriented instruction). If the measure cannot identify differences in these comparisons, the measure will need to be revisited, as either the differences do not exist or they exist but are not detected by the measure. The sensitivity of a measure can also be tested using methods comparable to those used to test for the concurrent validity of a measure. For example, if an expert coach who repeatedly observed a teacher's instruction identified a change, but this change was not detected by a practical measure (e.g., a student survey) that was used in the same lessons, the measure may not be sensitive enough to detect the change noted by the expert. In most cases, improvers want practical measures that can detect differences that are large enough to lead to an improvement in the intended outcome.

Attend to the Purpose, Context, and User Perspectives

The validity-in-use of practical measures requires a specific set of norms and social arrangements around interpreting and using the data produced. As noted previously, Takahashi and Norman (chapter 2) emphasize that it was important for users of the FAFSA data to make asset-based rather than deficit-based interpretations of why families were not filling out the financial aid forms for the data to be useful in helping increase completion rates. In the freshman ontrack indicators case, Allensworth (chapter 5) stresses that it was essential for users to understand why students were absent or failing courses if they were to use the data to help students get back on track for graduation.

The teams leading the PMRR, Pitt, and C3WP projects all addressed the challenge of users interpreting practical measures data in ways that are not aligned with their theory of improvement. They did this (1) by developing routines for when and how to interpret the data, and (2) by recommending that the data be analyzed in a professional learning context (coaching, professional development, common planning time led by an expert facilitator). All five cases highlight how the types of norms and social arrangements that are integral to validity-in-use can be built.

The PMRR case also illustrates that it can be important to consider the conditions in which practical measures are used when establishing validity-in-use. The team leading this improvement effort advised that the student surveys should be used only in districts and schools where the vision of high-quality instruction aligns with their research-based theory of improvement; that teachers receive adequate support (e.g., coaching, professional development, facilitated collaborative planning time) to interpret the data in ways aligned with the theory of improvement; and that the information is used to inform actions that will advance student learning equitably. By publishing conditions of use for its practical measures on its website, the PMRR team indicates to potential users the characteristics of contexts in which the use of the practical measures may not be useful because the inferences that users are likely to draw from the data would not support improvement. As improvement teams make their practical measures available (e.g., at conferences, in journals, on websites), they should consider the conditions of use that influence whether and how users attend to norms and social arrangements around interpreting and using the data produced by the measures.

CONCLUSIONS

Although practical measures may appear simple when reviewed in their final form, developing high-quality measures that meet the validity criteria described in this chapter is a complex process requiring improvement teams to have multiple skills, including content expertise, practical expertise, measurement expertise, and improvement expertise. I have described the qualities associated with validity-for-use (namely, whether an instrument measures what it was designed to measure) and validity-in-use (which focuses on whether the use of a measure is appropriate, given the intended purpose, context, and user perspectives). The improvement cases in chapters 2–6 provide detailed examples of how different improvement teams addressed these validity issues in the development, testing, and use of practical measures.

As described previously, a system of practical measures should operationalize a theory of improvement, linking processes, practices, and outcomes that should improve if organizational or instructional changes are successful. To be practical, a measure should be meaningful to users and minimally burdensome to them. Codesigning practical measures with practitioners, or at least involving them in an in-depth review of already designed measures, can help ensure that they are meaningful. For users who were not involved in the development process, the improvement team can describe how the measures were designed (e.g., by mapping individual items to research, showing their link to desired outcomes, and explaining how practitioners participated in their development). It can be quite useful to have this information on a website next to where the measures themselves are available, for future users to download.

In addition to being meaningful, practical measures need to be appropriately actionable. This requires that they meet validity-for-use and especially validity-in-use criteria and be sensitive enough to detect improvements reliably. A measure's sensitivity or signaling power can be addressed in the design process by attending to content and construct validity. Content validity can be enhanced by carefully reviewing the research literature on an improvement project's aim and involving practitioners in its development. To ensure construct validity, developers need to address enough aspects of the construct being measured to satisfy academic and practitioner experts that the measure adequately covers the relevant content. Having enough items to adequately represent the construct being measured must be balanced against the need for instruments to be short enough to fit into current work routines. The practical measure should also predict outcomes in the theory of improvement. Improvement teams can lean on prior research to make an argument about a measure's likely predictive validity. Using and modifying measures that have already been shown to correlate with desired outcomes (e.g., student achievement or high school graduation) or practices (e.g., high-quality literacy instruction) can help designers make an argument that their measure is likely to have predictive validity.

Routines for analyzing practical measures can also enhance validity-in-use. By making user-friendly representations of the data, the developers make it more likely that the data will be interpreted as intended and, as a result, have the potential to support improvement. The case studies in this book also suggest that support from an expert (e.g., a coach or professional development provider) is often required for users to interpret and use data in ways that are consistent with the theory of improvement.

As the improvement cases detailed in this book attest, continuous improvement methods are used to address various instructional and organizational challenges in schools. While calls to increase the flow of research to practice continue, off-the-shelf solutions to challenging educational problems tend to be less effective in contexts other than those where they were developed or initially tested. Adaptation to a local context is often required. Continuous improvement methods can help with this adaptive implementation, as improvement teams design or adapt instructional or organizational changes based on research and their knowledge of the context in which the changes are being tested. Continuous improvement methods such as PDSA cycles can help improvement teams initially test changes with small numbers of practitioners, then across contexts, and ultimately at scale. To know whether these changes lead to improvements, we need practical measures that meet the validity-for-use and validity-in-use criteria described in this chapter. The framework for examining the validity of improvement efforts detailed here is an accessible support for this continuous improvement work.

8

Practical Measurement in Action

Paul Cobb
Paul G. LeMahieu

In this chapter, we pull together important themes and insights from throughout the book. The five cases presented in chapters 2–6 and the discussion of validity of practical measurement for improvement (chapter 7) have much to offer practitioners and researchers who are considering using practical measures in their improvement work. Each of the cases explains how the development and use of one or more practical measures enhanced an educational improvement effort by enabling practitioners to monitor whether their improvement strategies are having the desired impact, and thus whether they needed to revise their strategies. Taken together, the cases illustrate how practical measurement enables practitioners to see whether focusing on the specific factors that they have identified enables them to make significant progress toward their chosen aims, and whether their efforts are leading to scalable improvements. In a very real sense, the educators in each of the cases were no longer flying blind; instead, they could see and better understand what they were trying to improve, as well as the consequences of their efforts to do so.[1]

The authors of each of the case chapters make it clear that they developed their measurements for improvement purposes rather than for accountability or research purposes. As they indicate, the intent of accountability measures is to enable an audience external to particular educational processes or practices—audiences such as state, district, or school leaders or the broader public—to determine whether processes or practices within the educational system truly measure up.[2] Accountability measures clearly have legitimate uses, but those uses do not include determining how to improve current processes or practices or whether new ones are improvements. This is because the findings do not explain how the outcomes that they document were produced, and thus why those outcomes rather than others were achieved. Ironically, absent effective measurement for improvement (together with well-conceived processes for their use), the practitioners who are held accountable for the outcomes have to fly blind when they attempt to improve them.

In the following pages, we draw on the cases to discuss five sets of issues that have implications for the development, implementation, and use of practical measures as a central element of an educational improvement effort. First, we consider the various educational problems addressed in the five cases and distinguish between two classes of problems. Second, we discuss essential characteristics of practical measures that the five cases illustrate. These include that measures assess what their developers conjecture makes a difference given the educational problem at hand, the measures are meaningful to and minimally burdensome for educators to use, and the measures yield actionable information in a timely manner. Third, we consider what the cases tell us about the process of creating practical measures, including the different types of expertise that are required to do so well. Fourth, we discuss what the cases illustrate about the role of practical measurement in reducing inequities in students' educational opportunities and accomplishments. Fifth and finally, we focus on the contextual conditions and types of support that practitioners will likely need if they are to use different types of practical measures productively.

FOCAL EDUCATIONAL PROBLEMS

Collectively, the five cases illustrate that practical measurement can enhance efforts to address a wide range of education problems. Two of the five cases focus on what might be termed "organizational or structural" issues. The goal of the improvement effort described in chapter 5 (Allensworth) is to improve high school graduation rates and the overall goal of the case presented in chapter 2 (Takahashi and Norman) is to increase the rate at which students complete the Free Applications for Federal Student Aid (FAFSA). In contrast, the remaining three cases all focus on improving instruction in particular content areas. The goal of the case described in chapter 3 (Jackson and colleagues) is to enable mathematics teachers to support their students' attainment of rigorous learning goals that include both conceptual understanding and procedural fluency. The focal problems in chapter 4 (Friedrich and Bear) and chapter 6 (Larbi-Cherif and colleagues) both focus on English language arts (ELA) instruction. Friedrich and Bear's goal is to enable teachers to teach students to write source-based arguments, whereas Larbi-Cherif et al.'s goal is to improve literacy outcomes in schools that serve a high proportion of students from historically marginalized groups. In all three of these instructionally focused cases, the issue is to support teachers to better provide for their students' learning.

We will refer to this distinction between organizationally focused and instructionally focused cases throughout this chapter. For now, we note that the goals of these two broad classes of improvement efforts are complementary. On the one hand, improvements in students' core content–learning will likely enhance their prospects for being accepted by and succeeding at a college or thriving in the world of work. On the other hand, improvements in students' content-focused learning will not pay off unless they graduate from high school and complete all the steps of the college application process (including access to the resources that allow them to matriculate). Together, they address complementary aspects of educational attainment. Up to this point, the bulk of the work on practical measurement in education has focused on organizational problems. The inclusion of three cases that focus on what Elmore called the "instructional core" marks a significant step forward for research and design in practical measurement.[3]

One further issue relating to the educational problems that motivate improvement efforts merits discussion. It is clearly important that both the researchers and practitioners involved in an improvement effort appreciate the significance of the focal problem. In some cases, this is quite straightforward. For example, it will likely be self-evident to all school and district personnel, as well as to parents and other stakeholders, that increasing high school graduation rates is significant for students' educational, economic, and civic future. However, in other cases, the significance of the focal problem might not be self-evident to all involved in an improvement effort. Thus, Friedrich and Bear (chapter 4) explain that many teachers do not initially appreciate the importance of teaching students to back up the claims that they make when writing arguments by drawing on multiple sources. An initial goal of the teacher professional development that they and their colleagues designed, therefore, was to support teachers in understanding just what source-based argumentation is and why it is an important capability for students to develop. This case and similar ones indicate that it is essential when preparing to deploy practical measures to assess whether the significance of the focal problem will be widely understood by users. Only then will they have the will and agency needed to engage fully in the improvement effort.

KEY CHARACTERISTICS OF PRACTICAL MEASURES

Takahashi and Norman (chapter 2) do us a great service by introducing five essential characteristics of practical measures. Smith (chapter 7) discussed these characteristics to clarify the range of issues that need to be considered when establishing the validity of a practical measure. We revisit these same characteristics to tease out implications for practitioners and researchers who are planning to integrate practical measures into their improvement work.

Practical Measurement Is Closely Tied to a Theory of Improvement

It is impossible to overemphasize the importance of this first characteristic. In each of our five cases, the development of the practical measures was guided from the outset by an evidence-based theory of improvement. A theory of this type indicates what makes a difference, given the educational problem being addressed, where and how to intervene to make the desired improvements, and thus what is important to measure. For example, in the organizationally focused case described by Allensworth (chapter 5), the existing research on the factors that influence whether students graduate was inadequate. In this situation, the team leading the improvement effort had to conduct a series of studies to figure out what makes a difference and thus needs to be measured. The initial studies conducted by Allensworth and her colleagues revealed that staying on track in ninth grade is a strong predictor of graduating from high school. Although this was a significant insight, it was not clear which of a myriad of possible factors influenced whether ninth graders stay on track. Allensworth and her colleagues therefore conducted additional studies that indicated that staying on track is primarily predicted by students' attendance and by their grades. The resulting theory of improvement makes clear both what needed to be measured and where school and district staff should direct their improvement efforts. In contrast, the theory of improvement in our second organizationally focused case reported by Takahashi and Norman (chapter 2) is more straightforward and orients school staff to focus directly on developing strategies that support students in completing FAFSA applications.

The theory of improvement for the three instructionally focused cases all involved working with teachers to improve their instruction and thus better support their students' learning. In the two cases reported by Friedrich and Bear (chapter 4) and Larbi-Cherif and colleagues (chapter 6), the substance of the theory of improvement was suggested by prior research, and the support for teachers' improvement of their instruction was supplied by the staff members of intermediary organizations, who were accomplished professional development leaders and coaches. The third instructionally focused case reported by Jackson et al. (chapter 3) was part of an extensive line of investigation that sought to understand how districts can increase their capacity for instructional improvement. The theory of improvement for this case, therefore, suggested an additional level of intervention as the researchers collaborated with members of the participating district's mathematics department. Together, they sought to provide professional development for mathematics coaches who worked with teachers to support their development of more effective instructional practices.

While these top-level descriptions of the theories of improvement for the instructionally focused cases are helpful, they do not indicate what needs to be measured. It is essential that these theories also specify key aspects of teachers' instruction, students' learning, or both that make a difference and need to be measured if teachers and the coaches working with them are to receive useful feedback on their improvement efforts. For example, the theory of improvement that grounded the work described by Jackson and colleagues (chapter 3) specifies aspects of classroom learning environments that prior research indicates make a difference for students' mathematical learning. These aspects include the level of cognitive demand of tasks as they are implemented by the teacher, what students perceive themselves to be accountable for, whether students can understand other students' explanations, and whether students feel that the teacher and other students value their ideas. Jackson and her colleagues therefore developed practical measures of these aspects, thereby enabling teachers and the coaches with whom they were working to assess whether the instructional changes that they made improved students' learning opportunities.

This case and that reported by Allensworth (chapter 5) differ in many respects, not least that Jackson et al. could draw on prior research, whereas Allensworth and her colleagues had to conduct several studies to determine what mattered and therefore had to be measured. However, both illustrate the critical role of an evidence-based theory of improvement in orienting an improvement team to focus on what might be termed "the right stuff," whether that stuff involves ninth graders' attendance and grades or key aspects of the classroom learning environment. As Smith makes clear in his discussion of validity in chapter 7, if the theory of improvement that underpins an improvement effort is solid, then valid measures based on it will predict subsequent outcomes, thus enabling educators to determine whether the changes that they have made are improvements.

Practical Measurement Is Meaningful to Key Stakeholders

Meaningfulness requires that users of practical measures understand both what is being measured and why it needs to be measured, given the educational problem at hand. It is therefore essential that they understand the theory of improvement that informed the development of the measures. As the case presented in chapter 2 (federal student aid) illustrates, the theory of improvement sometimes can be almost self-evident. However, it is clear from the remaining four focal cases that users of practical measures and others involved in an improvement effort will frequently require explicit support to understand the theory of improvement. For example, in the case reported by Allensworth (chapter 5), many teachers and school leaders initially believed that a wide range of factors influence whether ninth graders stay on track and initially questioned an exclusive focus on students' attendance and grades. Similarly, Jackson et al. (chapter 3) and Friedrich and Bear (chapter 4) explain in detail why they had to intentionally support the users of their practical measures in understanding both what was being measured (key aspects of classroom learning environments and of high-leverage argument skills, respectively) and why these measures were important, given the education problem being addressed (enable mathematics teachers to support their students' attainment of rigorous learning goals and enable ELA teachers to teach their students to write source-based arguments, respectively).

The focal education problem in the remaining case reported by Larbi-Cherif and colleagues (chapter 6) was to improve students' comprehension of complex texts. The primary improvement strategy was to support teachers to implement a sequence of student-centered activities in each lesson. Implementing these activities effectively was a significant departure from the teachers' current instructional practices and required significant learning on their part. Larbi-Cherif and colleagues anticipated and developed a practical measure for each major instructional change that teachers might make during this learning process. These measures took the form of short student surveys and were designed to give teachers prompt feedback on their improvement efforts. In this case, the grounding theory of improvement centered on the learning opportunities that would arise for students if teachers enacted each activity effectively with their students. As this theory of improvement was not self-evident to the teachers, they received professional development that included a focus on what the practical measures were designed to measure and why these aspects of effective enactment of the instructional activities mattered for students' learning. Only then would the practical measures be meaningful to the participating teachers.

Based on this review of the five cases, we contend that it is more productive to view meaningfulness as an accomplishment for users rather than as an inherent characteristic of practical measures in and of themselves. Taken together, the cases indicate that practical measures become meaningful to users and others involved in an improvement effort as they come to understand the grounding theory of improvement. This perspective is helpful because it orients the team leading an improvement effort to consider the types of support that users might need for specific practical measures to become meaningful.

Practical Measurement Yields Actionable Information

As Takahashi and Norman observe in chapter 2, it is essential that practical measures can inform the next steps in an improvement process. This implies that these steps are not merely changes in current practices or processes, but changes that have a reasonable likelihood of being improvements. It is clear from our focal cases that users of practical measures often require support if they are to identify potentially productive next steps. This is especially the case for the instructionally focused improvement efforts, as appropriate next steps may not be apparent or may be more nuanced than is the case with the organizational improvement problems.

Friedrich and Bear explain in chapter 4 that a major goal of the professional development program that they and their colleagues developed was to support teachers in using the Using Sources Tool (UST) practical measure to assess the quality of students' written arguments and, on that basis, identify feasible next steps for the development of their argument-writing capabilities. For their part, Larbi-Cherif and colleagues describe in chapter 6 how accomplished coaches supported teachers in interpreting their practical measures data (students' responses to a short survey) and in identifying instructional changes that would likely prove to be an improvement. Similarly, Jackson and colleagues explain in chapter 3 that school-based coaches supported teachers in identifying instructional changes that would likely improve their students' learning.

In contrast to these instructionally focused cases, users of the practical measures in the two organizationally focused cases did not, for the most part, require the direct support of more accomplished colleagues for the measures to become actionable. Takashi and Norman (chapter 2) and Allensworth (chapter 5) both indicate that it was sufficient to organize users and others involved in the improvement effort into school-based data analysis teams and to create mechanisms for teams to share successful improvement strategies across schools.

The relevant difference between the two sets of cases concerns the learning demands involved in identifying and skillfully enacting potentially productive changes. In the absence of support, teachers in the instructionally focused cases would have to reinvent new forms of professional practice on their own. It would not be sufficient for teachers to merely extend or elaborate their current instructional practices for their students to attain rigorous learning goals in ELA or mathematics. They would have to fundamentally reorganize those practices, and in the process reconceptualize what ELA or mathematics learning should be in school. We contend that the apprenticeship model of a teacher working with an accomplished coach is an appropriate type of support for teachers' development of new forms of professional practice.

Substantial practitioner learning is also involved in the two organizationally focused cases. For example, many of the practitioners in these cases have to revise their views about why students fail to complete the college application process or why ninth graders fail to stay on track.

However, they do not have to reconceptualize what it means to apply for college, attend school, or receive a grade. Furthermore, their deep knowledge of their school and district contexts is a relevant resource on which they can capitalize when addressing organizationally focused problems.

Our intent in drawing this contrast between the two sets of cases is not to minimize the contributions of the two organizationally focused improvement efforts. Improving the rate at which students from historically underserved communities graduate from high school and apply for college is a laudable achievement that addresses longstanding inequities in students' educational attainment. Moreover, every bit as much insight and creativity is needed to conceive of changes to organizational processes and structures as potential improvements in each of these types of problems. Our intent in drawing the contrast is instead to highlight the challenges involved in making the instructional improvements required for students to achieve rigorous learning goals in core content areas. One of these challenges is to provide users with the support necessary for practical measures to become both meaningful and actionable, thereby enabling them to receive evidence-based feedback that can inform the next steps in their ongoing improvement work.

Practical Measurement Is Minimally Burdensome and Provides Timely Feedback

The three characteristics of practical measurement that we have discussed thus far focus on the empirical grounding of practical measures and on ensuring that the measures become both meaningful and actionable to users. The remaining two characteristics discussed by Takahashi and Norman (chapter 2) concern the usability of the measures. The fourth characteristic is that the measures are minimally burdensome. This requires that educators can integrate them into current routines with little disruption. The final characteristic is that the measures can provide users with timely feedback. In this case, timeliness is meant in two senses: when the measures are administered and how long it takes before the data are returned for use. It is essential that data from the measures are available when users need to determine whether a change in current practices or processes is an improvement, and this requires timeliness in both senses of the word, as our five cases illustrate.

The question of when the measures are administered is self-evident in organizationally focused cases reported by Takahashi and Norman (chapter 2) and Allensworth (chapter 5), as both use data that districts typically collect: students' FAFSA completion and ninth graders' attendance and grades, respectively. However, the teams leading these improvement efforts created data dashboards that updated frequently, thereby ensuring that educators had access to current data when they met to assess the effectiveness of their current improvement strategies.

The practical measures used in the instructionally focused cases reported by Jackson et al. (chapter 3) and Larbi-Cherif et al. (chapter 6) were short student surveys that assessed students' perceptions of key aspects of a specific lesson. The surveys took students less than three minutes to complete, thereby minimizing disruptions to instruction, and were administered at the end of lessons before students' recollections began to fade. The data dashboards created as part of these improvement efforts gave teachers and the coaches supporting them access to the resulting data when they met to debrief on a lesson. The practical measure in the final case reported by Friedrich and Bear (chapter 4) was a tool that teachers used to analyze their students' written arguments. This measure was minimally disruptive, and access to the data was timely, because analyzing students' reasoning and planning future instruction on that basis are critical aspects of high-quality teaching.[4]

The last two defining characteristics of practical measures correspond to the second and fourth principles that Larbi-Cherif and colleagues propose for designing practical measures in chapter 6. Their discussion of these principles further clarifies the issues that need to be considered when creating minimally burdensome measures that can provide timely feedback.

CREATING PRACTICAL MEASURES

As Takahashi and Norman note in chapter 2, the term *practical measure* is often taken to mean that measures of this type are quick and easy to create. As we noted in chapter 1 of this book, creating measures that have the five defining characteristics discussed in the previous section is often challenging. Our five focal cases illustrate some of the challenges that can arise when first developing an evidence-based theory of improvement that indicates what needs to be measured, and then figuring out how to create an appropriate measure.

The first characteristics of practical measures, that they be tied to a problem-driven theory of improvement, emphasizes that having a solid, evidence-based understanding of the mechanisms and processes relevant to the educational problem being addressed is crucial.[5] For example, Jackson et al. were familiar with the current research on high-quality mathematics instruction in general and on productive whole-class discussions of students' solutions in particular. Similarly, Friedrich and Bear had a deep understanding of the current research on writing instruction, including the key features of high-quality written arguments. Allensworth and colleagues' work is particularly revealing, as it illustrates that figuring out what needs to be measured can itself be a major achievement. The research on which they could draw was inadequate, as there was no consensus about what made a difference in whether students graduated, and thus what needed to be measured. They therefore had to conduct an exemplary program of research that identified attendance and grades in ninth grade as the key factors.

The second step in creating practical measures is to figure out how to measure what needs to be measured. As we have noted, this step was straightforward in our two organizational focused cases, increasing the rate of applications for federal student aid (chapter 2) and increasing the graduation rate (chapter 5). Districts typically collect data on students' completion of federal student aid applications and on ninth graders' attendance and grades. However, it would be a mistake to overgeneralize and assume that the required types of data are always readily available in all organizational focused improvement efforts. Figuring out how to measure what needs to be measured can be as much of a challenge in organizationally focused improvement efforts as it was in the three instructionally focused cases.

Jackson et al. illustrate some of these challenges when they describe the iterative cycles they conducted to test and revise their practical measures of the classroom learning environment. Similarly, Friedrich and Bear clarify that their practical measure of students' current capabilities as argument writers, the UST, went through several iterations based on both their observations of teachers using the UST and on feedback from teachers. For their part, Larbi-Cherif and colleagues clarify that they approached the development of their practical measures of reading comprehension instruction as an improvement process involving iterative testing and refinement. The primary purpose in conducting these iterative cycles was to establish what Smith (chapter 7) termed the *validity-for-use* of a measure by ensuring that it measures what it is designed to measure and can detect improvements reliably.

We again stress that it will be necessary to conduct iterative cycles to develop measures that are valid for use in some organizationally focused improvement efforts, as well as for the vast majority of instructionally focused improvement efforts that aim to support students in attainment of rigorous learning goals in core content areas. Although schools and districts collect data on instruction and student learning, they usually do so primarily for accountability purposes. As discussed in chapter 1, these accountability measures are unlikely to be appropriate for improvement purposes, given the necessary characteristics that have been discussed and illustrated throughout this book. In our view, it is essential to develop an infrastructure of research-based practical measures of instruction and students' reasoning in specific content domains if improvement science is to contribute to ongoing improvements in the instructional core.

We noted in chapter 1 that creating measures that have all five characteristics is a tall order. It is clear from our focal cases that three complementary forms of expertise are required if this challenge is to be met. The first is content expertise, knowledge about the problem that is the focus of the improvement work. This includes a deep understanding of the extant relevant research and scholarship. The second is practical expertise, which includes having a deep understanding of local school and district contexts and how they affect (and perhaps even define) the problem. Certainly, knowledge of practice, its development, and its context can make critical contributions to the creation of successful improvement strategies. The third is technical or analytic expertise, which includes knowledge about assessment development (psychometrics) as might be necessary to ensure that measures are valid for use and to clarify the conditions necessary for measures to be valid in use. It also subsumes the expertise in conducting research and analytics to support the improvement process itself, including the research needed to fully understand the focal problem and to inform the creation of data displays that enabled practitioners to access timely feedback.

As Takahashi and Norman noted in chapter 2, there is a very real danger that a lethal power imbalance might emerge between researchers and psychometricians on one side and accomplished practitioners on the other. It is therefore crucial that all the participants in an improvement effort recognize others' forms of expertise. This can be facilitated by ensuring that they are committed to a common improvement goal, regularly engage in improvement work together, and institute routines that promote collaborative decision-making. This "colleagueship of expertise" is essential to productive improvement research. It is as participants honor each other's areas of expertise that they establish productive relationships grounded in mutual respect and trust.

REDUCING INEQUITIES IN STUDENTS' EDUCATIONAL OPPORTUNITIES AND ACCOMPLISHMENT

The five focal cases illustrate several ways that the use of practical measures can contribute to the more equal distribution of educational opportunities, and thus outcomes. These include the types of improvement problems that practical measurement makes tractable, users' development of an improvement disposition that foregrounds students' current strengths, and the development of data systems that enable users to focus on different groups of students, including traditionally underserved groups. The relevance of practical measurement to issues of equity should not be a surprise given Bryk and his colleagues' clarification that a primary goal of improvement-oriented research is to reduce variation in students' educational opportunities and outcomes.[6]

Focal Educational Problems Revisited

The problems addressed in all five of the focal cases have an equity dimension. This is readily apparent in the two organizationally focused cases, both of which aim to improve the future educational and economic opportunities and outcomes of students from traditionally underserved groups. Allensworth (chapter 4) focused on increasing graduation rates for these students, whereas the case reported by Takahashi and Norman (chapter 2) aimed to increase the rate at which they complete applications for federal student aid.

The equity dimension of the three instructionally focused cases becomes apparent when we note that they all sought to ensure that students from traditionally underserved groups have access to challenging learning opportunities that enhance their prospects of success in their subsequent educational pursuits and their lives beyond. Furthermore, all three improvement efforts aimed to support students' development of capabilities that, in Bruner's terms, have clout by enabling them to participate in significant out-of-school activities.[7] These capabilities include flexible mathematical reasoning and problem solving, together with the ability to make and critique mathematical arguments (Jackson and colleagues, chapter 3), writing evidence-based arguments by drawing on sources that represent a range of perspectives (Friedrich and Bear, chapter 4), and the ability to analyze complex texts and write analytically (Larbi-Cherif and colleagues, chapter 6).

Each of these cases aimed to facilitate students' development of these capabilities by supporting teachers to organize instruction around cognitively demanding tasks, maintain the level of challenge across classroom learning activities, and provide students who experience difficulties with the additional support that they need to participate fully in and learn from ambitious instruction.[8] In each case, practical measures played a crucial role by enabling teachers and those charged with supporting them to improve their instruction and thus their students' learning.

Disaggregating Practical Measures Data

Takahashi and Norman (chapter 2) and Allensworth (chapter 5) both discuss the value of disaggregating practical measures data, and in so doing emphasized the importance of intentionally designing data dashboards and associated data representations to support practitioners in detecting possible disparities in the impact of the improvement efforts. In both these organizationally focused cases, analyses that disaggregate practical measures data at the school and district levels are particularly relevant, given the improvement problems being addressed.

Disaggregating data can also be important in instructionally focused improvement cases, as they can give teachers feedback on their efforts to better support their students' learning. In this regard, Larbi-Cherif and colleagues (chapter 6) propose as one of their four principles for designing practical measures that it should be possible to identify any disparities in how an improvement effort is affecting different groups of students, including groups that are often underserved. They illustrate the value of disaggregating data by sharing sample analyses in which they identified differences between students who chose to respond to the Spanish-language and English-language versions of a short survey practical measure. Larbi-Cherif and colleagues also noted that disaggregating practical measures data at the classroom level can lead to difficulties when a school serves a very diverse student population and students actively participate in generating practical measures data by, for example, responding to survey items.

The improvement effort described by Jackson and colleagues (chapter 3) illustrates this difficulty. Jackson et al. translated their practical measures (which also took the form of short surveys) into twelve languages because their partner districts served students from multiple language groups. However, they decided not to disaggregate student responses because teachers might have been able to impute individual students' responses when there was only a small number of students from some language groups in a class. Crucially, prior findings revealed that when their responses were not anonymous, students frequently seek to please their teachers by giving survey responses that they believed their teachers desired, thereby threatening the validity-in-use of the measures. This is especially likely when teachers have yet to establish relationships of trust with their students. Thus, there is a trade-off in some instructionally focused cases when a school serves a linguistically diverse student population. On the one hand, disaggregating data by language group can become problematic, but on the other hand, students' active participation in the data-generation process gives them voice in decisions about how their teachers might better support their learning.

Developing an Improvement Disposition

Takahashi and Norman (chapter 2) set a tone that runs throughout the entire book when they observed that improvement work in general, and the productive use of practical measures in particular, require that all participants in an improvement effort take responsibility for what the data tell them about their ongoing improvement efforts. Users of practical measures who have developed an improvement disposition attribute critical or disconfirming feedback to limitations in their current improvement strategies rather than to perceived deficits in students and their families.[9] All five focal cases emphasize the importance of shifting from a deficit perspective, which scrutinizes students, to an improvement perspective, which scrutinizes the system and the current efforts to address the problem at hand.

In four of these cases, teachers and others involved in the improvement efforts made this transition in conjunction with their use of practical measures. For example, Friedrich and Bear (chapter 4) discuss how they intentionally designed their practical measure, the UST, to support teachers in identifying strengths and how they can build on students' current writing rather than on assessing how students' writing fails to measure up when compared with accomplished writing. Similarly, Allensworth (chapter 5) explained that when teachers examine data on ninth graders' attendance and class grades, some educators begin to ask why students are missing school and why their grades are unsatisfactory. In following up, many of these teachers realize that students who they previously assumed did not care about school could stay on track in ninth grade if they received specific types of targeted support.

In the remaining case, Jackson et al. (chapter 3) framed teachers' development of an improvement perspective as a precondition for the productive use of their practical measures of key aspects of the classroom learning environment. In taking this approach, they were influenced by prior work suggesting that teachers who do not believe that their students are capable of learning from ambitious mathematics instruction typically explain their students' responses on the practical measures in terms of student deficits rather than instructional limitations.[10] Jackson et al. therefore supported the coaches with whom they worked to assess teachers' views of their students' mathematical capabilities. If coaches found that a teacher's view was unproductive, they would intervene by modeling ambitious instruction in the teacher's classroom to show what the students were capable of doing mathematically when supported appropriately. Looking beyond the difference in approach between this and the other four cases, the major takeaway from all five cases is the importance of supporting the users of practical measures to develop an improvement disposition.

SUPPORTING PRACTITIONERS' PRODUCTIVE USE OF PRACTICAL MEASURES

In prior sections of this chapter, we have capitalized on the five focal cases to identify several aspects of users' perspectives, knowledge, and practice that are implicated in the effective use of practical measures:

- Understanding the significance of the problem that orients the improvement effort
- Developing an improvement disposition that is integral to improvement work in general, and to work that specifically targets inequities in students' educational opportunities in particular
- Understanding the theory of improvement that makes practical measures meaningful by indicating both what needs to be measured and why it is important to measure it
- Determining how to respond productively to feedback from practical measures, thereby making them actionable

This checklist of user capabilities can guide the deployment of practical measures in the context of an improvement effort. As an illustration, we saw that the significance of the problem being addressed was self-evident to users in four of our five focal cases. However, in the remaining case described by Friedrich and Bear, teachers needed support to understand why writing source-based arguments is an important student learning goal. The teachers might well have resisted, or at best gone through the motions of complying, had the team leading this improvement effort failed to anticipate that teachers would need support to understand that it was important to address the focal problem of improving instruction on argument writing. More generally, improvement efforts will probably not end well if the leadership team fails to anticipate the level of support that users might need to understand the focal improvement problem, develop an improvement disposition, understand the theory of improvement, and identify potentially productive changes. Practical measures for improvement can also serve a signaling function by illustrating what matters most and what good performance looks like. Collectively, the five focal cases illustrate several types of support for users including professional development sessions, social routines for analyzing practical measures data, coaching, and data systems and representations. We discuss each of these in turn now.

Professional Development Sessions

The supports provided for users in all three instructionally focused cases included a coherent sequence of professional development sessions. For example, a major goal of the professional development sessions described by Friedrich and Bear (chapter 4) was to help teachers understand the significance of the focal improvement problem (improving the teaching of argument writing) and to learn to use the UST practical measure to identify strengths in students' written arguments on which they could build. For their part, Larbi-Cherif and colleagues (chapter 6) anticipated that the theory of improvement that grounded their instructional improvement effort would not be self-evident to teachers. The professional development that teachers received, therefore, include a focus on what the practical measures assessed and why these aspects of ELA instruction were important. Similarly, the mathematics coaches who participated in the improvement effort described by Jackson et al. (chapter 3) received ongoing professional development designed to support them in understanding what was being measured and why these aspects of the classroom learning environment mattered for students' mathematical learning.

Professional development figured less prominently in the two organizationally focused cases. Allensworth (chapter 5) reported that myths about why students succeed or fail and what educators can do about it continued to be pervasive even after researchers had shared their findings that grades and attendance in ninth grade are what really matter. However, they also reported that it was sufficient for administrators to bring teachers back to this evidence. Looking across the five cases, professional development sessions would appear to be particularly appropriate when educators need support to understand the significance of the focal improvement problem, as well as to make practical measures meaningful by clarifying what is being measured and why it matters.

Social Routines and Coaching

It is as educators analyze practical measures data and identify potentially productive next steps in their ongoing improvement work that practical measures become actionable. A recurrent theme in the literature on practical measurement is that of educators working in groups or teams to analyze data. This includes routines for analysis and sensemaking, inferring potentially productive changes and how to develop them, as well as processes for evaluating those changes to determine whether they are improvements and for curating what has been learned, in order to delineate warranted practices that can orient and inform improvement efforts more broadly.

Takahashi and Norman (chapter 2) clarify that social routines also play a critical role in indicating who should participate in the improvement work and in specifying norms of participation that characterize productive data conversations in which there is space for multiple voices. Educators worked together to analyze data and identify potentially productive next steps without the support of accomplished facilitators in the two organizationally focused improvement efforts described by Takahashi and Norman (chapter 2) and Allensworth (chapter 5). However, the leaders of these improvement efforts sometimes had to press the school-based analysis teams to locate the source of the problem that they were addressing within the school system, and thus within their locus of control, rather than deflecting responsibility for the problem to students and their families. These interventions served to support members of the analysis teams in developing an improvement disposition. As we have seen, this development was essential from the point of view of equity.

Educators also worked collaboratively to analyze data in the instructionally focused case reported by Friedrich and Bear (chapter 4). However, the UST practical measure was introduced to teachers in a professional development session. The teachers then worked collaboratively in this and subsequent sessions to use the UST to analyze samples of students' writing. Friedrich and Bear make it clear that the support that the teachers received from the professional development facilitators was crucial, and clarified that these facilitators also conducted one-on-one coaching sessions with individual teachers. In the other two instructionally focused cases reported by Jackson et al. (chapter 3) and Larbi-Cherif et al. (chapter 6), the practical measures took the form of short student surveys. In both cases, coaches worked one on one with teachers to help them analyze their students' survey responses and identify potentially productive instructional changes. Looking across the five cases, we attribute the more substantial support that teachers in the three instructional focused cases received to the significant challenges involved in determining how they might modify their instruction to better support their students' learning. The realization that it is unreasonable to expect teachers to identify potentially productive changes on their own has led school districts across the country to create coaching positions in core content areas.

Data Systems and Data Representations

In four of the five cases, the improvement efforts included the development of data systems and associated data representation that provided educators with timely feedback on the changes that they have made. In the fifth case, reported by Friedrich and Bear (chapter 4), teachers used the UST to analyze their students' writing, thereby receiving immediate feedback on their instruction. This engagement with rigorous evidence for assessing and shaping practice is essential to improvement research. Yet statistical acumen or technical prowess cannot be a prerequisite for that engagement. What is needed are systems that manage and enable ready access to measurement for improvement, as well as displays and representations of the data that are intuitively meaningful to those who will use them.

It is clear from the descriptions of the four cases with data systems that considerable thought went into their development. As noted earlier, the development of measurement for improvement and its attendant infrastructure is often an improvement project in itself. The design of all the data dashboards was informed by the underlying theory of improvement and oriented users toward focusing on what matters, given the improvement problem being addressed. For example, the dashboard described by Jackson et al. (chapter 3) enabled coaches and their partner teachers to determine whether changes in the teachers' instruction improved one or more aspects of the classroom environment that matter for students' learning (e.g., whether more students could now understand other students' explanations during whole-class discussions). Similarly, the data system described by Allensworth (chapter 5) was designed to focus users' attention on ninth graders' attendance and grades, the two primary factors that prefigure whether they will graduate.

It is also evident that the representations used in all four data systems were specifically chosen to support users in addressing questions that were consequential for the improvement work. For example, the data system described by Takahashi and Norman (chapter 2) enables users to compare the rates at which different groups of students (e.g., based on ethnicity/race and gender) are completing financial aid applications, and thus to identify those that needed additional support. As Takahashi and Norman recount, a change in the way that data were presented on the dashboard, from a separate pull-down menu for each key subgroup to a single display that included a bar graph for each of the subgroups, proved more effective at enabling users to identify groups that were not being served adequately. While adjustments and tweaks of this type might seem relatively minor, such differences can really make a difference in users' improvement practices.

Implications

It is clear from our five cases that there is significant variation in the levels and types of support that educators might need if they are to use practical measures productively. While it is possible that they might need support to understand the significance of the education problem being addressed, they more likely require support to understand the theory that underpins an improvement effort and gives meaning to the practical measures. Our five cases suggest that professional development sessions might well be an appropriate form of support for addressing both these needs.

The five cases also indicate that educators could well need support to develop an improvement disposition. In four of the cases, it was sufficient for leaders of the improvement efforts to push the educators to focus on aspects of the school system and their current improvement strategies when they analyzed data. An alternative that might be necessary in some cases is to treat the development of an improvement disposition as a precursor to introducing practical measures.

There was a significant difference between the two organizationally focused cases and the three instructionally focused cases in the level of support that users needed to identify potentially productive next steps in their improvement work. In the organizationally focused cases, creating school-based analysis teams and supporting the establishment of productive social routines appeared to be sufficient. In both of these cases, the participating educators could identify potentially productive next steps by drawing on their current professional knowledge and their deep understanding of the school and district contexts in which they worked.

In contrast, the teachers who participated in the three instructionally focused improvement efforts required the support of an accomplished coach, along with the additional resources that a coach might bring to the efforts. This is understandable because all three instructional improvement efforts aimed to support teachers' development of classroom practices that aimed at rigorous student learning goals. One-on-one coaching is often a more appropriate form of support than large-scale professional development sessions because the practical measures data that the coaches and their partner teachers analyzed were specific to individual teachers' instructional practices and their students' learning.

Stepping back from the five cases, we see it as essential that the researchers and practitioners charged with leading improvement work involving practical measures assess the learning needs of users in advance and plan support accordingly. The checklist of perspectives, knowledge, and practices that we discussed at the beginning of this section should be helpful, as it indicates four broad capabilities that underpin the productive use of practical measures.

FINAL THOUGHTS

Chapter 1 underscored the danger of using practical measures for accountability rather than improvement purposes, a theme that runs through all the subsequent chapters. Smith brings this concern into sharp relief in chapter 7, when he observes that using practical measures for accountability purposes undermines their usefulness and threatens their validity. He goes on to note that in instructionally focused cases, teachers must work in district and school contexts that value the vision of high-quality instruction that motivated the development of the practical measures. In other words, it is not enough for school and district leaders to give teachers the space to use practical measures without interference. The valid use of practical measures requires that school and district leaders actively contribute to the instructional improvement efforts by ensuring that teachers receive the support that they need to develop an improvement disposition, to understand the underlying theory of improvement, and to identify and enact potentially productive instructional changes.

Allensworth makes it clear in chapter 5 that principal support can also be critical in organizationally focused improvement efforts. She explains that it was important for teachers to meet regularly to analyze data on their students' attendance and grades. She also observes that principals' support and encouragement for teachers to collaborate in this way was essential, and the extent to which teachers did so affected their schools' graduation rates. It therefore seems clear that using practical measures productively is a team sport in which the roles of both school leaders and district leaders to whom they report are often decisive.

In closing, we highlight the value of looking beyond individual practical measures to create systems of practical measures. The work of Allensworth and colleagues provides a helpful illustration of systems of this type. As we have seen, they first determined that staying on track in ninth grade is a strong predictor of graduating from high school, and then established that grades and attendance are the primary factors that influence whether ninth graders stay on track. The resulting measures of grades, attendance, and on-track status in ninth grade constitute a system of practical measures: graduation is strongly predicted by on-track status, which is in turn influenced by grades and attendance.

The approach that Allensworth illustrates in which improvement science methods are used to track down the primary factors that make a difference, and therefore need to be measured, is well established for organizationally focused cases. In comparison, work on practical measurement in instructionally focused cases is less well developed. However, Jackson et al. indicated that they intended to create a system of practical measures. Although they focus almost exclusively on classroom measures in chapter 3, they subsequently developed practical measures of coaching both when coaches work one on one with mathematics teachers in their classrooms and when they facilitate teacher collaborative meetings. The resulting system of practical measures is closely tied to the theory of improvement that guides many districts' efforts to improve students' learning in core content areas: support for coaches to work more effectively with teachers (individually in their classrooms and/or in groups in collaborative meetings) will result in improvements in teachers' classroom instruction, and consequently in their students' learning.

As a further illustration, it is not hard to imagine improvement efforts that might aim to foster students' interest, motivation, and engagement, or to develop productive academic identities, or to remove language barriers to learning. These and similar initiatives might collectively reveal interdependencies between a range of improvements such that some reinforce others, and collectively, they significantly enhance students' learning while reducing disparities. The practical measures created as an essential aspect of these improvement efforts would then constitute a system that could enable school and district leaders to monitor whether a multifaceted improvement effort is realizing its aim, and if it is not, pinpointing where it is breaking down.

As we look toward the future of improvement work in education and to the indispensable role of practical measurement in this work, we do so with considerable confidence. As we have noted, the bulk of improvement work to date has addressed organizationally focused problems and has compiled an impressive track record of success.[11] While the use of practical measures in efforts to address instructionally focused problems is relatively novel, the three instructionally focused cases in this book give us grounds for optimism. In our view, the appropriation and adaptation of improvement science methods that include using practical measures are essential if the field is to make progress in supporting teachers' development of ambitious instructional practices at scale. The growing number of researchers and practitioners who are well versed in improvement approaches that involve the use of practical measures, together with the rapid development of a material and social infrastructure to support them, bodes well for the future.

Notes

Chapter 1
1. Anthony S. Bryk et al., *Learning to Improve: How America's Schools Can Get Better at Getting Better* (Cambridge, MA: Harvard Education Press, 2015).
2. Donald J. Peurach et al., eds., *The Foundational Handbook on Improvement Research in Education* (New York: Rowman and Littlefield, 2022).
3. Paul G. LeMahieu and Anthony S. Bryk, eds., "Working to Improve: Seven Approaches to Quality Improvement in Education," *Quality Assurance in Education* 25, no. 1 (2017): 1–124.
4. See, for example, Paul G. LeMahieu and Richard C. Wallace Jr., "Up Against the Wall: Psychometrics Meets Praxis," *Educational Measurement: Issues and Practice* 5, no. 1 (1986): 12–16; Nancy S. Cole, "A Realist's Appraisal of the Prospects for Unifying Instruction and Assessment," in *Assessment in the Service of Learning: Proceedings of the ETS Invitational Conference*, ed. Eileen Freeman (New York: Educational Testing Service, 1988), 104; Paul G. LeMahieu and Elizabeth C. Reilly, "Systems of Coherence and Resonance: Assessment for Education and Assessment of Education," *Yearbook of the National Society for the Study of Education* 103, no. 2 (2004): 189–202; Edmund W. Gordon, "Toward Assessment in the Service of Learning," *Educational Measurement: Issues and Practice* 39, no. 3 (2020): 72–78.
5. Leif I. Solberg, Gordon Mosser, and Sharon McDonald, "The Three Faces of Performance Measurement: Improvement, Accountability, and Research," *Joint Commission Journal on Quality Improvement* 23, no. 3 (1997): 135–47.
6. Solberg et al., "The Three Faces of Performance Measurement."
7. Sola Takahashi et al., "Measurement for Improvement," in *Handbook on Improvement Research in Education*, ed. Donald J. Peurach et al. (Washington, DC: Rowman and Littlefield, 2022), 423; LeMahieu and Wallace, "Up Against the Wall."
8. Brandi Nicole Hinnant-Crawford, *Improvement Science in Education: A Primer* (Gorham, ME: Myers Education, 2020).
9. David Sherer et al., *Evidence for Improvement: An Integrated Analytic Approach for Supporting Networks in Education* (Stanford, CA: Carnegie Foundation for the Advancement of Teaching, 2020).

10. LeMahieu and Wallace, "Up Against the Wall"; Cole, "A Realist's Appraisal of the Prospects for Unifying Instruction and Assessment"; Gordon, "Toward Assessment in the Service of Learning."
11. See, for example, Samuel Messick, "Validity," in *Educational Measurement*, 3rd ed., ed. Robert L. Linn (New York: Macmillan, 1989); and Pamela A. Moss, Brian J. Girard, and Laura C. Haniford, "Validity in Educational Assessment," *Review of Research in Education* 30, no. 1 (2006): 109–62.

Chapter 2

1. We are grateful for the generosity of Stacey Caillier, Ben Sanoff, and Edgar Montes of HTH GSE, and Jeff Giles, Adrian Perez, and David Calderon Rodriguez of Warren High School in Downey, California, in sharing their stories of and insights about the Carpe Network.
2. This statistic was determined by the percentage of students who were eligible for free- and reduced-price lunch.
3. A "system" is a network of interdependent elements that work toward a common goal; for more, see W. Edwards Deming, *Out of the Crisis* (Cambridge, MA: Massachusetts Institute of Technology Press, 1986); Sarah L. Woulfin and C. Allen, "The Institution of Schooling," in *The Foundational Handbook on Improvement Research in Education*, ed. Donald J. Peurach et al. (Washington, DC: Rowman and Littlefield, 2022), 67. A system can include "formal structures and roles, social structures, technologies . . . relationships . . . and more that interact" (personal communication, Donald Peurach, March 21, 2021). They can include elements both within a system and outside it. Policies, laws, and social beliefs are just some of the elements in the surrounding environment of an organization that may be part of the system at hand. In this chapter, therefore, "systems" are associated with but not the same as "school districts," or even "organizations." Rather, it is a term that we use to acknowledge the broad array of factors that "(a) cause and institutionalize problems of practice and (b) support potential solutions" (personal communication, Donald Peurach, March 21, 2021).
4. Here and throughout the remainder of this chapter we use quotes from anonymous surveys to illustrate several of our points. Individual attribution is not possible given the conditions of data collection. However, we will describe the speaker's role when available.
5. Melanie Bertrand and Julie Marsh, "How Data-Driven Reform Can Drive Deficit Thinking," *Phi Delta Kappan* 102, no. 8 (2021): 35–39.
6. Sola Takahashi et al., "Measurement for Improvement," in *Handbook on Improvement Research in Education*, ed. Donald J. Peurach et al. (Washington, DC: Rowman and Littlefield, 2022), 423.
7. David Yeager et al., *Practical Measurement* (Stanford, CA: Carnegie Foundation for the Advancement of Teaching, 2013).
8. For instance, see Anthony S. Bryk et al., *Learning to Improve: How America's Schools Can Get Better at Getting Better* (Cambridge, MA: Harvard Education Press, 2015); Lloyd P. Provost and Sandra K. Murray, *The Health Care Data Guide: Learning from Data for Improvement* (Hoboken, NJ: Wiley, 2022).
9. HTH GSE is a network of sixteen charter schools in the San Diego area. Their teacher-credentialing program and graduate school of education provide professional

development opportunities for educators around the country and around the world. For further information, see https://www.hightechhigh.org/about-us/.
10. In the face of the rising costs of postsecondary education, financial support is essential for college attendance. In the 2017–2018 school year in the United States, 86 percent of full-time undergraduate students at four-year colleges received financial aid. See National Center for Education Statistics (NCES), "NCES Fast Facts," https://nces.ed.gov/fastfacts/display.asp?id=31 (accessed December 23, 2020).
11. Steven Bahr, Dianah Sparks, and Kathleen Mulvaney Hoyer, "Why Didn't Students Complete a Free Application for Federal Student Aid (FAFSA)? A Detailed Look, Stats in Brief, NCES 2018-061" (Washington, DC: National Center for Education Statistics, 2018).
12. While the federal deadline is June, the March deadline applies to state-based financial aid in California, including the Cal Grant. The Carpe Network considers March as the critical deadline for students in their schools.
13. These questions track the essential issues that characterize useful improvement knowledge: what works, for whom, and under what conditions (Bryk et al., *Learning to Improve*).
14. See Yeager et al., *Practical Measurement*; Bryk et al., *Learning to Improve*; Sola Takahashi et al., "Measurement for Improvement in Education," in *Oxford Bibliographies in Education* (Oxford: Oxford University Press, 2020).
15. This quote can be attributed to Dr. Paul Batalden. Its origins, which can be traced to Procter & Gamble, are discussed in this Institute for Healthcare Improvement blog post: http://www.ihi.org/communities/blogs/origin-of-every-system-is-perfectly-designed-quote (accessed January 14, 2021).
16. Brandon Bennett and Lloyd Provost, "What's Your Theory?," *Quality Progress* 48, no. 7 (2015): 36; Bryk et al., *Learning to Improve*.
17. The college application process is particularly challenging for students who are first-generation college goers and those who are from low-income backgrounds because there is a systemic lack of easily accessible information and support. Furthermore, these students tend not to receive the guidance and support that can lead them to apply to the best-suited colleges, leading to missed opportunities for students to attain their postsecondary degrees at more selective institutions. See Caroline Hoxby and Sarah Turner, "Expanding College Opportunities for High-Achieving, Low Income Students," *Stanford Institute for Economic Policy Research Discussion Paper* 12, no. 014 (2013): 7. FAFSA completion is associated with higher financial aid and college matriculation rates; see Eric Bettinger, Bridget Terry Long, and Philip Oreopoulos, *Increasing Postsecondary Enrollment among Low-Income Families: A Project to Improve Access to College Information and Financial Aid: The FAFSA H&R Block Experiment* (Cambridge, MA: Harvard University, 2009); Benjamin Castleman and Joshua Goodman, "Intensive College Counseling and the Enrollment and Persistence of Low-Income Students," *Education Finance and Policy* 13, no. 1 (2018): 19–41. Students from historically marginalized communities tend to experience a lesser sense of belonging in mainstream institutions such as colleges, which have traditionally underserved people from these backgrounds. These feelings of belonging have been connected to students' academic performance and health. See Gregory M. Walton and Geoffrey L. Cohen, "A Brief Social-Belonging Intervention Improves Academic and Health Outcomes of Minority

Students," *Science* 331, no. 6023 (2011): 1447–51. "Summer melt" is a phenomenon disproportionately affecting students from low-income backgrounds, in which students who have been accepted to a college and declare their intention to enroll fail to actually attend the school when the time comes. Simple communication strategies have been found to effectively reduce summer melt. See Benjamin L. Castleman and Lindsay C. Page, "A Trickle or a Torrent? Understanding the Extent of Summer 'Melt' among College-Intending High School Graduates," *Social Science Quarterly* 95, no. 1 (2014): 202–20.

18. See Bryk et al., *Learning to Improve*; Provost and Murray, *The Health Care Data Guide*; Brandon Bennett, "Branching Out," *Quality Progress* 51, no. 9 (2018): 18–23; Gerald J. Langley et al., *The Improvement Guide: A Practical Approach to Enhancing Organizational Performance* (Hoboken, NJ: Wiley, 2009).
19. While the predicted graduation rate does not represent all aspects of college quality, this indicator reflects some of the most essential characteristics that the Carpe teams hope for in the colleges that their graduates attend. Namely, the colleges that the graduates attend should have support structures and mechanisms in place that enable the greatest proportion of students to be successful and attain a postsecondary degree. Aside from being an indicator of college quality, for the Carpe Network, the attainment of the degree itself is a valued outcome, given the general quality of life effects that a degree may have (e.g., greater social and economic mobility). See Martha J. Bailey and Susan M. Dynarski, "Gains and Gaps: Changing Inequality in US College Entry and Completion," no. w17633 (National Bureau of Economic Research, 2011).
20. See Bryk et al., *Learning to Improve*; Provost and Murray, *The Health Care Data Guide*; and Bennett, "Branching Out." "Balancing measures" are also a part of a system of measures, and they indicate if and when changes in one part of the system offset another part of the system. Unintended consequences are captured by such balancing measures, which typically follow the identification of outcomes and process measures and are not a focus of this discussion.
21. Ann R. Edwards and Rachel L. Beattie, "Promoting Student Learning and Productive Persistence in Developmental Mathematics: Research Frameworks Informing the Carnegie Pathways," *NADE Digest* 9, no. 1 (2016): 30–39.
22. Carissa Romero, "What We Know about Belonging from Scientific Research," Mindset Scholars Network (Stanford, CA: Center for Advanced Study in the Behavioral Sciences, Stanford University, 2018). Retrieved from https://studentexperiencenetwork.org/wp-content/uploads/2018/11/What-We-Know-About-Belonging.pdf.
23. Yeager et al., *Practical Measurement*.
24. For a further discussion of this idea, see Pamela A. Moss, "Shifting the Focus of Validity for Test Use," *Assessment in Education: Principles, Policy & Practice* 23, no. 2 (2016): 236–51.
25. Lloyd Provost and Sandra Murray, leading thinkers in and practitioners of measurement work in quality improvement efforts in health care and other fields, make a distinction between "global project measures" and "Plan, Do, Study, Act (PDSA)" measures (the latter referring to the structure of rapid inquiry cycles commonly used in quality improvement efforts). They explain that "global measures focus at the project level and are maintained throughout the life of the improvement project," whereas "other measures are done on an as needed basis as part of PDSA Cycles for diagnosis

and for assessment of changes tested" (Provost and Murray, *The Health Care Data Guide*, 35). Investment in ensuring the rigor of practical measures is worthwhile for global project measures, and less so for short-lived, small-scale PDSA measures.
26. Geoffrey C. Bowker et al., "Toward Information Infrastructure Studies: Ways of Knowing in a Networked Environment," *International Handbook of Internet Research* (2010): 97–117.
27. Manuelito Biag and David Sherer, "Getting Better at Getting Better: Improvement Disposition in Education," *Teachers College Record* 123, no. 4 (2021): 1–42.
28. June Ahn et al., "Designing in Context: Reaching beyond Usability in Learning Analytics Dashboard Design," *Journal of Learning Analytics* 6, no. 2 (2019): 70–85.
29. Cynthia E. Coburn and Erica O. Turner, "Research on Data Use: A Framework and Analysis," *Measurement: Interdisciplinary Research & Perspective* 9, no. 4 (2011): 173–206.
30. We draw on elements of the data use framework developed by Coburn and Turner, "Research on Data Use."
31. Coburn and Turner, "Research on Data Use."
32. Shorter sprints of data collection and testing activity are another structure that has been used for concentrated improvement efforts.
33. Judith Warren Little and Marnie W. Curry, "Structuring Talk about Teaching and Learning: The Use of Evidence in Protocol-Based Conversation," in *Professional Learning Conversations: Challenges in Using Evidence for Improvement* (Dordrecht, Netherlands: Springer Netherlands, 2009), 29–42.
34. The Data for Equity protocol can be found on the High Tech High Graduate School of Education Protocol Library website, https://HTH GSEgse.edu/research-center/protocol-library/.
35. Coburn and Turner, "Research on Data Use."
36. Jeffrey R. Henig, "The Politics of Data Use," *Teachers College Record* 114, no. 11 (2012): 1–32.
37. Henig, "The Politics of Data Use."
38. Empathy strategies, such as empathy interviews, are utilized in human-centered design approaches, which aim to enhance the ability of improvers to solve the problem that they hope to solve. See, for example, Katja Battarbee, Jane Fulton Suri, and Suzanne Gibbs Howard, "Empathy on the Edge: Scaling and Sustaining a Human-Centered Approach in the Evolving Practice of Design," IDEO, http://www.ideo.com/images/uploads/news/pdfs/Empathy_on_the_Edge.pdf (2014).
39. To read more about the role of an "analytic partner" for an improvement effort, see David Sherer et al., *Evidence for Improvement: An Integrated Analytic Approach for Supporting Networks in Education* (Stanford, CA: Carnegie Foundation for the Advancement of Teaching, 2020). Furthermore, measurement and analytic expertise are listed together here, but they may reside in different individuals.
40. See Bryk et al., *Learning to Improve*; Provost and Murray, *The Health Care Data Guide*; Bennett, "Branching Out."

Chapter 3

1. Paul Cobb et al., *Systems for Instructional Improvement: Creating Coherence from the Classroom to the District Office* (Cambridge, MA: Harvard Education Press, 2018).

2. See https://www.pmr2.org/ for more information about the project.
3. Megan Loef Franke, Elham Kazemi, and Daniel Battey, "Mathematics Teaching and Classroom Practice," in *Second Handbook of Research on Mathematics Teaching and Learning*, ed. Frank K. Lester (Greenwich, CT: Information Age, 2007), 225–56.
4. "Common Core State Standards for Mathematics," 2010, http://www.corestandards.org/assets/CCSSI_Math%20Standards.pdf.
5. Melissa D. Boston and Anne Garrison Wilhelm, "Middle School Mathematics Instruction in Instructionally Focused Urban Districts," *Urban Education* 52, no. 7 (2015): 829–61, https://doi.org/10.1177/0042085915574528.
6. Mary Kay Stein, Barbara W. Grover, and Marjorie Henningsen, "Building Student Capacity for Mathematical Thinking and Reasoning: An Analysis of Mathematical Tasks Used in Reform Classrooms," *American Educational Research Journal* 33, no. 2 (1996): 455–88; Mary Kay Stein and Suzanne Lane, "Instructional Tasks and the Development of Student Capacity to Think and Reason: An Analysis of the Relationship between Teaching and Learning in a Reform Mathematics Project," *Educational Research and Evaluation* 2, no. 1 (1996): 50–80.
7. Kara Jackson et al., "Exploring Relationships between Setting up Complex Tasks and Opportunities to Learn in Concluding Whole-Class Discussions in Middle-Grades Mathematics Instruction," *Journal for Research in Mathematics Education* 44, no. 4 (2013): 646–82; Kara Jackson et al., "Launching Complex Tasks," *Mathematics Teaching in the Middle School* 18, no. 1 (2012): 24–29.
8. Paul Cobb, Erna Yackel, and Terry Wood, "Young Children's Emotional Acts While Engaged in Mathematical Problem Solving," in *Affect and Mathematical Problem Solving: A New Perspective*, ed. Douglas B. McLeod and Verna M. Adams (New York: Springer-Verlag, 1989), 117–48; Ilana S. Horn, *Strength in Numbers: Collaborative Learning in Secondary Mathematics* (Reston, VA: National Council of Teachers of Mathematics, 2012); Terry Wood and Erna Yackel, "The Development of Collaborative Dialogue within Small Group Interactions," in *Transforming Children's Mathematics Education: International Perspectives*, ed. Leslie P. Steffe and Terry Wood (Hillsdale, NJ: Lawrence Erlbaum, 1990), 244–52.
9. Mary Kay Stein et al., "Orchestrating Productive Mathematical Discussions: Five Practices for Helping Teachers Move beyond Show and Tell," *Mathematical Thinking and Learning* 10, no. 4 (2008): 313–40.
10. Stein et al., "Orchestrating Productive Mathematical Discussions."
11. Elham Kazemi and Deborah Stipek, "Promoting Conceptual Thinking in Four Upper-Elementary Mathematics Classrooms," *Elementary School Journal* 102, no. 1 (2001): 59–80; Stein et al., "Orchestrating Productive Mathematical Discussions."
12. Boston and Wilhelm, "Middle School Mathematics Instruction."
13. Kara Jackson, Ilana S. Horn, and Paul Cobb, "Overview of the Teacher Learning Subsystem," in *Systems for Instructional Improvement: Creating Coherence from the Classroom to the District Office*, ed. Paul Cobb et al. (Cambridge, MA: Harvard Education Press, 2018), 65–75.
14. Mary Kay Stein, Janine T. Remillard, and Margaret S. Smith, "How Curriculum Influences Student Learning," in *Second Handbook of Research on Mathematics Teaching and Learning*, ed. Frank K. Lester (Greenwich, CT: Information Age, 2007), 319–71; Erin Henrick, Mollie Appelgate, and Mahtab Nazemi, "Instructional Materials

as Tools for Instructional Improvement," in *Systems for Instructional Improvement: Creating Coherence from the Classroom to the District Office*, ed. Paul Cobb et al. (Cambridge, MA: Harvard University Press, 2018), 149–57.
15. See, for example, Deborah L. Ball and David K. Cohen, "Developing Practice, Developing Practitioners: Toward a Practice-Based Theory of Professional Education," in *Teaching as the Learning Profession: Handbook of Policy and Practice*, ed. Linda Darling-Hammond and Gary Sykes (San Francisco: Jossey Bass, 1999), 3–32; Pamela Grossman et al., "Teaching Practice: A Cross-Professional Perspective," *Teachers College Record* 111, no. 9 (2009): 2055–2100.
16. Deborah L. Ball, Mark H. Thames, and Geoffrey C. Phelps, "Content Knowledge for Teaching: What Makes It Special?," *Journal of Teacher Education* 59, no. 5 (2008): 389–407.
17. Jackson et al., "Overview of the Teacher Learning Subsystem."
18. Cobb et al., *Systems for Instructional Improvement*.
19. Jackson et al., "Overview of the Teacher Learning Subsystem."
20. Laura M. Desimone and Kerstin Carlson Le Floch, "Are We Asking the Right Questions? Using Cognitive Interviews to Improve Surveys in Education Research," *Educational Evaluation and Policy Analysis* 26, no. 1 (2004): 1–22.
21. Margaret S. Smith and Mary Kay Stein, *Five Practices for Orchestrating Productive Mathematics Discussions*, 2nd ed. (Reston, VA: National Council of Teachers of Mathematics, 2018), 11.
22. Stein and Lane, "Instructional Tasks"; Boston and Wilhelm, "Middle School Mathematics Instruction."
23. Franke et al., "Mathematics Teaching and Classroom Practice."
24. Franke et al., "Mathematics Teaching and Classroom Practice."
25. Deborah L. Ball, "Teaching, with Respect to Mathematics and Students," in *Beyond Classical Pedagogy: Teaching Elementary School Mathematics*, ed. Terry Wood, Barbara Scott Nelson, and Janet Warfield (Mahwah, NJ: Erlbaum, 2001), 11–22.
26. Paul Cobb, "Theorizing about Mathematical Conversations and Learning from Practice," *For the Learning of Mathematics* 18, no. 1 (1998): 46–48.
27. Kazemi and Stipek, "Promoting Conceptual Thinking"; Horn, *Strength in Numbers*.
28. Indigo Esmonde, "Ideas and Identities: Supporting Equity in Cooperative Mathematics Learning," *Review of Educational Research* 79, no. 2 (2009): 1008–43; Victoria M. Hand, "The Co-construction of Opposition in a Low-Track Mathematics Classroom," *American Educational Research Journal* 47, no. 1 (2010): 97–132; Danny Bernard Martin, Celia Rousseau Anderson, and Niral Shah, "Race and Mathematics Education," in *Compendium for Research in Mathematics Education* (Reston, VA: National Council of Teachers of Mathematics, 2017), 607–36; Niral Shah and Zeus Leonardo, "Learning Discourses of Race and Mathematics in Classroom Interaction," in *Power and Privilege in the Learning Sciences: Critical and Sociocultural Theories of Learning*, ed. Indigo Esmonde and Angela N. Booker (New York: Routledge, 2017), 50–69.
29. Melissa D. Boston, "Assessing the Quality of Mathematics Instruction," *Elementary School Journal* 40 (2009): 119–56; see also Mary Kay Stein et al., *Implementing Standards-Based Mathematics Instruction: A Casebook for Professional Development* (New York: Teachers College Press, 2000).
30. Jackson et al., "Overview of the Teacher Learning Subsystem."

31. Henrick et al., "Instructional Materials."
32. Boston and Wilhelm, "Middle School Mathematics Instruction."
33. Ilana S. Horn and Britnie Delinger Kane, "Opportunities for Professional Learning in Mathematics Teacher Workgroup Conversations: Relationships to Instructional Expertise," *Journal of the Learning Sciences* 24, no. 3 (2015): 373–418.
34. Nicholas Kochmanksi, "Aspects of High-Quality Mathematics Coaching: What Coaches Need to Know and Be Able to Do to Support Individual Teachers' Learning," doctoral dissertation, Vanderbilt University, Nashville, 2020.
35. For an elaboration on this case, see Marsha Ing et al., "When Should I Use a Measure to Support Instructional Improvement at Scale? The Importance of Considering Both Intended and Actual Use in Validity Arguments," *Educational Measurement: Issues and Practice* 40, no. 1 (2021): 92–100, https://doi.org/10.1111/emip.12393.
36. At the time of the Curriculum Guide Writing Initiative, our team had yet to develop the practical measure of a launch of a cognitively demanding task.
37. Anthony S. Bryk et al., *Learning to Improve: How America's Schools Can Get Better at Getting Better* (Cambridge, MA: Harvard Education Press, 2015); David Yeager et al., *Practical Measurement* (Stanford, CA: Carnegie Foundation for the Advancement of Teaching, 2013).
38. Lindsay Clare Matsumura et al., "Online Content-Focused Coaching to Improve Classroom Discussion Quality," *Technology, Pedagogy and Education* 28, no. 2 (2019): 191–215, https://doi.org/10.1080/1475939X.2019.1577748; Jennifer Lin Russell et al., "Mathematics Coaching for Conceptual Understanding: Promising Evidence Regarding the Tennessee Math Coaching Model," *Educational Evaluation and Policy Analysis* 42, no. 3 (2020): 439–66, https://doi.org/10.3102/0162373720940699.
39. Kochmanski, *Aspects of High-Quality Mathematics Coaching*.
40. Kochmanski, *Aspects of High-Quality Mathematics Coaching*.
41. Kochmanski, *Aspects of High-Quality Mathematics Coaching*.
42. Hilda J. Borko et al., *Mathematics Professional Development: Improving Teaching Using the Problem-Solving Cycle and Leadership Preparation Models* (New York: Teachers College Press, 2015); Horn and Kane, "Opportunities for Professional Learning."
43. Fred M. Newmann et al., "Instructional Program Coherence: What It Is and Why It Should Guide School Improvement Policy," *Educational Evaluation and Policy Analysis* 23, no. 4 (2001): 297–321.
44. Susan Leigh Star and James R. Griesemer, "Institutional Ecology, 'Translations' and Boundary Objects: Amateurs and Professionals in Berkeley's Museum of Vertebrate Zoology, 1907–39," *Social Studies of Science* 19, no. 3 (1989): 387–420; Etienne Wenger, *Communities of Practice: Learning, Meaning, and Identity* (New York: Cambridge University Press, 1998).
45. For examples, see Hannah Nieman et al., "Student Surveys Inform and Improve Classroom Discussion," *Mathematics Teacher: Learning and Teaching PK–12* 113, no. 12 (2020): 91–99, https://doi.org/10.5951/MTLT.2019.0141.
46. Sakinah S. J. Alhadad, "Visualizing Data to Support Judgement, Inference, and Decision Making in Learning Analytics: Insights from Cognitive Psychology and Visualization Science," *Journal of Learning Analytics* 5, no. 2 (2018): 60–85; Tamara Munzner, *Visualization Analysis and Design*, A. K. Peters Visualization Series (Boca Raton, FL: CRC, 2014).

47. June Ahn et al., "Designing in Context: Reaching beyond Usability in Learning Analytics Dashboard Design," *Journal of Learning Analytics* 6, no. 2 (2018): 70–85, https://doi.org/10.18608/jla.2019.62.5.
48. Ahn et al., "Designing in Context"; June Ahn, Ha Nguyen, and Fabio Campos, "From Visible to Understandable: Designing for Teacher Agency in Education Data Visualizations," *Contemporary Issues in Technology and Teacher Education* 21, no. 1 (2021): 155–86; Fabio Campos et al., "Making Sense of Sensemaking: Understanding How K-12 Teachers and Coaches React to Visual Analytics," *Journal of Learning Analytics* (2021): 1–21, https://doi.org/10.18608/jla.2021.7113.
49. Edward Haertel, "Expanding Views of Interpretation/Use Arguments," *Measurement: Interdisciplinary Research and Perspectives* 11, no. 1–2 (2013): 68–70; Pamela A. Moss, "Shifting the Focus of Validity for Test Use," *Assessment in Education: Principles, Policy & Practice* 23, no. 2 (2016): 236–51; Michael T. Kane, "Validating the Interpretations and Uses of Test Scores," *Journal of Educational Measurement* 50, no. 1 (2013): 1–73; Pamela A. Moss, Brian J. Girard, and Laura C. Haniford, "Validity in Educational Assessment," *Review of Research in Education* 30, no. 1 (2006): 109–62.
50. See, for example, American Educational Research Association, American Psychological Association, and National Council on Measurement in Education, *The Standards for Educational and Psychological Testing* (Washington, DC: Author, 2014).
51. Ing et al., "When Should I Use a Measure?"
52. See, for example, Lee J. Cronbach, "Five Perspectives on Validity Argument," in *Test Validity*, ed. Howard Wainer (Hillsdale, NJ: Erlbaum, 1988), 3–17; Samuel Messick, "Test Validity: A Matter of Consequence," *Social Indicators Research* 45 (1998): 35–44; and Lorrie A. Shepard, "The Centrality of Test Use and Consequences for Test Validity," *Educational Measurement: Issues and Practice* 16 (1997): 5–8.
53. Ing et al., "When Should I Use a Measure?"
54. Kara Jackson et al., "Making Sense of Teachers' Varied Responses to Representations of Practice," paper presented at the annual meeting for the National Council of Teachers of Mathematics Research Conference, San Diego, 2019.
55. Kara Jackson, Lynsey Gibbons, and Charlotte Sharpe, "Teachers' Views of Students' Mathematical Capabilities: Challenges and Possibilities for Ambitious Reform," *Teachers College Record* 119, no. 7 (2017), https://doi.org/10.1177/016146811711900708.
56. Paul Cobb and Anne Garrison Wilhelm, "Classroom Teaching and Learning as the Focus of Improvement Research," in *The Foundational Handbook on Improvement Research in Education*, ed. Don Peurach et al. (New York: Rowman and Littlefield, 2022), 139–63.
57. Kara Jackson, Anne Garrison Wilhelm, and Charles Munter, "Specifying Goals for Students' Mathematics Learning and the Development of Teachers' Knowledge, Perspectives, and Practice," in *Systems for Instructional Improvement: Creating Coherence from the Classroom to the District Office*, ed. Paul Cobb et al. (Cambridge, MA: Harvard Education Press, 2018), 43–64.
58. Bryk et al., *Learning to Improve*.

Chapter 4

1. National Governors Association Center for Best Practices, *Common Core State Standards* (Washington, DC: Council of Chief State School Officers, 2010).

2. *Common Core State Standards*, appendix A, 24.
3. Arthur N. Applebee and Judith A. Langer. "'EJ' Extra: A Snapshot of Writing Instruction in Middle Schools and High Schools," *English Journal* 100, no. 6 (2011): 14–27.
4. Steve Graham, "Changing How Writing Is Taught," *Review of Research in Education* 43, no. 1 (2019): 277–303, https://doi.org10.3102/0091732X18821125/.
5. Julia H. Kaufman et al., "What Supports Do Teachers Need to Help Students Meet Common Core State Standards for English Language Arts and Literacy? Findings from the American Teacher and American School Leader Panels" (Santa Monica, CA: RAND Corporation, 2016), 5, https://www.rand.org/pubs/research_reports/RR1374-1.html.
6. Laura M. Desimone, "A Primer on Effective Professional Development," *Phi Delta Kappan* 92, no. 6 (2011): 68–71, https://lfp.learningforward.org/handouts/Dallas2018/8133/Effective%20PD%20DeSimone.pdf.
7. Joseph Harris, *Rewriting: How to Do Things with Texts* (Denver: University Press of Colorado, 2017).
8. Barbara Heenan et al., "Deep Changes in Classroom Practice: Teachers' Perspectives on the Effects of Participation in the C3WP" (Inverness, CA: Inverness Research, 2017), https://inverness-research.org/reports/nwp-portfolio2017/C3WP-DeepChanges-FINAL.pdf.
9. N. L. Arshan and C. J. Park, "Research Brief: SRI Finds Positive Effects of the College, Career, and Community Writer's Program on Student Achievement" (Menlo Park, CA: SRI International, 2021), https://www.sri.com/publication/research-brief-sri-finds-positive-effects-of-the-college-career-and-community-writers-program-on-student-achievement/.
10. Heenan et al., "Deep Changes in Classroom Practice."
11. Linda Friedrich, Rachel Bear, and Tom Fox, "For the Sake of Argument: An Approach to Teaching Evidence-Based Writing," *American Educator* 42, no. 1 (2018): 18.
12. Paul Black and Dylan Wiliam, "Assessment and Classroom Learning," *Assessment in Education: Principles, Policy and Practice* 5, no. 1 (1998): 7–74, https://doi.org/10.1080/0969595980050102; Edmund W. Gordon, "Toward Assessment in the Service of Learning," *Educational Measurement: Issues and Practice* 39, no. 3 (2020): 72–78.
13. Sonja Brookins Santalesis, "Checking In: Do Classroom Assignments Reflect Today's Higher Standards?" (Washington, DC: The Education Trust, 2015), https://edtrust.org/wp-content/uploads/2014/09/CheckingIn_TheEducationTrust_Sept20152.pdf; *The Opportunity Myth* (New York: The New Teacher Project, 2018), 49, https://tntp.org/assets/documents/TNTP_The-Opportunity-Myth_Web.pdf.
14. The NWP staff collected surveys from Writing Project site leaders about their use of the UST in professional learning in 2014–2015 and 2015–2016. Site leaders submitted for each district with which they were working. In 2014–2015, we collected five surveys to which the twelve local Writing Project sites working with all twenty districts, and a sixth survey representing sixteen of twenty (80 percent) districts. This was the second year that districts had participated in C3WP professional development, and the first year that the UST was used projectwide. In 2015–2016, when local Writing Project sites were working with a new set of twenty districts, we collected four surveys, with response rates that ranged from a low of eight out of twenty (40 percent) responding in

February 2016 and a high of twenty out of twenty responding in December 2015. We summarized themes about site leaders' observations about what they were seeing in students' writing and counted how many sites shared a similar observation. We wrote site leaders' comments about what teachers were taking up in a chart and color-coded them as: teachers' actions based on analyzing student writing—yellow, comments about teachers seeing growth or evidence of teaching in students' writing—pink, and teachers' attitudes toward their students' ability to write changed—blue. More than half of Writing Project site leaders' comments focused on recurrent patterns that they saw in students' writing.

15. Quotes taken from the sources identified in endnote 14.
16. Quotes taken from the sources identified in endnote 14.
17. The AWC-SBA derives from the NWP's Analytic Writing Continuum (AWC), which was developed based on the 6+1 Traits framework as a measure for use in assessing writing for program evaluation and as a prompt and writing type agnostic. See Sherry Swain and Paul LeMahieu, "Assessment in a Culture of Inquiry: The Story of the National Writing Project's Analytic Writing Continuum," in *Writing Assessment in the 21st Century: Essays in Honor of Edward M. White*, ed. Norbert Elliot and Les Perelman (New York: Hampton, 2012), 45–66. Over an eight-year period, the AWC was continuously refined and has demonstrated strong technical qualities, including strong interrater agreement (e.g., ranging from .85 to .95) across all six attributes of writing, consistency of scoring across time, and a strong internal structure for the attributes of writing measured. Hee Jin Bang, "Reliability of National Writing Project's Analytic Writing Continuum Assessment System," *Journal of Writing Assessment* 6, no. 1 (2013). Because of the centrality of the use of source material in evidence-based argument writing, the AWC-SBA adapts four of the original AWC attributes to allow for more particular assessment of this type of writing. The original AWC leadership team worked closely with NWP research staff to develop a revised rubric, select new anchor papers, and write detailed score descriptions for the AWC-SBA. The central processes that were part of the original AWC scoring system (extensive training of scorers, calibration exercises, expert table and room leadership, processes for measuring interrater agreement) remain intact. The AWC-SBA uses a six-point scale to measure four attributes of writing: Content (including Quality of Reasoning and Use of Evidence), Structure, Stance, and Conventions. The AWC-SBA system across three scorings has achieved interrater agreement levels that are comparable to the original AWC.
18. Expert UST and AWC raters independently provided ratings on a set of pilot, on-demand writing samples similar to those used in the efficacy studies of C3WP. Writing samples were collected from a convenience sample of students in schools that were not part of the C3WP evaluation. However, the convenience sample included teachers with and without C3WP or NWP professional development experience. For middle school samples, r = 0.57 (df = 256, $p < 0.001$); and for high school samples, r = 0.58 (df = 386, $p < 0.001$). The Pearson's Product-Moment Correlation varied by prompt. For middle school prompts, the range was r = 0.44 to r = 0.72; for high school prompts, the range was r = 0.35 to r = 0.74.
19. Arshan and Park, "Research Brief."
20. *The Opportunity Myth.*

21. Daniel Showalter et al., "Why Rural Matters 2018–2019: The Time Is Now. A Report of the Rural School and Community Trust" (Washington, DC: Rural School and Community Trust, 2019), https://files.eric.ed.gov/fulltext/ED604580.pdf; Santalesis, "Checking In."
22. N. L. Arshan, C. J. Park, and H. A. Gallagher, "Supporting Source-based Argument Writing Instruction: Effects of National Writing Project's College, Career, and Community Writers Program," (unpublished manuscript).
23. Heenan et al., "Deep Changes in Classroom Practice."

Chapter 5

1. I am not a neutral observer in this story. This is my recollection of the unfolding of the freshman ontrack story in which I actively participated. As one of the researchers at the University of Chicago Consortium on School Research, I conducted some of the research described here and also met extensively with district leaders and district principals in Chicago and other districts, interacted with staff and leaders in school support organizations such as GEAR UP and the Network for College Success (NCS), and interviewed students and teachers as part of a qualitative study of the transition to high school. My descriptions of teacher and administrator perceptions of the ninth-grade and high school graduation rates come from those experiences. In addition, staff at the NCS regularly provided insight to guide research at the Consortium and described the issues and questions that they encountered in schools in their work with high school leadership teams. Instrumental to this story was the work of district leaders, including Carmita Vaughn and Page Ponder at the Department of Graduation Pathways, many innovative school principals who figured out strategies that others copied, and CEOs from Arne Duncan forward, who kept freshman ontrack as a district priority; the NCS staff, including Sarah Duncan, Mary Ann Pitcher, Jacqueline Lemon, Sarah Howard, and Eliza Moeller; and Consortium researchers who were instrumental to this work, including John Easton, Melissa Roderick, and Shazia Miller.
2. This is based on district reported data, available at https://www.cps.edu/about/district-data/metrics/. An interactive data report on trends over the last several years is available at https://toandthrough.uchicago.edu/tool/cps/.
3. Elaine M. Allensworth et al., *High School Graduation Rates through Two Decades of District Change: The Influence of Policies, Data Records, and Demographic Shifts* (Chicago: University of Chicago Consortium on School Research, 2016).
4. Allensworth et al., *High School Graduation Rates through Two Decades of District Change*.
5. Allensworth et al., *High School Graduation Rates through Two Decades of District Change*.
6. Jenny Nagaoka and Alex Seeskin, *The Educational Attainment of Chicago Public Schools Students: 2017* (Chicago: University of Chicago Consortium on School Research, 2018); Jenny Nagaoka et al., *The Educational Attainment of Chicago Public Schools Students: 2019 Research Report* (Chicago: University of Chicago Consortium on School Research, 2020).
7. Jeremy D. Finn, "Withdrawing from School," *Review of Educational Research* 59, no. 2 (1989): 117–42; Russell W. Rumberger, "Why Students Drop out of School," in *Dropouts*

in America: Confronting the Graduation Rate Crisis, ed. Gary Orfield (Cambridge, MA: Harvard Education Press, 2004), 131–56; Russell W. Rumberger and Katherine A. Larson, "Student Mobility and the Increased Risk of High School Dropout," *American Journal of Education* 107, no. 1 (1998): 1–35, https://doi.org/10.1086/444201.
8. Philip Gleason and Mark Dynarski, "Do We Know Whom to Serve? Issues in Using Risk Factors to Identify Dropouts," *Journal of Education for Students Placed at Risk* 7, no. 1 (2002): 25–41, https://doi.org/10.1207/S15327671ESPR0701_3.
9. Elaine M. Allensworth, *Graduation and Dropout Trends in Chicago: A Look at Cohorts of Students from 1991 through 2004* (Chicago: Consortium on Chicago School Research at the University of Chicago, 2005).
10. Elaine M. Allensworth and John Q. Easton, *What Matters for Staying On-Track and Graduating in Chicago Public High Schools: A Close Look at Course Grades, Failures, and Attendance in the Freshman Year* (Chicago: University of Chicago Consortium on Chicago School Research, 2007).
11. Melissa Roderick and Eric Camburn, "Academic Difficulty during the High School Transition," in *Charting Reform in Chicago: The Students Speak*, ed. Penny Bender Sebring et al. (Chicago: Consortium on Chicago School Research, 1996), 47–65.
12. Shazia Rafiullah Miller et al., *How Do [Your School] 8th Grade Graduates Perform in CPS High Schools?* (Chicago: Consortium on Chicago School Research, 1999).
13. Shazia Rafiullah Miller and Elaine M. Allensworth, "Progress and Problems: Student Performance in CPS High Schools, 1993 to 2000," in *Reforming Chicago's High Schools: Research Perspectives on School and System Level Change*, ed. Valerie E. Lee (Chicago: Consortium on Chicago School Research, 2002), 51–87.
14. Elaine Allensworth and John Q. Easton, *The Ontrack Indicator as a Predictor of High School Graduation* (Chicago: University of Chicago Consortium on School Research, 2005), http://www.consortium-chicago.org/publications/p78.html.
15. Allensworth and Easton, *What Matters for Staying On-Track and Graduating in Chicago Public High Schools*.
16. K. Ali et al., *Freshmen On-Track: A Guide to Help You Keep Your Freshmen On-Track to Graduate* (Chicago: Chicago Public Schools, Department of Graduation Pathways, 2010).
17. Ali et al., *Freshmen On-Track*.
18. Ali et al., *Freshmen On-Track*.
19. For further information on using teams, see the University of Chicago Network for College Success, "Implementing School-based Teams," https://ncs.uchicago.edu/toolkit-component/implementing-school-based-teams.
20. For example, see Nicholas Montgomery and Melissa Roderick with Alissa Bolz, *Getting On-Track: Understanding Freshman Performance at [Your School]* (Chicago: University of Chicago Consortium on School Research, 2009).
21. Anthony S. Bryk et al., *Learning to Improve: How America's Schools Can Get Better at Getting Better* (Cambridge, MA: Harvard Education Press, 2015).
22. These observations come from reports of staff at NCS and from attending NCS meetings of school leadership teams.
23. Information about the NCS, including the Freshman Ontrack toolkit, is available at https://ncs.uchicago.edu/.

24. Melissa Roderick et al., *Preventable Failure: Improvements in Long-Term Outcomes When High Schools Focused on the Ninth Grade Year* (Chicago: University of Chicago Consortium on Chicago School Research, 2014).
25. Camille A. Farrington et al., *Teaching Adolescents to Become Learners: The Role of Noncognitive Factors in Shaping School Performance—A Critical Literature Review* (Chicago: Consortium on Chicago School Research, 2012).
26. This section provides a summary that is elaborated further in Mary Ann Pitcher et al., *A Capacity-Building Model for School Improvement* (Chicago: Network for School Success, 2016).
27. Farrington et al., *Teaching Adolescents to Become Learners*.
28. Elaine Allensworth, James Sebastian, and Molly Gordon, "Principal Leadership Practices, Organizational Improvement, and Student Achievement," in *Exploring Principal Development and Teacher Outcomes: How Principals Can Strengthen Instruction, Teacher Retention, and Student Achievement*, ed. Peter Youngs, Jihyun Kim, and Madeline Mavrogordato (Oxfordshire, UK: Routledge, 2020), 189–203.
29. For an example of one successful high school and how its staff has dramatically increased its students' progress to graduation, see the featured segment on Hancock High School at http://chicagotonight.wttw.com/2013/11/21/american-graduate-special.
30. For more on networked improvement communities, see Paul G. LeMahieu et al., "Networked Improvement Communities: The Discipline of Improvement Science Meets the Power of Networks," *Quality Assurance in Education* 25, no. 1 (2017): 5–25.
31. For more information about the use of data to improve practices, see Eliza Moeller, Alex Seeskin, and Jenny Nagaoka, *Practice-Driven Data: Lessons from Chicago's Approach to Research, Data, and Practice in Education* (Chicago: University of Chicago Consortium on School Research, 2018); and Elaine M. Allensworth, Jenny Nagaoka, and David W. Johnson, *High School Graduation and College Readiness Indicator Systems: What We Know, What We Need to Know. Concept Paper for Research and Practice* (Chicago: University of Chicago Consortium on School Research, 2018).
32. Elaine Allensworth, "The Use of Ninth-Grade Early Warning Indicators to Improve Chicago Schools," *Journal of Education for Students Placed at Risk* 18, no. 1 (2013): 68–83, http://dx.doi.org/10.1080/10824669.2013.745181.
33. Indicators with similar predictive properties as freshman ontrack include growth in math scores or grade point average from seventh to twelfth grade, and grades of D or lower in grades 7–12. Alex J. Bowers, Ryan Sprott, and Sherry A. Taff, "Do We Know Who Will Drop Out? A Review of the Predictors of Dropping out of High School: Precision, Sensitivity, and Specificity," *High School Journal* 96, no. 2 (2012): 77–100, https://doi.org/10.1353/hsj.2013.0000.
34. Allensworth, "The Use of Ninth-Grade Early Warning Indicators."
35. Gleason and Dynarski, "Do We Know Whom to Serve?"; Bowers et al., "Do We Know Who Will Drop Out?"
36. Allensworth and Easton, *The Ontrack Indicator as a Predictor of High School Graduation*.
37. Elaine M. Allensworth and Kallie Clark, "High School GPAs and ACT Scores as Predictors of College Completion: Examining Assumptions about Consistency across High Schools," *Educational Researcher* 49, no. 3 (2020): 198–211, https://doi.org/10.3102/0013189X20902110.

38. Allensworth et al., *High School Graduation Rates through Two Decades of District Change*.
39. Alex Seeskin, Shelby Mahaffie, and Alexandra Usher, "The Forgotten Year: Applying Lessons from Freshman Success to Sophomore Year" (Chicago: University of Chicago Consortium on School Research, 2020).
40. Robert Balfanz and Vaughan Byrnes, "Closing the Mathematics Achievement Gap in High-Poverty Middle Schools: Enablers and Constraints," *Journal of Education for Students Placed at Risk* 11, no. 2 (2006): 143–59; Bowers et al., "Do We Know Who Will Drop Out?"
41. See examples in Marcia Davis, Liza Herzog, and Nettie Legters, "Organizing Schools to Address Early Warning Indicators (EWIs): Common Practices and Challenges," *Journal of Education for Students Placed at Risk* 18, no. 1 (2013): 84–100.
42. Todd Rosenkranz et al., "Free to Fail or On-Track to College: Why Grades Drop When Students Enter High School and What Adults Can Do about It" (Chicago: University of Chicago Consortium on School Research, 2014).
43. Elaine M. Allensworth and Stuart Luppescu, "Why Do Students Get Good Grades, or Bad Ones? The Influence of the Teacher, Class, School, and Student," *Sign*, 773 (2018), https://consortium.uchicago.edu/sites/default/files/2018-10/Why%20Do%20 Students%20Get-Apr2018-Consortium.pdf.
44. For example, clear grading systems and keeping up with grading so that students (and their parents) always know where their grade stands support student work efforts. Supports that are opt-out—where students automatically get help when they fall behind rather than expecting students to ask for help—are more effective than those where students have to ask for help proactively (Rosenkranz et al., "Free to Fail or On-Track to College").
45. The idea of "helping students who want to succeed" would come up when talking with some teachers about how they support students and why some students fail during our qualitative study of the ninth-grade transition.
46. Roderick et al., *Preventable Failure*.
47. Allensworth et al., *High School Graduation Rates through Two Decades of District Change*.
48. Nagaoka et al., *The Educational Attainment of Chicago Public Schools Students: 2019 Research Report*.

Chapter 6

1. The vast majority of the students in network schools are economically disadvantaged, and 90 percent identify as Latinx or Black. In addition, more than one-third of the students are classified as Emergent Multilingual Learners (EMLs), with Spanish being the predominant language outside of English. Anthony S. Bryk et al., *Learning to Improve: How America's Schools Can Get Better at Getting Better* (Cambridge, MA: Harvard Education Press, 2015); David Sherer et al., "Conceptualizing, Measuring, and Evaluating Improvement Networks," in *Oxford Bibliographies in Education* (Oxford: Oxford University Press, 2021), https://www.oxfordbibliographies.com/view/document /obo-9780199756810/obo-9780199756810-0271.xml (accessed April 25, 2021).
2. Adrian Larbi-Cherif et al., "Digging Deeper: A Framework for Conducting Equity-Focused Root Cause Analyses in Education" (under review).

3. Network teachers were provided with several supports to aid in developing student-centered ELA pedagogies through the development of tools that embodied the change ideas (e.g., comprehension task sheets). Each school had improvement teams composed of school coordinators (who were typically ELA coaches), eighth- or ninth-grade ELA teachers, specialist teachers (e.g., English learner teachers and/or special education teachers), and school administrators who oversaw ELA instruction. Each team had weekly collaborative meetings and attended monthly network professional development meetings to support teacher learning. IFL coaches introduced new instructional practices and change ideas in network professional development sessions and also made follow-up visits to each school to support school teams in adapting and implementing change ideas and practical measures.
4. Ms. Green is a composite persona based on our interactions with many network teachers and their experiences with practical measures.
5. Typically, it took at least twenty-four hours for a critical mass of students to respond to the exit ticket (at least five responses) after the teacher had assigned it. It then generally took less than twenty-four hours after that to generate and send the teacher an exit ticket report.
6. Joshua L. Glazer et al., "District-Led School Turnaround: Aiming for Ambitious and Equitable Instruction in Shelby County's iZone. CPRE Research Report #RR 2020-1" (Philadelphia: Consortium for Policy Research in Education, 2020); Pamela A. Moss, "Shifting the Focus of Validity for Test Use," *Assessment in Education: Principles, Policy & Practice* 23, no. 2 (2016): 236–51.
7. Change ideas can focus on a number of innovations in school settings. This chapter will present change ideas and practical measures that are implemented in lessons for instructional improvement.
8. Sola Takahashi et al., "Measurement for Improvement in Education," in *Oxford Bibliographies in Education* (Oxford: Oxford University Press, 2020), https://www.oxfordbibliographies.com/view/document/obo-9780199756810/obo-9780199756810-0247.xml (accessed March 19, 2021); David Yeager et al., *Practical Measurement* (Stanford, CA: Carnegie Foundation for the Advancement of Teaching, 2013).
9. Dana L Mitra, "The Significance of Students: Can Increasing 'Student Voice' in Schools Lead to Gains in Youth Development?," *Teachers College Record* 106, no. 4 (2004): 651–88; Jean Rudduck and Julia Flutter, "Pupil Participation and Pupil Perspective: 'Carving a New Order of Experience,'" *Cambridge Journal of Education* 30, no. 1 (2000): 75–89.
10. Gloria Ladson-Billings, "Toward a Theory of Culturally Relevant Pedagogy," *American Educational Research Journal* 32, no. 3 (1995): 465–91, https://doi.org/10.3102/00028312032003465; Gloria Ladson-Billings, "Culturally Relevant Pedagogy 2.0: Aka the Remix," *Harvard Educational Review* 84, no. 1 (2014): 74–84; H. Richard Milner, "Culturally Relevant Pedagogy in a Diverse Urban Classroom," *Urban Review* 43, no. 1 (2011): 66–89.
11. Takahashi et al., "Measurement for Improvement in Education"; Yeager et al., *Practical Measurement*.
12. Bryk et al., *Learning to Improve*.
13. Gloria Ladson-Billings, "From the Achievement Gap to the Education Debt: Understanding Achievement in US Schools," *Educational Researcher* 35, no. 7 (2006): 3–12.

14. Geneva Gay, *Culturally Responsive Teaching: Theory, Research, and Practice* (New York: Teachers College Press, 2018).
15. Although we designed practical measures that were rather general in terms of the cultural responsiveness of a text, we found that teachers and coaches had rich conversations about these measures. It helped teachers to reflect more deeply on which texts would be more responsive to and engaging for their students. Furthermore, schools had either majority Latinx students or majority Black students. Conversations around cultural responsiveness thus were contextualized based on students' race and teachers' understandings of their students' experiences.
16. Takahashi et al., "Measurement for Improvement in Education"; Yeager et al., *Practical Measurement*.
17. Bryk et al., *Learning to Improve*; Jennifer Lin Russell et al., "A Framework for the Initiation of Networked Improvement Communities," *Teachers College Record* 119, no. 7 (2017): 1–36.

Chapter 7

1. Gregory J. Cizek, "Defining and Distinguishing Validity: Interpretations of Score Meaning and Justifications of Test Use," *Psychological Methods* 17, no. 1 (2012): 31; Daniel Koretz, "Making the Term 'Validity' Useful," *Assessment in Education: Principles, Policy & Practice* 23, no. 2 (2016): 290–92.
2. Pamela A. Moss, "Shifting the Focus of Validity for Test Use," *Assessment in Education: Principles, Policy & Practice* 23, no. 2 (2016): 236–51; Marsha Ing et al., "When Should I Use a Measure to Support Instructional Improvement at Scale? The Importance of Considering Both Intended and Actual Use in Validity Arguments," *Educational Measurement: Issues and Practice* 40, no. 1 (2021): 92–100.
3. David Yeager et al., *Practical Measurement* (Stanford, CA: Carnegie Foundation for the Advancement of Teaching, 2013).
4. Anthony S. Bryk et al., *Learning to Improve: How America's Schools Can Get Better at Getting Better* (Cambridge, MA: Harvard Education Press, 2015).
5. The PDSA cycle is a systematic process for gaining the knowledge needed to continually improve a product, process, or service. It is, in essence, a bounded experiment—small enough that it can be easily conducted iteratively as a change idea is tested and refined until it is either adopted as a warranted improvement, adapted for further testing and refinement, or abandoned as not able to be used as an improvement. In the Plan phase, improvers identify a goal or purpose, formulate a theory of improvement, prototype a change of interest, and define measures relevant to testing that change. In the Do phase, the components of the plan or change idea are implemented. In the Study phase, improvers monitor the measures to test whether the change led to improvement. In the Act phase, improvers adopt the change idea, further adapt it and test it again, or abandon it as a means of achieving the desired improvement. Improvers run additional PDSA cycles until the change leads to the intended outcome reliably, across contexts, and at scale. See Bryk et al., *Learning to Improve*; and Gerald J. Langley et al., *The Improvement Guide: A Practical Approach to Enhancing Organizational Performance* (Hoboken, NJ: Wiley, 2009).
6. While measurement experts have expressed the need to address both validity-for-use (measurement validity) and validity-in-use (consequential validity) when making an

argument about the validity of a measure, many research methods textbooks address only the former.
7. Validity-for-use is also referred to as *measurement validity*.
8. In the signal-to-noise ratio, the signal represents the true underlying construct, while noise is the random error or irrelevant information that can cloud the results.
9. Concurrent and predictive validity are often described as forms of criterion validity.
10. Laura M. Desimone and Kerstin Carlson Le Floch, "Are We Asking the Right Questions? Using Cognitive Interviews to Improve Surveys in Education Research," *Educational Evaluation and Policy Analysis* 26, no. 1 (2004): 1–22.
11. Validity-in-use is also referred to as *consequential validity*.
12. Donald T. Campbell, "Assessing the Impact of Planned Social Change," *Evaluation and Program Planning* 2, no. 1 (1979): 67–90, https://doi.org/10.1016/0149-7189(79)90048-X.
13. For descriptions of continuous improvement tools, see Bryk et al., *Learning to Improve*; and Langley et al., *The Improvement Guide*.
14. WestEd, "Math Practical Measurement," https://mpm.wested.org/.

Chapter 8

1. Anthony S. Bryk et al., *Learning to Improve: How America's Schools Can Get Better at Getting Better* (Cambridge, MA: Harvard Education Press, 2015).
2. Leif I. Solberg, Gordon Mosser, and Sharon McDonald, "The Three Faces of Performance Measurement: Improvement, Accountability, and Research," *Joint Commission Journal on Quality Improvement* 23, no. 3 (1997): 135–47.
3. Richard Elmore, *School Reform from the Inside Out* (Cambridge, MA: Harvard Education Press, 2004).
4. Paul Black and Dylan Wiliam, "Assessment and Classroom Learning," *Assessment in Education: Principles, Policy and Practice* 5, no. 1 (1988): 7–74.
5. Sola Takahashi et al., "Measurement for Improvement," in *Handbook on Improvement Research in Education*, ed. Donald J. Peurach et al. (Washington, DC: Rowman and Littlefield, 2022), 423–42.
6. See Bryk et al., *Learning to Improve*, in which the authors assert that improvement research should focus on variability in performance as the problem to solve. This, they make clear, includes identifying and remediating variability in the performance of historically underserved or marginalized students.
7. Jerome Bruner, *Actual Minds, Possible Worlds* (Cambridge, MA: Harvard University Press, 1987).
8. Jonee Wilson and Denice Kelley, "Supplemental Supports for Currently Struggling Students," in Paul Cobb et al., *Systems for Instructional Improvement: Creating Coherence from the Classroom to the District Office* (Cambridge, MA: Harvard Education Press, 2018), 169–79.
9. Manuelito Biag and David Sherer, "Getting Better at Getting Better: Improvement Disposition in Education," *Teachers College Record* 123, no. 4 (2021): 1–42. Biag and Sherer identify six dispositions that are integral to continuous improvement work in education, including a shift from seeing deficits in students and their families as the cause of poor outcomes to seeing current educational processes and practices as needing improvement.

10. Kara Jackson, Lynsey Gibbons, and Charlotte Sharpe, "Teachers' Views of Students' Mathematical Capabilities: A Challenge for Accomplishing Ambitious Reform," *Teachers College Record* 119, no. 7 (2017): 1–43.
11. Anthony S. Bryk, *Improvement in Action: Advancing Quality in America's Schools* (Cambridge, MA: Harvard Education Press, 2020), shares the stories of six successful improvement effforts.

About the Editors and Contributors

EDITORS

Paul G. LeMahieu is the Senior Advisor to the President at the Carnegie Foundation. Previously as Carnegie's Senior Vice President for Programs, he managed the Foundation's programmatic work and directed the work of the Carnegie Hub, which supported the networked improvement communities the Foundation convened to engage persistent problems of education practice in the field. He is also on the graduate faculty at the University of Hawai'i at Mānoa. Previously, he served as Superintendent of Education for the State of Hawai'i, the Chief Educational and Executive Officer of the only state system in the United States that is a unitary school district. LeMahieu's professional interests and contributions have focused on assessment and measurement, including the design and development of innovative forms of assessment, data representation and analysis, as well as the use of data and research to inform and improve policy, programs, and practice. LeMahieu has held top educational research and policy positions for the state of Delaware and in the Pittsburgh Public Schools, and he is a coauthor, along with Anthony S. Bryk, Louis M. Gomez, and Alicia Grunow, of *Learning to Improve* (Harvard Education Press, 2015).

Paul Cobb is Professor Emeritus at Vanderbilt University, and was a principal investigator of the Practical Measures, Routines, and Representations

(PMRR) project. His recent work focuses on improving the quality of mathematics teaching and student learning on a large scale, and on issues of equity in students' access to significant mathematical ideas. Cobb has published widely in peer-reviewed journals and is the coauthor or coeditor of eight books, including *Systems of Instructional Improvement* (Harvard Education Press, 2018). He received the Hans Freudenthal Medal for cumulative research program over the prior ten years from the International Commission on Mathematics Instruction (ICMI) in 2005, and the Sylvia Scribner Award from American Educational Research Association in 2010 for research over the past ten years that contributes to our understanding of learning and instruction. Cobb is an elected member of the National Academy of Education and is an Invited Fellow of the Center for Advanced Studies in the Behavioral Sciences.

CONTRIBUTORS

June Ahn is a Professor of Learning Sciences and Research-Practice Partnerships at the University of California, Irvine (UCI). Ahn is also Senior Associate Dean at the UCI School of Education. He conducts research at the intersection of participatory design, technology, education, and community partnerships.

Elaine Allensworth is the Lewis-Sebring Director of the UChicago Consortium, where she conducts research on educational policy and practice.

Rachel Bear is the Director of Professional Learning at the National Writing Project, where she provides leadership and support for NWP-developed teacher professional development efforts. She previously served as a secondary English teacher in the Boise School District.

Starlie Chinen is a Teaching Academy and Education Careers Teacher in Seattle Public Schools. She worked in various roles related to teacher education while completing her doctorate at the University of Washington.

Linda D. Friedrich is the Director of Literacy at WestEd where she leads the agency's Reading Apprenticeship team as well as literacy research and technical assistance projects. Previously, she served as the Director of Research and Evaluation at the National Writing Project (NWP), as well as Research Director at the Coalition of Essential Schools and as a program officer at the Philadelphia Education Fund.

Marsha Ing is an Associate Professor of Educational Psychology in the School of Education at the University of California, Riverside. Her research focuses on measuring mathematics and science teaching and learning.

Kara Jackson is a Professor of Mathematics Education at the University of Washington. Her research focuses on specifying forms of teaching practice that advance equity, and understanding how district and school systems can enable teachers to develop such forms of practice.

Nicholas Kochmanski is an Assistant Professor at the University of North Carolina at Greensboro. His research focuses on mathematics coaching and instructional improvement at scale.

Adrian Larbi-Cherif is a Senior Program Associate and Research Director at the Manhattan Strategy Group (MSG), where he supports the National Center for Education Statistics on analysis and release of National Assessment of Educational Progress results. Prior to MSG, he was an Associate Scholar at the University of Pittsburgh. His research focuses on improving student outcomes at scale through research practice partnerships.

Angel Yee-lam Li is an Associate on the Evidence and Improvement Lab team at the Carnegie Foundation. Prior to joining the Foundation, Angel worked for Denver Public Schools (DPS) as an innovation and improvement specialist, holding the position of analytics lead of the College Ready On Track Network for School Improvement.

Hannah Nieman is a Research Consultant and Teaching Associate at the University of Washington, Seattle. Her research focuses on teacher education, professional learning, and mathematics education.

Jon Norman is Chief Research and Evaluation Director for Jewish Family and Children's Services of San Francisco. He previously served as Managing Director for Evidence and Analytics at the Carnegie Foundation for the Advancement of Teaching.

Anna Premo is a Postdoctoral Fellow studying educational approaches to misinformation in the Professorship for Research on Learning and Instruction at ETH Zurich. She was previously a doctoral student in the University of Pittsburgh's Learning Research and Development Center.

Jennifer Lin Russell is a Professor of Leadership, Policy and Organizations at Vanderbilt University's Peabody College. Her research focuses on organizing educational systems for improvement, inter-organizational collaboration, and research-practice partnerships.

Christian Schunn is a Professor of Psychology and a Senior Scientist in the Learning Research and Development Center at the University of Pittsburgh. His work and research focus on STEM learning, peer interaction and instruction, engagement and learning, and improvement science for education reform.

Thomas M. Smith is Dean of the School of Education at the University of California, Davis. Prior to joining UC Davis, he was a professor of public policy and education in Vanderbilt University's Peabody College and he held several leadership roles at UC Riverside, including interim provost and executive vice chancellor, dean of the Graduate School of Education, and interim vice chancellor for Student Affairs. His research focuses on how policy and context impact teacher learning, teaching, and retention—primarily in research-practice-partnerships.

Sola Takahashi is a Senior Research Associate with the Improvement Science team at WestEd, where she leads improvement analytics work. She develops and uses measurement and analytics to improve educational systems through a continuous improvement approach, with a focus on equitable and just systems and instructional improvement.

Index

academic writing, 97, 161. *See also* writing
accomplished coach, 67, 217–18, 221, 235. *See also* coach/coaching
accountability, 60
   assessment, 12
   freshman ontrack indicator for, 201
   improvement and, 11–13
   indicator for, 152
   measurement for, 12
   in whole-class discussion survey, 60
action/actionable information, 29–30, 150–51, 191–92, 213–38
Advanced Placement (AP), 130, 152
Allensworth, Elaine M., 201, 204, 208, 217–19, 221, 223–24, 227, 229, 232, 233, 236–37
ambitious and equitable teaching, 52–56, 66–67, 86, 89
American Educator, 103
American Psychological Association (APA), 105
analytical writing, 159, 161. *See also* writing
analytic/technical expertise, 45, 225
Analytic Writing Continuum for Source-Based Argument Writing (AWC-SBA), 123–24
annotated student writing, 109, 116, 124. *See also* writing
annual evaluative/performance assessment, 2, 6. *See also* assessment
argument
   components of, 206
   high-quality, 97, 103, 107, 113, 115
   moves, 98–99, 108, 110, 116, 119, 124, 126
   public/civic/civil, 103
   sound, 95
argument writing, 108–10
   debatable/defensible claims in, 105
   definition of, 97, 100, 108–10
   development of, 221
   key aspects of, 108
   quality of, 119–20
   shared vision of, 97
   skills, 99–100, 105, 112, 127, 198, 219
   source-based, 93–94, 123–24, 192–93, 215–16, 231
   students, impact on, 122–24
   theory of action for, 94–96, 107, 121
   traditional approaches to, 98
   See also College, Career, and Community Writers Program (C3WP); instructional resources; Using Sources Tool (UST); writing
assessment
   accountability, 12
   annual evaluative/performance, 2, 6
   of cognitive demand task, 71
   ELA, 157
   formative, 102
   forms of, 5–6, 9
   of/for learning, 106
   MAP, 185
   purpose of, 7–8
   summative, 105, 115, 117
   traditional educational, 48
attendance, 141–43
   college, 22, 26, 34, 191, 198

attendance (cont.)
  CPS, 147
  grades and, 137–38, 147, 149–51, 201, 218–19, 223–24, 236–37
  students, 150–51

Barron's selectivity index, 28
Bear, Rachel, 215–17, 219–20, 223–24, 229, 231, 233
belongingness measure, 29–30.
  See also measure/measurement
Bill and Melinda Gates Foundation, 22
Black, Latinx, Indigenous, and/or experiencing poverty, 18, 21, 26
Bryk, Anthony S., 4, 91, 140, 190, 226
burdensome data, 30–31. *See also* data; minimally burdensome measurement

Caillier, Stacey, 23–24, 35, 39–40, 43, 50
Carnegie Foundation's Community College Pathways Project, 174
Carnegie Math Pathways (CMP) program, 29
Carpe College Access Network (Carpe Network), 17–29, 31, 36, 43–44, 191, 193, 200, 207
  aim of, 26
  for college application, 22, 26
  FAFSA data in, 19–20, 23–24
  outcomes of, 27–28
  for students. *See* students
Center for Urban Education, 159
Chicago Public Schools (CPS), 129–55
  attendance/grades, 147
  data tools for, 135–41
  graduation rates in, 129–32, 134
  NCS model, 139–41, 143–47
  ninth-grade in, 134, 136
  off-track students of, 153–54
  reports, 136–37
  research/practice in, 132–35
  See also freshman ontrack indicator; school
chief executive officer (CEO), 134
claims. *See* debatable/defensible claims; nuanced claims
classroom, 3, 53, 113, 151, 186, 218, 237
  characteristics of, 151
  instruction, 79, 85, 174, 192, 237
  learning environment, 56–57, 63–66, 76–80, 90, 191, 218, 227, 232
  literacy activities in, 159
  measures, 56–57, 66, 70, 84–89, 201, 237
  norms, 62
  validity of, 84–88
  See also improvement; students

clearly indicated paraphrasing, 105, 108
coach/coaching, 2, 33, 75, 113, 167, 235
  accomplished, 67, 217–18, 221, 235
  calls, 41
  cycles, 67–70
  for data interpretation, 203
  IFL, 159, 161–62, 164, 167, 173, 175, 179, 181–82, 186
  individual, 111, 113
  mathematics, 191, 218
  one-on-one, 52, 55, 66, 79, 89, 113, 233, 235
  phases of, 67
  professional development of, 75
  school-based, 221
  social routines and, 232–33
  See also teacher/teaching
Coburn, C. E., 40, 42
cognitive interview, 59, 63, 196, 204–6
cognitively demanding tasks, 53–56, 59–60, 80, 89, 218, 227
collaborative meetings, 52, 55–57, 66, 78, 80, 86, 89–90, 237
college, 18–19, 95, 130, 190–91, 222
  access, levers of, 22, 43, 48
  application/matriculation, 18–19, 26–29, 199, 224
  attendance, 22, 26, 34, 191, 198
  balanced list of, 49–50
  Carpe Network for, 22, 26
  mathematics courses in, 29
  See also Free Application for Federal Student Aid (FAFSA)
College, Career, and Community Writers Program (C3WP), 93–127, 192–93, 202–3
  to argument writing, 97–99
  core principles of, 100
  effectiveness of, 102
  evaluations, 93–94
  improvement problem/theory of action, 94–96
  instructional resources.
    See instructional resources
  PD, 94, 96, 103, 107, 197
  to practical measurement, 97, 102–7
  qualitative analysis of, 127
  See also Using Sources Tool (UST)
Common Core State Standards for Mathematics, 53
community expertise, 45
Comprehension Task Sheet, 158–62, 164, 166–67, 175, 177, 180–82
concurrent validity, 198–99, 206–8
consequential validity, 183–84

construct validity, 197–99, 206, 210
content expertise, 11, 45, 209, 225
content-focused learning, 215.
   See also learning
content validity, 196–97, 205, 210
continuous improvement. *See* improvement
conversational norms, 42
coplanning phase, 67
Curriculum Guide Writing Initiative, 66, 70, 80–83

data, 13
   attendance and grade, 142
   burdensome, 30–31
   collection, 14, 36–37, 50, 223–25
   conversation protocols, 42
   dashboards, 223, 227, 234
   disaggregating, 227–29
   elements, 132, 147, 198
   FAFSA, 19–20, 23–24
   for inequities, 176–79
   infrastructure, 36–39
   for mathematics improvement, 80–83
   myths, 13
   NCS, 146
   physical aspects of, 36
   real-time/right-time, 132, 150
   reports, 136–37
   role in improvement, 24
   sensemaking, 40–41
   social and analytical aspects of, 37
   systems/representations, 80–83, 233–34
   technical aspects of, 36
   tools, 135–41
   use of, 40, 80–83
"Data for Equity" protocol, 42
debatable/defensible claims, 105, 108, 121
debrief phase, 67, 75–77, 81–82, 87, 223
deep learning, 12. *See also* learning
deficit-thinking, 42, 115–16, 120
Denstaedt, Linda, 113, 121, 126
depression, 153. *See also* mental health; stress
design/analysis/revision, 58–59
design principles, 169–84, 187.
   See also instructional improvement
diagnostic data reports, 132, 140
disaggregating data, 227–29. *See also* data
distribute leadership, 144.
   See also leader/leadership
district, 6, 55–57, 96, 125, 182, 217, 236–38
   accountability policy, 134
   administrators, 195
   data collection by, 223–25
   instructional improvement in, 218

   leader/leadership, 151–52, 182
   mathematics specialists, 58, 67, 70–74, 78–83, 85, 89–90, 192
   PMRR for, 201–2
   school context and, 86–87, 201–3

Early-Warning Indicator (EWI) system, 135–38, 147, 151
education, 4, 40, 91, 137, 170–71, 214, 238
   attainment, linkage to, 149
   data use in, 40
   equity issues in, 91
   focal problems, 215–16, 226–27
   improvement, core principles of, 4–5
   system levels, 7
   See also school; students; teacher/teaching
Education Trust West, 125
Emergent Multilingual Learners (EMLs), 157–58, 167, 170, 177–78
English language arts (ELA), 96, 112, 125, 157–59, 161, 170, 215, 219, 221, 231
equity
   centered system, 157–87
   perspective, 54, 62
   reflections and UST, 124–27
   in school, 44, 153–54
   See also instructional improvement
exit tickets, 158, 162, 164, 167, 170–71, 175, 177–80, 183–86, 192, 197
expertise. *See* specific expertise

face validity, 195–96. *See also* validity
feedback. *See* timely feedback
fluency measure, 13. *See also* measure/measurement
focal educational problems, 215–16, 226–27
formative assessment, 97, 102, 175, 195.
   See also assessment
For the Sake of Argument (Friedrich, Bear, & Fox), 103
Free Application for Federal Student Aid (FAFSA), 33–36, 39–40, 47–49, 195, 203–4, 215
   aim of, 191
   college attendance, determinant of, 34
   completion data, 19–20, 23–24, 190–91, 194, 200, 223
   for students. *See* students
freshman ontrack indicator, 129–55
   as accountability measure, 201
   actionability, 150–51
   data elements in, 147, 198
   educational attainment, linkage to, 149
   end-of-year, 132, 134, 143, 147–49, 194, 198

freshman ontrack indicator (cont.)
  graduation rates/data reports/attendance, 141–43
  predictiveness/reliability of, 147–48
  pushback and criticisms to, 151–53
  real-time/right-time, 150
  sustainable improvements in, 144
  usability and clarity, 149–50
Freshmen Success Report, 138–42, 145, 151, 194–96
Friedrich, Linda, 215–17, 219–20, 223–24, 229, 231, 233

GEAR UP program, 133
General Education Diploma (GED), 130
grades, 137–38, 141–45, 149–51, 201, 218–19, 223–24, 236–37
graduation rates, 129–32, 141–43, 149, 152–53, 207, 215–16, 227, 236
Gray, James R., 1–4, 6, 8–9, 11, 13

Harris, Joseph, 97, 113
high-quality arguments, 97, 103, 107, 113, 115
High Tech High Graduate School of Education (HTH GSE), 18–19, 22–23, 26–27, 31, 34–36, 39–43, 49

improvement, 5–7, 52, 68, 94, 147, 168, 200, 227–28
  accountability and, 11–13
  classes of, 215
  continuous, 2, 7, 18, 21–22, 24–26, 30, 39–41, 43–49
  core principles of, 4–5
  data role in, 24
  disposition, 229–30
  experts/expertise, 45–46, 173, 209
  initial problem of, 94–96
  mathematics, 51–91
  practical measurement for, 5–7
  productive goals of, 77
  sound measurement for, 5, 9, 15
  teachers learning and, 70–74
  theory of, 2, 8, 25–28, 45–46, 49, 90, 114, 190, 204, 217–19, 236–37
  See also instructional change; instructional improvement; validity
inequities, 16, 20, 70, 153, 169, 176–79, 226
inquiry-oriented instruction, 202
Institute for Learning (IFL), 159, 161–62, 164, 167, 173, 175, 179, 181–82, 186

instructional change, 80, 88, 158, 162, 203, 221, 236
  determination of, 66–74, 191–92
  students' experiences of, 170–74, 206
instructional decision-making, 110–14, 122
instructional expertise, 173
instructional improvement, 66–74, 78–80, 157–87
  challenges of, 222
  change ideas for, 161–62
  coherence of, 78–80
  design principles, 169–82
  district capacity for, 218
  goals of, 77
  inequities in, 176–79
  networked approach to, 158–62
  PMRR/C3WP/Pitt projects, 203
  practical measures in, 174–76
  students' experiences of, 170–74
  teacher learning for, 162–69
  timely feedback, 179–82
  validity for, 182–85
instructionally focused cases, 215, 223–24, 231, 235–38
instructional practice, 52–54, 120–22, 173, 197–98, 202–3, 236
instructional program coherence, defined, 79
instructional resources, 96, 107, 110–11, 122, 124–25
  components, 99
  importance of, 102
  for PD, 110–11, 122, 124
  sets of texts, 100
  See also Using Sources Tool (UST)
intractable problem, 155
Inverness Research, 102, 127
iterative cycles, 58–59, 224–25

Jackson, Kara, 200–201, 218–19, 221, 223–24, 228–34, 237

lack of financial aid, 23
Larbi-Cherif, Adrian, 200, 215, 217, 219–21, 223, 225, 227–28, 231, 233
leader/leadership
  C3WP, 96
  distribute, 144
  district, 151–52
  HTH GSE, 35, 39, 41, 43
  principal, 145
  school, 10, 33, 79, 139–40, 214, 236–38
  site, 111–13, 119–20

learning, 4, 78, 95, 127, 171, 201, 232
    of/for assessment, 106
    cognitive processes and, 47
    content-focused, 215
    deep, 12
    environment, 56–57, 63–66, 76–80, 90, 191, 218, 227, 232
    networked, 146–47
    practitioners, 21, 221
    professional, 2, 64–65, 94–97, 107, 118, 169, 209
    shared, 39
    socioemotional, 206
    See also students; teacher/teaching
Learning Research and Development Center, 159
Learning to Improve (Bryk), 4, 190
lesson
    enactment phase, 67, 75, 80, 220
    launch, 53–54, 56–57, 64, 91, 192, 196, 198
    phases of, 53–54
local Writing Project, 93, 95–97, 100–101, 106–8, 115–16, 192
logical reasoning, 109
"Look For" protocols, 186–87
Louisville Writing Project, 108

MAP assessment, 185. *See also* assessment
mathematics
    coach/coaching, 191, 218
    courses, 29, 34
    district specialists, 58, 67, 70–74, 78–83, 85, 89–90, 192
    reasoning, 52, 60, 227
    research in, 53
mathematics improvement, 51–91
    ambitious and equitable, 52–56, 66–67, 86, 89
    data use for, 80–83
    design/analysis/revision, 58–59
    instructional change, 66–74
    instructional practices for, 52–54
    The PMRR project, 56–57
    set of items, 57–58
    survey items, 57–58
    validity-for-use, 84–85
    validity-in-use, 85–88
    whole-class discussion survey, 59–64
    See also instructional improvement
Math Practical Measurement Repository, 206
matriculation process, 19, 22, 26–27, 29, 40
meaningful measure, 28–29, 192–93, 219–20.
    See also measure/measurement

measure/measurement, 5, 47, 82, 123, 167, 190, 209–11, 233
    for accountability, 12
    belongingness, 29–30
    expertise, 173, 206, 209
    fluency, 13
    meaningful, 28–29
    minimally burdensome, 30
    power issues of, 42–43
    process, 22
    for research, 6
    sensitivity of, 208
    sound, 5, 9, 15
    system of, 48
    targeted, 18
    types of, 22, 47
    See also practical measure/measurement
mental health, 154. *See also* depression; stress
minimally burdensome measurement, 30, 174, 193, 222–23. *See also* measure/measurement
modeling, 122, 126
Modeling the Quickwrite, 164, 167, 180, 182, 184
Modern Language Association (MLA), 105
Montes, Edgar, 23–24, 29, 39, 50
myths, 7–13
    accountability/improvement purposes, 11–13
    data, 13
    "Quick and Dirty," 8–9
    researchers design, 9–11
    succeed or fail, 144

The National Writing Project (NWP), 93–127. *See also* College, Career, and Community Writers Program (C3WP); Using Sources Tool (UST)
networked learning, 146–47. *See also* learning
Network for College Success (NCS), 139–41, 143–47
The New Teacher Project (TNTP), 124–25
ninth-grade, 130–54. *See also* Chicago Public Schools (CPS); freshman ontrack indicator
nonfiction texts, 97
Norman, Jon, 66, 85, 190, 193, 204–5, 208, 216–17, 220–23, 226–27, 229, 232, 234
norms
    classroom, 62
    conversational, 42
    of openness/transparency/innovation, 41–42
    of participation, 25

Northwest Evaluation Association, 185
nuanced claims, 108, 111, 118, 122

off-track students, 153–54
one-on-one coaching, 52, 55, 66, 79, 89, 113, 233, 235. *See also* coach/coaching
ontrack coordinators, 139. *See also* freshman ontrack indicator
openness/transparency/innovation norms, 41–42

pedagogical content knowledge, defined, 55
plagiarism, 108
Plan, Do, Study, Act (PDSA) cycle, 67, 211
positive impacts indicator, 122–24
power, 3, 171, 226
    predictive, 9
    signaling, 195, 210
    social and political, 42–43
practical data reports, 132, 141–43, 145–47, 151–52, 154, 198
practical expertise, 173, 209, 225
practical measure/measurement, 17–50, 57, 64–66
    actionable information, 29–30, 191–92, 220–22
    aim of, 13–16
    burdensome data for, 30–31
    Carpe Network. *See* Carpe College Access Network (Carpe Network)
    challenges/encouragements, 44–48
    characteristics of, 25–34, 81, 216–23
    components of, 177–78
    data infrastructure. *See* data
    defined, 5–7, 21–22
    degree to, 34–35
    effective use of, 230–31
    exit tickets as, 158, 175
    focal educational problems, 215–16, 226–27
    foundational concepts, 17–50
    implications, 235–36
    inequities, 226
    instruments, 9, 46, 195
    iterative process of, 9, 132–35
    meaningful, 28–29, 192–93, 219–20
    minimally burdensome, 30, 174, 193, 222–23
    myths, 7–13
    PD sessions, 231–32
    practitioners and, 9–11, 34, 48
    purpose of, 200–201
    in research improvement. *See* research
    social routines/coaching, 39–44, 232–33
    steps for creating, 223–26
    theory of improvement, 26–28, 97, 217–19
    timely feedback, 31–34, 194, 222–23
    use/development of, 57, 64–66
    See also validity
Practical Measures, Routines, and Representations (PMRR), 51–52, 196–99, 201–4, 209
    in districts, 201–2
    goals of, 56–57
    instructional change, determination of, 191
    measures of, 198
    research-practice partnerships, 52
    student surveys, 191–94, 209
    validity, testing of, 199
practice expertise, 45
practitioner, 6–11, 48, 78–82, 155, 183, 196–99, 213–14
    learning, 21, 221
    practical measurements and, 9–11
    school, 130, 135, 146
    supporting, 230–31
predictiveness, 147–48
predictive power, 9
predictive validity, 122, 195, 198, 205–7, 211. *See also* validity
principal leadership, 145. *See also* leader/leadership
problem solving, 52, 64, 154, 227
process measures, 22. *See also* measure/measurement
professional development (PD), 7
    C3WP, 94, 96, 103, 107, 197
    district-level, 74
    goal of, 67, 75, 216, 220, 231
    improvement as, 70
    instructional resources for, 110–11, 122, 124
    for mathematics coaches, 218
    sessions, 47, 55, 67, 78, 82, 231–32
    of teacher. *See* teacher/teaching
professional learning, 2, 64–65, 86–89, 94–97, 107, 118, 169, 203, 209. *See also* learning
psychometrics, 225–26
purpose/context/user perspectives, 208–9

"Quick and Dirty" myth, 8–9

RAND Corporation, 95
real-time/right-time data, 13, 132, 150
reasoning. *See* logical reasoning; mathematics
reliability, 147–48
research
    data in education, 40

design for practical measurements, 9–11
engage in, 143–44
exemplary program of, 224
improvement, 1–16
iterative process of, 132–35
in mathematics education, 53
measurement for, 6
PMRR, 52
psychometrics and, 225–26
reports, 132
Rewriting: How to Do Things with Texts (Harris), 97
Roderick, Melissa, 133, 139
routine argument-writing resources, 113

Sanoff, Ben, 23–24, 28, 31, 36–37, 39, 50
scale-point definitions, 108, 115, 126
school, 17
  data sensemaking in, 40–41
  district context and, 86–87, 201–3
  early-warning data tools for, 135–38
  equity issues in, 44, 153–54
  leaders, 10, 33, 79, 139–40, 214, 236–38
  literacy outcomes in, 215
  meaningful measures for, 28–29
  network, 158
  practitioners, 130, 135, 146
  safety, 140
  staff, 153–54
  teams, 19–20, 23–24, 35–36, 43, 139–40, 146–47
  See also education; students; teacher/teaching
school-based coaches, 221
set of items, 57–58
shared learning, 39. *See also* learning
signaling power, 195, 210
site leaders, 111–13, 119–20.
  See also leader/leadership
skills. *See* technical skills; writing
Smarter Balanced Assessment Argumentative Rubric, 106
Smith, Thomas M., 216, 218–19, 225, 236
social and political power, 42–43
social routines, 39–44, 94, 232–33
socioemotional learning, 206.
  See also learning
sound argument, defined, 95
sound measurement, 5, 9, 15.
  See also measure/measurement
source-based argument, 93–94, 123–24, 192–93, 215–16, 231

SRI International (SRI), 102, 123, 125
stakeholders, 28–29, 39, 42, 44, 46
stress, 225
student-centered literacy instruction, 158–62
students, 17
  Carpe Network for, 17–29, 31, 36, 43–44
  change ideas, sensemaking of, 171–72
  disagreements of, 63
  English-speaking, 177
  experiences, design principles for, 170–74
  FAFSA, 18–20, 23–24
  failed, 137
  grades and attendance of, 150–51
  health of, 153–54
  ideas/opportunities, 60, 62
  in individual/small group work, 54
  inequities in, 16, 20, 70, 153, 169, 176–79, 226
  laziness in, 39–40
  learning, 44, 59, 78, 115, 174, 182–85, 208
  mathematical ideas, role of, 52, 55
  ontrack reports of, 204
  percentage tracking of, 23
  perspective of, 62, 76, 87–88, 171
  success conditions for, 124
  survey, 58–59, 191–94, 209
  task-sheet lessons for, 161
  test scores, 131, 135, 139–40, 148, 152, 201
  See also argument writing; teacher/teaching
summative assessment, 105, 115, 117.
  See also assessment
survey. *See* whole-class discussion survey
sustainability, 30, 144

Takahashi, Sola, 66, 85, 190, 204–5, 208, 216–17, 220, 222–23, 226–27, 229, 232, 234
targeted measurement, 18.
  See also measure/measurement
tasks
  cognitively demanding, 53–56, 59–60, 80, 89, 227
  sheets, 158–62, 164, 166–67, 175, 177, 180–82
  types of, 64
teacher/teaching
  ambitious and equitable, 52–56, 66–67, 86, 89
  of argument writing, 97–99
  centered instruction, 159
  coaches and, 75–78

teacher/teaching (cont.)
  collaborative meetings of, 52, 55–57, 66, 78, 80, 86, 89–90, 237
  as curriculum guide writers, 70
  individualized, 41
  in instructional improvement. *See* instructional improvement
  learning, 74–78, 162–69
  in mathematical problems, role of, 53–55
  modeling, 122, 126
  PD of, 55, 88–90, 93–96, 117–18, 179–80, 196–97, 231–32
  positional authority of, 44
  practices, 54–56
  primary goal of, 201
  site leaders and, 119–20
  support for, 55–56, 70–78
  timely feedback to, 179–82
  UST for, 119–20
technical skills, 35
technological support, 30
test scores, 131, 135, 139–40, 148, 152, 201
text comprehension, 159, 161, 167, 180
theory of improvement, 2, 25–28, 26–28, 45–46, 90, 114, 190, 204, 217–19, 236–37
  action, 94–96, 107, 121
  components of, 107
  factors in, 189
  refined, 97, 99, 102, 107
timely feedback, 31–34, 179–82, 194, 222–23
Turner, E. O., 40, 42

The University of Chicago Consortium on School Research, 131
University of Pittsburgh (Pitt), 159, 164, 193–94
users' perspectives, 87–88, 203–5, 208–9, 230
Using Sources Tool (UST), 93, 107–27
  application of, 108
  for argument writing, 108–10, 114, 122–24
  AWC-SBA and, 123–24
  collaborative use of, 114
  C3WP approach, 102–7
  data, 112–13
  debatable/defensible claims, 105
  instructional change, 191–92
  instructional decision-making, 110–14
  instructional practice, 120–22
  as leading indicator, 122–24
  in professional learning session, 112
  questions, 103–5, 108
  reflections on equity and, 124–27
  scale-point definitions, 108, 115, 126
  for students writing, 115–18, 233
  for teachers/site leaders, 119–20
  theory of action, role of, 107
  validity issues. *See* validity

validity, 13–15, 52, 84, 118, 183, 216, 236
  balancing, 205–7
  of classroom, 84–88
  concurrent, 198–99
  consequential, 183–84
  construct, 197–99
  content, 196–97
  design measures, 208
  face, 195–96
  framework for, 205
  for instructional improvement, 182–85
  practical measures, relation to, 190–94
  predictive, 198
  purpose/context/user perspectives, 200–201, 208–9
  schools and districts contexts, 86–87, 201–3
  technical quality and, 189–211
  types of, 195
  for UST, 118
validity-for-use, 84–85, 195–99, 202, 206–7, 210–11, 225
validity-in-use, 85–88, 200–205, 209–10, 228
  challenges to, 202–3
  purposes and uses, 85–86
  users' perspectives, 87–88, 203–5
variability in performance, 4–5, 11–12

Warren High School, 17–19, 24
WestEd, 206
whole-class discussion survey, 59–64, 68, 71–73, 76, 81, 84, 196, 224
  aspects of, 59–60, 62–63
  for mathematics improvement, 59–64
  purpose of, 72, 84
  students' responses to, 63–65, 71–72
Wolph, Jean, 108, 110, 120
writing
  academic, 97, 161
  annotated student, 109, 116, 124
  argument, 93–127
  of curriculum, 57, 66
  dimensions of, 106
  nonfiction sources in, 103
  skills, 115
  of students, 2–3, 33
  teaching of, 1, 97–99
Writing into the Day to Jumpstart Argument, 100